Yankees in
the Hill City

Yankees in the Hill City

The Union Prisoner of War Camp in Lynchburg, Virginia, 1862–1865

CLIFTON W. POTTER, JR.

McFarland & Company, Inc., Publishers
Jefferson, North Carolina

LIBRARY OF CONGRESS CATALOGUING-IN-PUBLICATION DATA

Names: Potter, Clifton W., author.
Title: Yankees in the Hill City : the Union prisoner of war camp in Lynchburg, Virginia, 1862–1865 / Clifton W. Potter, Jr.
Description: Jefferson, North Carolina : McFarland & Company, Inc., Publishers, 2024. | Includes bibliographical references and index.
Identifiers: LCCN 2024029702 | ISBN 9781476695884 (paperback : acid free paper) ∞
ISBN 9781476653891 (ebook)
Subjects: LCSH: Prisoner-of-war camps—Virginia—Lynchburg—History—19th century. | Lynchburg, Battle of, Lynchburg, Va., 1864—Casualties—Registers. | United States—History—Civil War, 1861-1865—Prisoners and prisons. | United States—History—Civil War, 1861-1865—Casualties—Registers.
Classification: LCC E612.L96 P68 2024 | DDC 973.7/72—dc23/eng/20240730
LC record available at https://lccn.loc.gov/2024029702

BRITISH LIBRARY CATALOGUING DATA ARE AVAILABLE

ISBN (print) 978-1-4766-9588-4
ISBN (ebook) 978-1-4766-5389-1

© 2024 Clifton W. Potter, Jr. All rights reserved

No part of this book may be reproduced or transmitted in any form or by any means, electronic or mechanical, including photocopying or recording, or by any information storage and retrieval system, without permission in writing from the publisher.

Front cover image: Edward Beyer's 1855 panoramic view of Lynchburg from the Amherst County side of the James River (courtesy of the Lynchburg Museum System).

Printed in the United States of America

McFarland & Company, Inc., Publishers
 Box 611, Jefferson, North Carolina 28640
  www.mcfarlandpub.com

To the Boys in Blue,
1861–1865

Table of Contents

Acknowledgments	ix
Preface	1
Chapter 1. Tobacco City	9
Chapter 2. The Decline of Richmond	28
Chapter 3. The Lynchburg System	52
Chapter 4. Vermin and Vespers	78
Chapter 5. The Lynchburg Campaign	100
Chapter 6. The Convenience of Memory	119
Appendix A: Burial Records for POWs, 1862–1865	143
Appendix B: Lynchburg Campaign Casualties, KIA/MIA	166
Chapter Notes	171
Bibliography	185
Index	213

Acknowledgments

Perhaps the most important key to understanding the anomaly that was the Union POW camp at the Lynchburg, Virginia, Fair Ground is the "Diuguid Soldiers Book," which is part of the collection housed in the offices of the Old City Cemetery. Over the years, the help and advice of the staff there have been indispensable. Other local institutions that were essential to this research were the Jones Memorial Library with its manuscript collection and Historic Sandusky, Lynchburg's Civil War center, which is part of the University of Lynchburg and home to the largest collection of printed sources on the Civil War to be found in central Virginia. The staff of the Knight-Capron Library at the University of Lynchburg obtained essential materials for this project through interlibrary loans. Other libraries that provided valuable manuscript resources were the Washington and Lee University Special Collections & Archives in Lexington, Virginia; Virginia Polytechnic Institute and State University Libraries in Blacksburg, Virginia; University of Virginia Libraries in Charlottesville, Virginia; and James Madison University Libraries in Harrisonburg, Virginia.

Outside the Old Dominion, appreciation is expressed to the staff members of the Filson Historical Society in Louisville, Kentucky; Special Collections Library at Western Kentucky University in Bowling Green, Kentucky; University of Rochester Libraries in Rochester, New York; Silver Special Collections, University of Vermont Libraries in Burlington, Vermont; and the James S. Schoff Civil War Collection at the William L. Clements Library, University of Michigan at Ann Arbor. With their expertise, patience, and guidance, it was possible to access and study irreplaceable references without which this book could not have been written.

The resources to tell the story of the POW camp at the Lynchburg, Virginia, Fair Ground were not readily accessible a generation ago for a number of reasons. Relevant manuscripts were scattered among

Acknowledgments

various libraries across the country, and using them required funded travel, time, seemingly endless correspondence, and patience. Many of the books published between the 1860s and World War I were printed on wood pulp paper that degraded over time and could not be borrowed through interlibrary loan because they were too fragile, thus requiring more travel if they were even available for use. Some newspapers had been microfilmed, but they were not always accessible by interlibrary loan. A few publishers were printing facsimiles of works dealing with particularly noteworthy regiments and individuals, but these were expensive as well as printed to order.

Thanks to the digital revolution, diaries, correspondence, memoirs, newspapers, and regimental histories are obtainable with a few clicks of a mouse. Most of the items found in the bibliography of this book—except for current publications—were first accessed on the internet. In recent years, the appearance of websites like the *American Civil War Database, Fold3, Ancestry.com,* and *Archives* has made research not only more productive but also more pleasurable.

When this project was in its early planning phase, James I. "Bud" Robertson, Jr.—one of the foremost Civil War scholars of his generation—offered some sage advice that has proven invaluable. He believed that the men who survived the harrowing ordeal of imprisonment told their stories better than historians from another generation. The closer in time to the event, the more reliable the account was. Time tempers memories, even of the most traumatic events.

Finally, sincere gratitude is due three scholars who have shepherded this project from its beginning to its completion: my wife, Dr. Dorothy Potter, professor emerita of history, University of Lynchburg, who served as a reliable critic and editor; our son, Dr. Edmund D. Potter, artist, photographer, and museum curator, whose advice on all these disciplines has proven invaluable; and award-winning author/historian of naval literature Dr. M. Ernest Marshall, who offered guidance that allowed me to navigate the shoals of modern publishing to a safe harbor.

Preface

To understand the American Civil War better—its causes and consequences—many contemporary scholars have chosen to explore the reactions of individual communities to the crisis that convulsed our republic between 1861 and 1865. Lynchburg voters initially supported the preservation of the Union, but when Virginia seceded, most of its white citizens zealously embraced the Confederacy. Within a year of armed conflict, Lynchburg was selected as the location for a POW camp, and that is perhaps one of the best-kept secrets among scholars. Fortunately, one aspect of the struggle between the North and the South that finally has received some in-depth attention from historians is the question of the fate of the POWs held by the federal government and the Confederacy. Mention Union prisons of war to a Virginian and the names that come to mind are Libby Prison, Castle Thunder, and Belle Isle, each one a reminder of a dark chapter in Richmond's past. By contrast, from June 1862 until April 1865, a series of events in Lynchburg allowed those in charge to fashion a complex that provided Union POWs with temporary shelter, adequate medical care, and for those who did not survive their wounds or illnesses, what Victorians considered "a good death" and burial. This is the story of the Union POW camp at Lynchburg, Virginia.

During the war and in the years immediately after its end, the plight of POWs filled newspaper columns, and in the 52 years between Lee's surrender at Appomattox on April 9, 1865, and the entry into World War I by the United States on April 6, 1917, a number of regimental histories and memoirs from survivors of the Civil War appeared in print. Often, the histories were written by the chaplain of a regiment and varied in length from slim books with a modicum of details to large volumes in several parts filled with minutiae. The initial printings were small, usually intended for veterans or the families of the men who had died during the war. Often, they were produced by local printers or publishers using wood pulp–based paper, which was less expensive than paper made with linen or cotton fibers. They were bound with cardboard or inexpensive buckram covers. Wood pulp paper tended to deteriorate quickly as it underwent a chemical change, and within several decades, these fragile works were no longer available to scholars. The memoirs that began to appear toward the end of the 19th century also had short runs and were printed usually on cheaper paper with simple bindings. Fortunately, many of these works have been reprinted and are also accessible in digital form.

Many of these faded pages contain passages that refer to the treatment of Union POWs in Lynchburg. Many of the original reports have been lost or destroyed, rendering these brief citations as pieces of a puzzle which, when assembled, reveal the story of a system for handling prisoners that might have saved both lives and money if it had become the norm and not the exception in a system mismanaged from its inception.

In 1880, the first installment of *The War of the Rebellion: A Compilation of the Official Records of the Union and Confederate Armies* appeared. Published under the direction of successive secretaries of war, it eventually comprised 130 volumes by the time it was completed in 1891. Eight of these were devoted to the incarceration of military personnel of all ranks and all service branches. The official records first mentioned the Lynchburg camp in volume 4 of series 2. The extant documents consisted of official correspondence as well as invoices dealing with supplies for the men detained in Lynchburg. These published manuscripts were not used to any extent until 1930 when a Virginian rediscovered the Lynchburg POW camp and placed it in its proper setting among similar Confederate installations.

William Best Hesseltine, a native of Brucetown, Virginia, received his bachelor of arts from Washington and Lee University in 1922 and his master of arts from the University of Virginia in 1925 before entering Ohio State University where he earned a doctorate in history in 1928. In his dissertation, he sought either to prove or debunk the long-held assumption that the Confederate government actively pursued a policy that ensured the deaths of a majority of the Union soldiers held as POWs.

When Hesseltine began his research, this was the accepted Northern view, but after interpreting the material available to him, he concluded that the Confederacy's poor planning, bureaucratic incompetence, and a critical lack of resources were the real root causes of the cruelty recorded in painful detail for more than six decades. Among the documents used to establish his case were the references to the Lynchburg camp found in *The Official Records*.[1] In 1930, Hesseltine's dissertation was published by Ohio State University Press as *Civil War Prisons: A Study in War Psychology*.[2] It was a seminal work in the study of the treatment of POWs on both sides of the Mason-Dixon line. While Hesseltine's work absolved the Confederate government of institutional brutality, there was still a public fascination with the experiences of the inmates of Civil War prison camps.

The publication in 1955 of MacKinlay Kantor's Pulitzer Prize–winning novel *Andersonville* rekindled interest in everything dealing with mid–19th-century America. Hesseltine wrote a scathing review of *Andersonville* in the *Georgia Review* in which he accused Kantor of ignoring current scholarship by relying on works such as *Narrative of Privations and Sufferings of United States Officers and Soldiers While in the Hands of the Rebel Authorities*, published by the United States Sanitary Commission in 1864.[3]

Unfortunately, Hesseltine died unexpectedly in 1963, thereby missing most of the Civil War centennial and the birth of Civil War reenacting as a means of preserving history. Forty-one years after the publication of Kantor's novel, John Frankenheimer received an Emmy for his television film *Andersonville*. It was not based on Kantor's work, but both men used some of the same sources in fashioning their narratives. Regrettably, as Hesseltine had predicted, in the public mind all Civil War prisons were like Camp Sumter in Georgia—the official name of Andersonville—and increasingly, the term "concentration camp" began to be used to describe the horrors endured by both Union and Rebel soldiers who were POWs.

The debate that began among scholars with the appearance of *Civil War Prisons: A Study in War Psychology* continues, and during the last 30 years, a number of works have been published that follow the pattern developed by Hesseltine while seeking to give this aspect of Civil War studies greater depth. Many of the recent books dealing with the problem of POWs provide information on the Lynchburg camp that is incomplete, incorrect, or negligible. Lonnie R. Speer attempted to expand on Hesseltine's work. Speer's data on Lynchburg were certainly minimal, but the same may be true of other camps mentioned in *Portals to Hell: Military Prisons of the Civil War*, which appeared in 1977. He referred to the use of the Lynchburg jail, the Fair Ground, and converted buildings, but he did not attempt to identify them or their respective locations.

Preface

However, he correctly attributed the creation of the Lynchburg facilities to overcrowding in the Richmond prisons before the establishment of the Dix-Hill Cartel in July 1862, which provided a means for prisoner parole and exchange between the two sides.[4]

Speer later listed Lynchburg among the major Confederate POW camps—which included those in Richmond and Danville in Virginia; Charleston and Columbia in South Carolina; the camp for Union officers in Macon, Georgia, and Camp Sumter—but his statistics on the Lynchburg camp were inadequate.[5] He was not certain the camp still existed in 1864 or 1865. Speer correctly identified its capacity at 500, but he had no idea of the maximum number incarcerated there, and he had no data on the number of Union prisoners who died in Lynchburg or whether any soldiers had attempted to escape.[6]

Charles W. Sanders, Jr.'s *While in the Hands of the Enemy: Military Prisons of the Civil War*, published in 2005, simply repeated the information gleaned from *The Official Records*, the same data Hesseltine had used in 1930. Frances H. Casstevens in her 2005 study, *"Out of the Mouth of Hell": Civil War Prisons and Escapes*, merely included Lynchburg in a list of Virginia camps with Danville, Petersburg, and the three Richmond facilities.[7]

Relying on official sources, regimental histories, and unpublished diaries, Roger Pickenpaugh fashioned one of the most useful works on POWs—*Captives in Blue: The Civil War Prisons of the Confederacy*—published in 2013. The references to the Lynchburg camp are valuable because they were based not only on official correspondence but also on a number of personal observations made by prisoners which Pickenpaugh carefully evaluated.[8] In 2015, *Transforming Civil War Prisons: Lincoln, Lieber, and the Politics of Captivity* by Paul J. Springer and Glenn Robins replaced Hesseltine as the preferred introduction to the study of incarceration during the "Great War of the Rebellion."[9]

Initially, Lynchburg was chosen as the site for an auxiliary camp because of its location. Until the beginning of the French and Indian War, the site of the future Hill City was just another relatively safe place to ford the treacherous James River. From 1756 until 1763, thousands of settlers moved into that contested wilderness, and the Lynch family responded by establishing a ferry service that gave safe passage across the river. The counties of central Virginia were well suited to the cultivation of tobacco. Many pioneers settled near Lynch's Ferry, and in 1786, this Quaker enterprise was granted a town charter. Tobacco was a labor-intensive crop, and in the late 18th century that meant slavery.

Preface

Nicotiana tabacum made Lynchburg the second wealthiest city in the United States by 1855, but it bound the Hill City and the Piedmont region to Richmond and the eastern counties where slavery was an established source of labor and wealth. Initially, the tobacco was sent to the wharves of Richmond in hogsheads latched to rapid-taming bateaux, then later barges on the James River and Kanawha Canal, and finally in the 1850s by railroad. Although Lynchburg was serviced by several turnpikes, the canal, and three railroads in 1861, it was still remote from the major fields of battle. The Hill City was already well on the way to becoming the second largest hospital center in the Upper South when the city council was ordered to prepare for the establishment of a transit camp in Lynchburg for Union POWs.

Any study of the Lynchburg POW camp must begin with a thorough understanding of the evolution of enemy incarceration in Richmond. The conundrum of POWs and how the Confederate government failed to meet that challenge starts with a consideration of poor planning, limited resources, and, especially, incompetent management. The assumption that the war would not last very long led those in charge to choose Richmond as the sole location for captured Union soldiers. As the original "prison" quickly filled to capacity, multiple locations in Richmond were requisitioned and adapted for that same purpose, including Libby, Castle Thunder, and eventually Belle Isle. Even with this expansion, the situation deteriorated so quickly that even someone trained to deal with inmates, vital services, and organization might have been unable to find solutions to all these problems. Unfortunately, President Jefferson Davis chose the wrong man for this crucial job.

Born in 1800, Brevet Lieutenant Colonel John Henry Winder was at the end of his lackluster career when he journeyed to Richmond in the spring of 1861 to seek a military commission from Davis. A graduate of West Point, class of 1820, Winder was teaching there in 1827 when he befriended Davis and another cadet, Robert E. Lee. Davis commissioned Winder a brigadier general and, in a series of appointments, made him virtual "Dictator of Richmond," thus promoting him far beyond his level of competence. Winder was particularly inept when it came to dealing with POWs. He stumbled from one expedient to another while inadvertently becoming entangled in the bureaucratic inertia that plagued the Confederate government. Unused to the demands of command, Winder often selected subordinates who were either unfit for the responsibilities heaped on them or exploited their positions for personal gain. Some were simply sadists. The exception to the rule was Colonel George C. Gibbs.

Preface

By the end of 1861, the euphoria with which the citizens of Richmond greeted the news that their city was to be the capital of the new Confederate States of America had worn thin. Prices had inflated, the city's population had more than doubled, every available living space was filled, the streets were no longer safe, and Union POWs were consuming supplies that should have been available to loyal Confederates. In desperation, those in charge of the system suggested scattering Union captives throughout the Confederacy. When Winder was tasked by his superiors with finding a solution to the "Yankee problem," the exhausted "Old Man of Richmond" endorsed the idea of auxiliary camps as a reasonable solution. Initially, they were the perfect response to a growing crisis, but Winder could not leave well enough alone; the ultimate auxiliary camp was Fort Sumter near Andersonville, Georgia. However, in December 1861, that disaster lay in the future. In a matter of weeks, Gibbs turned an abandoned factory in Salisbury, North Carolina, into a POW camp. His next assignment was Lynchburg, the "Tobacco City."

The Lynchburg POW camp was supposed to house 500 Union soldiers, but by April 1862, the city council had done absolutely nothing to plan for the first internees who could arrive at any moment. Diaries kept by three of the first inmates of the Lynchburg auxiliary camp described the steps Colonel George Gibbs took to make the best of a bad situation. When Gibbs arrived in the Hill City with the men of the Forty-Second North Carolina Infantry whom he had trained to manage POWs, all that local authorities could offer as a possible site was a portion of the 30-acre Fair Ground just outside the city limits. The first Union soldiers captured during General Stonewall Jackson's Shenandoah Valley Campaign were already on their way when Gibbs and his men, aided by slaves from Lynchburg, began to clean and prepare their share of the Fair Ground. By the time the first prisoners were moved into the camp on June 17, 1862, the 500 had become 3,000. With a talent for using all his resources as well as knowing whom to contact for more support, Gibbs made the impossible possible.

When American soldiers died in the Richmond prisons, they were stacked like cordwood until they could be collected and dumped into a common grave—but not so in Lynchburg. The firm of George A. Diuguid daily collected the bodies of Confederate soldiers from the hospitals and camps, and Union dead were accorded that same regard. Placed in coffins (their personal data recorded by Diuguid staff members), the deceased were buried in the City Cemetery. Each day, a local minister read the service of Christian burial over the newly interred. This practice continued until June 1865 when the last of the "Boys in Blue" was laid to rest. Although a local firm provided this service, the Confederate government paid the fees for soldiers from both sides. While Colonel Gibbs was in command of the POW camp at the Fair Ground, the prisoners received the same rations as their Confederate counterparts. Within days of their arrival, they were provided with tents and a field hospital. Between mid–June and mid–August, approximately 5,000 men were held at the Fair Ground POW camp, but only 79 died from wounds or illness, which was a death rate of roughly 1.56 percent.

Initially, all Union soldiers were detained at the Fair Ground, although the officers were physically separated from the ordinary "Boys in Blue." As tobacco factories became available in August 1862 to be used as hospitals, one was reserved as a prison for officers. Until the Dix-Hill Cartel was suspended, prisoners remained only briefly in Lynchburg unless they were recovering from wounds or illness. Lynchburg was the second largest hospital center in the Upper South after Richmond, and Union soldiers were accorded the same care available to sick and wounded Confederates. This was not the case in Richmond where Union captives died waiting to be admitted to the substandard hospital reserved for them, or they expired shortly after they arrived there. In Lynchburg, all soldiers, regardless of the color of their uniforms, often were treated in the same facilities. Inevitably and unfortunately as the war progressed, conditions deteriorated in Lynchburg for both Union and Rebel forces but never to the level of the Richmond facilities.

The most serious threat to the Hill City occurred in June 1864 when Brigadier General David Hunter launched his Lynchburg Campaign. Only then did those in charge of the Union prisoners seem overwhelmed, but the crisis passed and the "Lynchburg system" functioned until the surrender at Appomattox. However, if Hunter had followed General Grant's orders to the letter to take Lynchburg, he might have reduced the city to ashes, destroyed its transportation network, and liberated the Union prisoners. Chapter 5 is devoted to the Battle of Lynchburg, which could have been a Union victory if General Hunter had not indulged repeatedly his penchant for burning the property of those who irritated him. Many historians have debated the details of the Lynchburg Campaign, while others have examined the legends of empty trains accompanied by brass bands hauling phantom soldiers into the city's railroad depots. However, the key to Hunter's failure at Lynchburg was time management—or the lack of it. Brigadier General Jubal A. Early has been given credit for rescuing Lynchburg, but the honor for saving the city belongs to the smoldering ruins of the Virginia Military Institute (VMI). If Hunter had bypassed Lexington, Virginia, General Grant's objective of possessing Lynchburg for at least a single day might have been achieved.[10]

With the restoration of peace, the facilities used to care for prisoners quickly returned to their previous functions, in part because Lynchburg was the only major urban center in Virginia unharmed by the war. The camp was forgotten because it was repurposed time and again, but the manuscripts, diaries, memoirs, and regimental histories contain the data that clarified what the "Lynchburg system" was and how it functioned need only to be examined to discover another piece of the puzzle that is the American Civil War. All that remains of the Lynchburg POW camp are the sentinel oaks on the campus of E.G. Glass High School. They were saplings in the summer of 1862 when, in their shade, the first Union captives, weary and longing for home, sought shelter from the sun.

Chapter 1

Tobacco City

Virginians who ventured beyond the Blue Ridge Mountains before 1756 risked their lives at the hands of the French and their Indian allies. The English were viewed as interlopers because they destroyed the habitats of beaver, lynx, and otter as they cleared the land for farming. It is impossible to estimate the number of Britons who were killed, kidnapped, or had their farms destroyed. They were not protected on land claimed by the French and were repeatedly warned by the government in London that once they crossed the invisible yet ever-changing boundary, they were at the mercy of Great Britain's rival for empire. Then suddenly with the outbreak of the French and Indian War in 1756, the territory between the mountains and the Mississippi was in dispute, and an increasing number of settlers were willing to risk their lives for a chance to lay claim to a homestead beyond the Cumberland Gap or in the Ohio Country. This war was the catalyst for the creation of Lynchburg.

One of the most convenient routes westward from Tidewater Virginia lay through central Virginia. The Lynch brothers, led by 17-year-old John, facilitated this migration with their ferry service. From 1756 until 1763, thousands of settlers crossed the river and continued up the muddy trail above the water's edge. The Lynches' simple hostelry and storage facilities near their ferry landing grew into a thriving business run by men with a reputation for efficiency and fair dealing. There were no strictures against Quakers acquiring wealth through honest work—they saw the revenue that could be gained by providing safe passage, food, and lodging for those on their way west as income fairly earned. At the war's end in 1763, Great Britain was the most powerful nation in Europe, and its loyal subjects in North America looked forward to enjoying their share of its prosperity, but those living near Lynch's Ferry were also concerned with the closing of the frontier. Beginning in 1762, pioneers were forbidden to occupy land beyond the sources of the rivers that flowed into the Atlantic Ocean; suddenly, the Ohio Country was once again off-limits to settlers. Meant to placate the tribes in the newly acquired French territories and to encourage immigration by English-speaking colonists to Canada and Florida, the policy seemed sound and reasonable to those in London who formulated it. British colonials saw it as yet another attempt by absentee authorities to regulate their lives.

Many of the settlers who had traversed the mountains into the Ohio Country during the French and Indian War now died defending their homesteads. The number of persons crossing at Lynch's Ferry dropped but never stopped altogether. Some continued along well-worn tracks that led to the west and the southwest despite imperial regulations; others saw central Virginia as a final destination because it was safer to remain in the new counties of Amherst, Bedford, and Campbell where the soil was well suited to the cultivation of tobacco. Among these pioneers were artisans whose skills were essential to the survival and growth of a settlement. Carpenter, blacksmith, joiner, cooper, tailor, cobbler, tinker—all were welcomed. Most were not Quakers, or members of the Religious Society of Friends to use their official name, but the majority was nominally Protestant. Ironically, 13 years later in 1776, Virginia would be in a struggle with the mother country that eventually included the formerly despised French as allies.

Between 1756 and 1776, the population of Virginia almost doubled. Whereas some of that quarter of a million inhabitants were native born, many were immigrants, especially Scots and Scotch-Irish from Ulster. Accustomed to hardships and distrustful of any governmental authority, they tended to gravitate to the unregulated frontier. These settlers brought the area's first slaves but not in numbers found in the Chesapeake. A family might own one or two slaves who worked in the house, fields, workshop, or forge along with their master or mistress. During this same 20-year period, Virginia's African American population increased by about 65 percent to around 200,000, or 40 percent of the total population. On the frontier, it was easier to attempt to escape the bonds of slavery, and sometimes Blacks found refuge among Native Americans, including the Monacan of central Virginia, who felt no obligation to return them to their white owners.

Slavery was one of three great concerns that began to threaten the orderly existence that the Friends tried to maintain among their members and with their neighbors. The most immediate crisis—armed rebellion against the British government—had clearly unacceptable

Chapter 1. Tobacco City

implications; Friends did not take up arms, no matter how just a cause might seem to others. Virginia law exempted Quakers from militia duty, but even though their moral stance was legal, they were not spared the anger and contempt of their fellow citizens. This increased as Friends refused to engage in any activity related to the war, such as using continental currency. Some even refrained from voting since both sides were in conflict. Pacifists are generally a despised minority in wartime. The revolution's end in 1783 removed one stress from Quaker life. However, the issue of slavery was not to be resolved in a few years' time. Some Quakers found the economic sacrifices and social isolation that were part of emancipation efforts simply too difficult, so they kept their slaves, were disowned, and joined other denominations. Many became Methodists or Baptists and remained in Lynchburg after their more resolute brothers and sisters moved westward to territories that became Indiana, Ohio, Kansas, Oregon, and California.

Lynchburg, and indeed all of Virginia, might have avoided the angst over the issue of slavery if in 1832, the General Assembly had been able to adopt the plan for gradual emancipation set forth by a number of members of the House of Delegates. In the aftermath of the slave rebellion led by Nat Turner which swept through Southampton County in August 1831, at least 40 petitions—some from Quakers—were sent to members of the lower chamber of the General Assembly offering solutions ranging from the expulsion of all free Blacks from Virginia, a revival of the colonization scheme of the 1820s, and finally, to a plan for gradual emancipation, which eventually failed on a vote of 65 to 58 in January 1832. The Richmond Junto and its allies in the Piedmont had proven that the interests of that portion of Virginia always took precedence over those who lived west of the Blue Ridge Mountains.

A third problem that Quakers found increasingly difficult to combat as it began impinging on their numbers was marrying a non–Quaker. Although records of the Cedar Creek and South River Meetings indicate that both male and female Friends married out of their faith, disownments listed in J.P. Bell's *Our Quaker Friends of Ye Olden Time* show nearly twice as many women as men chose non–Quaker marriage partners.[1] The modesty and gentleness of young Quaker women were attractions, and for some female Friends, a desire for a less restrictive life was obviously as alluring as thoughts of love. Regardless of the reasons, the results were serious: a dwindling reproductive population dooms any social group to potential extinction. Although the Quakers of the central Piedmont slowly disappeared, some influences remained.

The grid pattern of the streets in the town and the municipal water system were based on those of Philadelphia, which was at the heart of William Penn's great experiment. Although they were no longer Quakers, many of the early leaders of Lynchburg were descendants of the Friends who formed the South River Meeting.

By the late 1770s, Lynch's Ferry was well established not only as a gateway to the west but also as a center of western Virginia's tobacco trade. In 1785, the Lynch brothers built near their original enterprise the first tobacco warehouse for the storage of hogsheads—the device used to transport tobacco. Every year, farmers and their teams braved the hills that tumbled down to the water's edge, bringing their golden leaf for inspection, and if it passed examination, the hogshead was resealed and prepared for shipment. Substandard tobacco was burned. In 1786, the Virginia General Assembly acknowledged the importance of the 29-year-old settlement on the south bank of the James River by granting it a town charter. Lynch's Ferry was now Lynchburg, a recognized political entity. The fortunes of the new town that was expanding along the terraced bluffs above the James River were linked to the growing of tobacco as the area's main cash crop. In time, tobacco made Lynchburg one of the wealthiest communities in the nation, but every step from placing the seedlings in the ground to taking the hogsheads to market involved slaves, and that shackled Lynchburg to the Richmond Junto.

Because there were no substantial roads from Lynchburg to Richmond—only rutted tracks that turned to mire in the rain—the best highway to the capital was the James River. A decade before Lynch's Ferry was established, a resident of Nelson County, Robert Rose, improvised a catamaran by linking two large canoes together; this cumbersome craft was capable of carrying a dozen hogsheads of tobacco down the James to the fall line above Richmond. These so-called tobacco canoes were in regular service until 1771 when the entire fleet was destroyed in a record flood. To solve the problem of shipping tobacco to Richmond, two brothers from Amherst County, Anthony and Benjamin Rucker, designed and built the first "James River bateau," which could carry the same number of hogsheads as its predecessor. Tightly packed in these enormous barrels, the wealth of the Piedmont rode the swiftly moving river down to market in the sleek, rapid-taming bateaux which were easier to maneuver than the cumbersome tobacco canoes. This new mode of transport also gave rise to the bateaux men who navigated the James River from Lynchburg to Richmond until the 1840s. Both freedmen and slaves, they ruled the river as they delivered hogsheads to

Chapter 1. Tobacco City

the capital and poled home to Lynchburg, their bateaux laden with consumer goods for the citizens of the growing town.

A savvy investor in real estate, George Washington was particularly interested in the Ohio Territory, which experienced a tremendous influx of settlers during the French and Indian War and after the revolution. One of his concerns was that the Ohioans might choose to buy, sell, or trade with their Canadian neighbors or with the Spanish who controlled the Mississippi Valley rather than their fellow countrymen on the other side of the Allegheny Mountains. Washington was familiar with the positive impact on commerce and manufacturing of the ever-expanding network of canals in Great Britain. He hoped that a similar system built across Virginia could link Tidewater with Ohio, while stimulating the growth and development of the communities along the route from the sea to the mountains and thence to the west, which was rich in fertile soil and minerals such as coal. Using his influence to lobby prominent Virginia politicians, Washington enjoyed the satisfaction of learning in January 1785 that the General Assembly had chartered the James River Company whose purpose was to link eastern Virginia with the Ohio River. The initial phase included the construction of a canal system with locks around the falls of the James near Richmond. It was the first such construction in the United States, predating the Erie Canal in New York State by 30 years. In 1791, during his first term in office, President Washington sailed through the lower canal in a James River bateau.[2]

Fifty-five years separated the chartering of the James River Company in 1785 and the arrival of the first canal boat in Lynchburg in 1840, and 30 of those years saw the national economy either in recession or depression, factors that surely had a profound effect on the progress of realizing George Washington's vision. The terminus of the first phase was opened in the Great Basin in the heart of Richmond in 1800, but the work that had begun with such promise was not continued when the national economy slipped into recession two years later. Finally, the James River and Kanawha Canal Company was chartered by the General Assembly in 1832, replacing the James River Company, which quickly faded into history. With the completion of the James River–Kanawha Canal to the wharves of Lynchburg in 1840, commerce between the capital and the heart of the commonwealth quickened, but another mode of transport already had captured the attention of the political and commercial leaders of Virginia—the steam locomotive.

With the enthusiastic support of the voters, the Lynchburg and

New River Railroad was incorporated on April 5, 1831, only to be killed by the canal faction in the General Assembly the following year.[3] It took 18 years of pressure and lobbying from central and western Virginia, until finally in 1848, the General Assembly chartered the Lynchburg and Tennessee Railway; however, the following year, the politicians in Richmond changed its name to the Virginia and Tennessee.[4] The first locomotive arrived in Lynchburg in 1852, and by 1856, there was regular service to Bristol, Virginia. During the Civil War, this rail line became vital for the shipment of supplies, soldiers, the wounded, and POWs. In 1854, the Southside Railway reached Lynchburg, thus linking the Hill City to Richmond via Petersburg, and in 1860, the Orange and Alexandria Railway gave freight and passengers access to the entire railroad system of the northeast. From Charlottesville, it was possible to access the Virginia Central Railway. Its eastern terminal was Richmond and Covington its western terminal. This line provided an alternate link to the capital and access to the entire lower Shenandoah Valley. These multiple rail connections served Lynchburg well. Lynchburg became a city in 1852 and, within three years, was the second wealthiest community in the United States. Its fortunes were built on the sale and processing of tobacco, which in all its forms garnered $3 million per annum, and per-capita wealth was $1,623.31.[5] Within five years, the secession crisis placed all this progress in jeopardy, but for Lynchburg, 1855 was a banner year not easily forgotten.

In 1805, John Lynch donated a 60-foot lot for a courthouse on the crest of the hill that rose above the site of the 1757 ferry landing. Completed in 1813, the modest two-story brick structure, which measured 24' × 40',[6] was adequate to the purpose and pleasing in its simplicity to the devout Quakers who approved it. However, there was one slight problem: it was built outside the corporate limits of the town. To ensure that all the cases heard in the town's courthouse were legally binding, the General Assembly allowed Lynchburg to annex its own courthouse on February 9, 1813.[7] Forty years later, Lynchburg citizens wanted something better. A courthouse of weathered brick with a wooden addition to the second floor propped with slender columns might do for a frontier community, but Lynchburg was now a city that needed a seat of justice worthy of its new status.

The March 19, 1853, edition of the *Lynchburg Daily Virginian* announced that the proposal of Andrew Ellison, Jr., had been chosen as the design for the new courthouse.[8] The following month, the Common Council authorized the razing of the old courthouse and the

Chapter 1. Tobacco City

construction of the new one on the same site. Andrew Ellison was the principal assistant engineer of the Virginia and Tennessee Railroad, and although his concept was chosen, it was his brother William S. Ellison who was ultimately credited with the finished project, which is an impressive example of the vernacular classicism that was so popular in the antebellum South. The portico features four massive, fluted Doric columns surmounted by an unadorned entablature and pediment. This simplest of the Greek orders of architecture symbolized strength and masculinity. Some citizens who had received an education based on the classics embraced the notion that the site of the courthouse was Lynchburg's acropolis, and Ellison's masterpiece was its Parthenon—that perfect representation of the Doric order. While Greece, particularly Athens, was regarded by the educated elite as the birthplace of democracy, they also admired the virtues of the early Roman Republic, and so Ellison crowned his creation with a Roman-style dome supporting a cupola resting on eight slender Ionic columns, symbolizing grace and femininity. The main structure was built of brick covered with a layer of stucco, which was scored and painted to resemble large sandstone blocks. The interior was spacious, modern, functional, and beautiful.

By 1850, the congregation of St. Paul's Episcopal Church had outgrown their red brick building constructed in 1826 on the south corner of 7th and Church streets. It was razed and replaced by a much larger church in the fashionable neo–Perpendicular Gothic style as interpreted by the same architect, William S. Ellison.[9] One of the elements from the old church not incorporated into the new structure was a large clock. Over the decades, it had become the town clock, and when the plans for the new courthouse were made public, a number of citizens suggested that it be taken out of storage[10] and set in the pediment of the new courthouse. The building committee objected because it was too big and might destroy the symmetry of the design, but public opinion forced them to change their vote.[11]

In the 19th century, it was fashionable to link towns and cities to ancient sites. The capital of the future Roman Empire was born on the bank of the Tiber River; Lynchburg had its genesis on the bank of the James River. Rome was the City of Seven Hills, and so one of Lynchburg's nicknames became the Hill City. While local pundits delighted in using attributions familiar to those schooled in the classics to describe their new seat of justice, they conveniently ignored the fact that like the architectural monuments of the ancient world, Lynchburg's new courthouse was for the most part created by slave labor.

There were a number of private schools in Lynchburg where those who could afford the tuition and fees might send their children, but there was no institution of higher education closer than Charlottesville, Hollins, Lexington, Salem, or Staunton where Lynchburg's sons and daughters could complete their education. A canal, railroads, new churches, elegant private homes, and a new courthouse were certainly symbols of status, but Lynchburg also needed a college. In 1855, that dream became a reality but under very unusual circumstances.

With its charter, Madison College, located in Uniontown, Pennsylvania, also received the assets of Union Academy, which had been founded in 1792.[12] In 1841, the Cumberland Presbyterian Church accepted jurisdiction over the college from the Methodist Episcopal Church.[13] One important goal of the new administration and faculty was that Madison College become a bridge over the growing chasm that separated the North and the South. With that in mind, professors and students from the South, especially from Virginia, were actively and successfully recruited. In 1852, the hierarchy of the Cumberland Presbyterian Church decided to devote their energy and the funds of the church to Allegheny College, a Presbyterian institution founded in Meadville, Pennsylvania, in 1815.[14] That same year, the Methodist Protestant Church assumed control of Madison College, which was described as "flourishing."[15]

However, the northern branch of the Methodist Protestant Church, organized in 1828, was aggressively opposed to slavery. Faculty members and students from the South as well as parents began to fear that Madison College might follow the example of Oberlin College in Ohio, which had admitted Black students in 1835 and women in 1841. Shortly after the end of the 1855 academic session, an unfounded rumor began to circulate that a wealthy Pittsburgh merchant who was a devout member of the Methodist Protestant Church was ready to make a large contribution to Madison College if the administration agreed to admit Black students.[16] Believing that the racial integration of the college was only a matter of time, five professors—including Samuel K. Cox, DD, a Yale graduate and president of the college—and 88 students decided to leave Uniontown and found a college below the Mason-Dixon line.[17] This action quickly led to the demise of the college, and in 1858, the sheriff of Fayette County, Pennsylvania, sold what was left of the physical assets of Madison College at a public auction.[18]

For over 165 years, local historians have assumed Lynchburg was chosen as the location of the new college because of its climate,

Chapter 1. Tobacco City

its transportation system, and the generous support of the Methodist Protestant Church, but they have ignored the prime reason for the pro-southern exodus from Madison College—racial integration was illegal in Virginia. Dr. Cox also chose Lynchburg because of his friendship with the Rev. Alexander Doniphan who was the pastor of a local church during the early 1850s and eventually spent the rest of his life in the Hill City.[19] Editor Charles Button used the pages of his *Lynchburg Daily Virginian* to lobby support for a college in central Virginia. When Cox and his faculty arrived in Lynchburg in July and began to negotiate with local leaders about the feasibility of opening a college for men in the fall of 1855, they met with an enthusiastic public response as well as the promise of backing from the Methodist Protestant Church. The business community also reacted favorably; in other Virginia communities, a college had proven to be a financial asset because it fostered growth and brought a new source of revenue into the local economy, not to mention cultural benefits and prestige. Until buildings forming a permanent campus were erected, a recently completed three-story tenement on Court Street between 6th and 7th streets served as dormitory and academic building.[20] It was not a residential campus like VMI, and hence, day students from Lynchburg and the surrounding counties who lived at home or with relatives in the city were welcome to enroll.

Button gave Dr. Cox the opportunity to use the pages of the *Lynchburg Daily Virginian*, and the latter wasted no time making his case for opening a college in Lynchburg, outlining a curriculum to prepare young men to enter college as well as courses that led to a bachelor of arts or bachelor of science degree. He needed $20,000 to construct a building containing 15 large classrooms, 36 dormitory rooms for faculty and students, a mess hall, a chapel, and quarters on campus for the college steward.[21] He also requested $10,000 for general expenses. Despite these financially ambitious proposals, enthusiasm for the project was high. Alexander Doniphan, working with William W. Walker, a prominent Methodist layman, secured the funds in cash and pledges in one week.[22] This permitted Lynchburg College, the first college sponsored by the Methodist Protestant Church south of the Mason-Dixon line,[23] to open on October 1, 1855. The General Assembly granted Lynchburg College its charter on December 17, 1855.

The first graduation at Lynchburg College was held on June 25, 1856, and the following day, the cornerstone for the main college building was laid by the members of Marshal Lodge #39, A.F. & A.M.[24] In March 1856, Cralle Place, two plots of land just outside the city limits, was purchased as the site for the main campus of Lynchburg College. "College Hill," as it is still known, was bordered by 10th, Floyd, 11th, and Wise streets. The architect of the building was James T. Murfee, professor of mathematics and natural science and head of the School of Design. He had graduated first in the class of 1853 at VMI and was a student while the buildings designed by Alexander Davis Jackson were still under construction in Lexington.[25] Finished in the summer of 1857, Murfee's Gothic revival academic block on College Hill was conceived to honor his alma mater and A.D. Jackson. During the war, it served as one of the main hospitals for soldiers from both armies—an architectural mirror of the main building on the campus in Lexington, which was burned in June 1864.

The Panic of 1857 sent shock waves through the financial structure of the United States. It was true that the South recovered quicker than the other segments of the nation, but the holdings of the four banks in Lynchburg as well as the portfolios of the city's wealthiest citizens were diversified, and a deepening recession was not the time to make donations to a newly chartered college. With the secession of Virginia from the Union in April 1861, Lynchburg College closed its doors as most of its students marched off to war.[26] Thirty-two years passed before college classes were offered again in Lynchburg with the opening of Randolph-Macon Woman's College and 58 years before the name Lynchburg College was heard again. Old Lynchburg College did not survive in part because many of its students and faculty members supported secession. The second Lynchburg College was founded in 1903 by Josephus and Sarah LaRue Hopwood as Virginia Christian College. Supported by the Disciples of Christ Church, its name was changed in 1919 to Lynchburg College. Ninety-nine years later, it became the University of Lynchburg. Josephus Hopwood was a Union veteran who had been a POW twice. He espoused coeducation, inclusion, temperance, and that Christian education was the "hope of the world."[27]

Springhill Cemetery was opened on October 18, 1855.[28] The previous year, a group of interested citizens led by Bishop John Early had purchased a large tract of land on the New London Road just outside the city limits and formed an association to establish a new burying ground since they assumed that two graveyards inside the city limits were not large enough to accommodate future interments. They also had another motive: the City Cemetery, which was a gift from John Lynch, was as old fashioned as the courthouse he had endowed with land, and the 30-year-old Presbyterian Cemetery was also passé. Scottish-born

Chapter 1. Tobacco City

architect John Notman had set the standard for cemetery design in 1832 with one of his first commissions, Philadelphia's Laurel Hill Cemetery, and in 1847, Notman designed the Hollywood Cemetery along the bank of the James River in Richmond. Lynchburg also needed a "garden cemetery," and on April 2, 1855, Notman was engaged to design it. Springhill Cemetery was yet another symbol of Lynchburg's arrival as a major urban center in the commonwealth.

In 1830, Anne Royall, regarded by many as the first American female journalist, visited Lynchburg. The indomitable Mrs. Royall, who was known for her candor as well as her anticlericalism, took Lynchburg to task for its plethora of churches and ministers, but she was captured by its beauty. "What distinguishes the scenery of Lynchburg, from any I have met with is, that such a number of images are drawn within so narrow a compass. The rough, the smooth, the sublime and the beautiful are thickly mingled, and combines every catalogue of the picturesque, and the fanciful. Whether we regard the boldness of the figures, or the variety they assume from different points, it certainly is the most finished picture of spontaneous, or studied beauty, to be met with perhaps in the world; and appeals most powerfully to the feelings."[29] Mrs. Royall used the printed word to express what the leaders of business and government wanted the rest of the country to learn about Lynchburg, and the renowned German artist Edward Beyer captured that beauty. In the summer of 1855, he completed the drawings for his panoramic view of Lynchburg from the Amherst side of the James River, without a doubt the most important representation of antebellum Lynchburg. It was included in his *Album of Virginia*, a portfolio of 41 unbound color plates and a 40-page pamphlet published in Dresden, Saxony, between 1857 and 1858. The plate shows all the major features of Lynchburg's cityscape including perhaps the very first representation of the newly dedicated courthouse.

While celebrating the recognition of Lynchburg's beauty and prosperity, few citizens paused to recognize that slave labor had made all this possible. Nowhere was this more evident than in the tobacco industry that dominated the city's economy. In 1860, there were 45 factories in Lynchburg and neighboring Campbell County[30] where the majority of the men, women, and children engaged in fabricating various products from tobacco were slaves. Some of the skilled jobs were held by free Blacks, while the managerial positions were occupied by whites. The slaves who worked in the larger firms, like Saunders' tobacco factory, were the property of the owners.[31] Those proprietors who did not own

Yankees in the Hill City

Edward Beyer's 1855 panoramic view of Lynchburg from the Amherst County side of the James River (courtesy Lynchburg Museum System).

their labor force could rent slaves on a yearly lease. Those slaves who were willing to do extra labor were paid bonuses that they were allowed to keep.[32]

Lynchburg tobacco merchants were very aggressive about marketing their merchandise, especially plug tobacco, which by 1850 was preferred by working-class consumers because of its taste and convenience; it did not require fire to be enjoyed. Richmond, Petersburg, and Lynchburg were the three main manufacturing centers in Virginia for tobacco products, but by sheer volume, Lynchburg claimed the antebellum moniker "The Tobacco City."[33] In 1843, the American poet William Cullen Bryant visited a tobacco factory in Richmond where plug or chewing tobacco was being processed. It was a multistep process requiring skilled laborers who often sang hymns while they worked not merely to relieve the tedium of their repetitive tasks but also to establish a rhythm that ensured the production of a standard product.[34] In the dozens of factories in Lynchburg where all forms of chewing tobacco were fabricated, the process was the same. Snuff and smoking tobacco were also produced in Lynchburg. The city's prosperity was dependent on the worldwide tobacco trade which was based on slave labor, but Lynchburg had been both an economic and political hostage of the Richmond Junto for too long. Its place among the wealthiest cities in the nation was threatened by the looming crisis that might tear the nation apart, but either the white elite did not understand their dilemma or perhaps they were blind to it.

Chapter 1. Tobacco City

J.W. Champney's engraving "Scene in a Lynchburg Tobacco Factory" first appeared in 1875, but it could be 1855, so little had changed (from Edward Kings' *The Great South*, 1875).

Since the mid–20th century, historians have made a strong case that the Civil War was multifaceted, with not only heroes and battles, causes just or lost but numerous quandaries that threatened to tear families, communities, and states apart. The Commonwealth of Virginia was a perfect example of this impasse. The agony of deciding whether to secede or remain in the Union eventually led to the formation of the state of West Virginia in 1863, but before that event occurred, there were numerous regiments in the Union Army that were raised in Virginia, units filled with men who were born in the commonwealth, Virginians as much as their brothers in gray. On December 20, 1860, barely six weeks after Lincoln's election, when South Carolina seceded from the Union, Susan Blackford reflected the feelings of many of her fellow Lynchburgers when she wrote in her journal, "South Carolina acted before cooling time had been given her people."[35] Throughout January, the Lynchburg newspapers were filled with commentary on the forthcoming election of delegates to the special convention to be held in Richmond to discuss secession. When most eligible voters went to the polls on Saturday, February 2, Lynchburg's pro–Union candidates, John M. Speed and Charles R. Slaughter, beat their secessionist opponents by a three-to-one majority.[36]

On March 4, 1861, Abraham Lincoln was inaugurated as the 16th president of the United States without incident. The Confederate States of America was organized in Montgomery, Alabama, the following day. The hopes of the states that remained in the Union seemed to hang in the balance in Richmond. Reporters from all over the nation converged on Virginia's capital to glean what information they could from the public sessions of the convention. The Lynchburg papers faithfully reported the deliberations, but their editors were not privy to the bitter debates that revealed the widening rupture between the eastern Virginia counties where slavery drove the economy and the western Virginia counties where it was less vital. The representatives of the future West Virginia resented the financial advantages given to slave owners. The western counties paid the difference, and they railed against it. Several times, delegates came close to duels, and at one point, former governor Henry Wise laid a loaded pistol on the podium to intimidate his audience.[37] On April 4, the secessionists forced a vote and lost 88 to 45. Eight days later on April 12, General P.G.T. Beauregard ordered the firing on Fort Sumter, which was under the command of Major Robert Anderson.

It was not the attack on the unfinished fort in Charleston's harbor but President Lincoln's call for 75,000 volunteers to crush the rebellion that led to Virginia's departure from the Union. Governor John Letcher refused the president's request for 2,340 soldiers, although the western counties mustered far more than that number to wear Union blue. On April 17, the convention delegates voted 88 to 55 to submit to the voters on May 23 a resolution proposing separation from the Union. It was a mere formality; only the western part of Virginia offered any real opposition to it. On April 22, a mass meeting held in Clarksburg led to the first session of the Wheeling Convention on May 13; the western counties had taken the first steps toward the formation of the state of West Virginia in July 1863. The protection of slavery and a false perception that Virginia shared a special kinship with the states of the Lower South had finally ended the agony of indecision. Virginia's reward was the designation of Richmond as the capital of the Confederacy; the price it paid for that "honor" was the loss of West Virginia and becoming the major battleground.

At the time of John Brown's raid on Harpers Ferry, militia units had been formed in most Virginia communities, and Lynchburg was no exception. Almost immediately after the news of the convention's final vote reached Lynchburg, members of the local militia, which included students and faculty from Lynchburg College, prepared for the attack on the "Yankee capital." Poignantly, many of their grandfathers had

Chapter 1. Tobacco City

marched north to save Washington City from the British; now their generation hoped to help capture it for the Confederacy. Males under the age of 18 were expected to aid their elders over the age of 45 in defending their city, while all men between 18 and 45—unless they purchased a substitute—were expected to enlist. It is ironic that all over Virginia, there were units named in honor of Henry Wise, who had successfully accomplished what John Brown had failed to do—seize the federal arsenal at Harpers Ferry illegally before Virginia seceded from the Union; thus technically, he too committed an act of treason.[38]

These local militia units were equipped fully and had been training for 18 months—in short, they were ready to march. On April 22, three Lynchburg companies were ordered to report to Richmond the following day to aid in the defense of Virginia. Unfortunately, some recruits did not possess the basic kit needed for service, but the women of Lynchburg quickly supplied the items that were lacking.[39] In addition to a rifle, a soldier's ideal kit consisted of a gray sack coat and trousers, two blankets, three gray flannel shirts, two pairs of cotton socks, two pairs of cotton underpants, a pair of shoes, a pair of boots, and various toiletries. Except for the fancy battle shirts worn by the members of the home guard, the uniforms produced by Nat Guggenheimer, a Lynchburg haberdasher, were adequate for a summer campaign.[40]

In his 1900 history, *Lynchburg and Its People*, W. Aubrey Christian described the events of Tuesday, April 23, through the veil of sentiment that was so much a part of the lost cause. Surrounded by their friends and loved ones, the volunteers listened to a sermon by the Rev. Jacob D. Mitchell, minister of Second Presbyterian Church, who was known for his extreme secessionist views. Although it was expected that he must encourage them to trust in God and be brave, his frequent references to the necessity to preserve and defend the institution of slavery sounded a discordant note to an otherwise solemn and ennobling event.[41] Far more telling was the entry William M. Blackford made in his diary on that date, the warmest of the season: "There was scarcely a dry eye to be seen. I certainly thought none the less of our gallant men when I saw their cheeks moistened by manly tears. I had my confidence in their courage even increased.... The cars were very uncomfortable, and wanted air; they were only box cars, and the men soon ventilated them by knocking out the planks. It was shameful to put them in such boxes. It was a scene never seen here before, and I hope will never be witnessed again."[42] Ironically, that is how the first Union POWs arrived in Lynchburg in June 1862. When the Lynchburg recruits reached

Richmond late in the afternoon of April 23, they found intolerable living arrangements—vermin-infested lodgings, leaking tents, and spoiled food. While the soldiers faced the challenges of army life, their families tried to meet the difficulties of separation.

To encourage men to enlist in the army, the city council offered to any man who formed a company of one hundred $1,000 to supply their needs. The flood of volunteers soon exhausted the supplies of uniforms and equipment. The citizens of Lynchburg raised $20,000 to equip these new units, and Lynchburg women devoted their sewing skills to supply the needed uniforms, shirts, socks, underwear, blankets, and even tents. They sewed and knitted at home, but the center of their activities was the Masonic Hall at the corner of 9th and Church streets where they worked from dawn to dark.[43]

On May 23, Virginians overwhelmingly voted for secession; the vote in Lynchburg was 1,486 in favor. Although there were no negative votes cast, the total was 102 less than in the presidential election the previous November. The secret ballot was not in general use in the United States until the end of the 19th century; therefore, even though there were obviously a number of eligible voters who opposed secession, many fearing retribution either did not vote or cast their ballots for leaving the Union.

Once Virginia officially joined the Confederacy, soldiers from all over the South began to pour into the Hill City. Two camps, one for Virginians and the other for all other soldiers, were created as the population of the city seemed to double overnight. Camp Davis, which was close to the city's center, accommodated both officers and soldiers from Virginia. Temporary buildings were erected for the officers, while enlisted men spent their first nights in tents. Sleeping quarters were later built to house them and those who followed over the next four years. Similar arrangements were made at the Fair Ground, which was on the outskirts of the city where soldiers from all over the Confederacy ate, slept, and trained.

The presence of large numbers of soldiers in Lynchburg put a tremendous strain on the city's resources. Within a few weeks, food was in short supply, and from time to time, these shortages were a problem until the end of the war. In some cases, residents simply lived without certain commodities or they made substitutions for products no longer obtainable. However, there were other difficulties—most notably crime—that the city fathers had not envisioned when they welcomed the "Boys in Gray" to make Lynchburg their temporary home.

Chapter 1. Tobacco City

Many soldiers on both sides were from rural backgrounds, unused to urban life and the many temptations it held. Lynchburg's police force dated from 1806, but its officers were unable to stem the increase in violence, which began in May 1861. Robberies were an everyday occurrence. Before an incident could be reported and investigated, the felon was often miles from the scene. Most thefts were committed at night—in fact, the streets were almost devoid of civilians after dark. Homes were also targeted by soldiers seeking food and small articles that they could sell once they were on the march. Then there was the problem of Buzzard's Roost.

Located on what is now Jefferson Street and extending to the edge of the canal was a collection of brothels, gambling dens, and saloons that had catered to locals for years. Suddenly, a flood of young men just entering their prime, far from home for the first time, and ready to succumb to a variety of attractions flooded the Buzzard. Public drunkenness became almost epidemic, and the officers in charge of these men either could not control them or joined them in the district that slowly slinked up the hills above the river and spilled onto the lower end of Main Street. Local ministers preached against the tide of vice, but that was not enough. Once one group of soldiers left the city bound for the battlefields of Virginia, another took its place, and the cycle began all over again. The pleasures to be experienced in Lynchburg were reported far and wide—it was a "liberty town" in every sense of the word.

As active recruitment continued in the city, shops began to close as their owners or managers and employees joined the army. There was a widely held belief that after one decisive battle, which would be a Confederate victory, the conflict would end. At the peace conference that followed this military triumph, Southern independence would be recognized, and life would return to normal. Between May and December 1861, there were 15 clashes between Union and Confederate forces on Virginia soil, but the most important were those that occurred in Prince William and Fairfax Counties. On July 18, 35,000 Union soldiers under Brigadier General Irvin McDowell encountered 22,000 Confederates under Brigadier General P.G.T. Beauregard, who was charged with guarding the fords of Bull Run. At Blackburn's Ford, McDowell's superior force was repulsed with a loss of 83 men. There were 68 Confederate casualties. Three days later on July 21, McDowell crossed Sudley Ford and attempted to turn the Confederate left flank located on Matthews Hill. Slowly, the Southern forces were pushed from their position as the fighting raged through the summer heat. Then, late in the afternoon, fresh Confederate reinforcements arrived, some by rail from the Shenandoah Valley. They shattered the Union right, and then the rout of McClellan's green volunteers began. Some did not stop running until they reached Washington City the following morning. It was on July 21 that General Thomas J. Jackson earned the name "Stonewall," and General Irvin McDowell lost his command. There were 2,950 Union casualties and 1,750 Confederate dead, including the first Lynchburg soldiers.[44] The *Lynchburg Daily Virginian* celebrated the victory with banner headlines, and many who read the stirring account of Southern arms hoped that this was the beginning of the end of the war, but it was not. On June 30, a bright comet appeared in the night sky, which some thought it foretold a long conflict. The failure of the Confederate Army to complete its victory by pursuing the fleeing Union forces seemed to fulfill the superstitious prophecy. In Washington, President Lincoln appointed Major General George B. McClellan as the commander of the Union Army. It would be a long and costly war, both in lives and money, and Lynchburg was beginning to pay the price of battle.

The national financial system had not fully recovered from the Panic of 1857 when the secession crisis broke in December 1860, and the effectiveness of the Union blockade of the Atlantic coast, which began in April 1861, immediately had an adverse effect on the Southern economy. Until 1857, the U.S. government permitted the use of foreign gold and silver coins for all transactions. Merchants had special scales on which to weigh these pieces as well as techniques to determine their fineness, and they were more than willing to accept gold and silver in any form before it vanished from circulation. Unfortunately, the recoinage had just started when the Civil War began.[45] Gold coins—the perfect hedge against inflation—vanished from circulation first, then the silver coins, and finally, the new copper-nickel cents.

When Virginia joined the Confederacy, all U.S. postage stamps and coins were no longer legal instruments of exchange. The stamps were only paper, and it was easy to substitute Confederate versions of the most useful denominations. Coinage was another matter. Bullion supplies seemingly vanished overnight, forcing the three mints in the South to close. Those at Charlotte, North Carolina, and Dahlonega, Georgia, which only struck gold coins, would never reopen, while new coins bearing the New Orleans mint mark would not reappear until 1892. On October 25, 1861, the Lynchburg City Council authorized the printing of $50,000 worth of paper notes. Since the Confederate government permitted state and local governments to print their own money, counterfeiting quickly became a major problem fueling the inflation that was already eroding the Confederate dollar.[46] Many Union soldiers were armed not only with weapons that could fire but also with fake Confederate bills to weaken the Southern economy. In April 1861, the exchange rate of the Confederate dollar was $0.95 to its U.S. counterpart; by April 1865, it was worth only $0.33.

As the holiday season of 1861 approached, some of the churches in Lynchburg offered their bells for the war effort. Bronze was in great demand as supplies of strategic metals dwindled. The gift of the bells was welcomed by the local firm of F.B. Deane and Son, which was engaged in making shot and shells. In Lynchburg, there was little to celebrate that first Christmas of the war. There were 3,000 sick and wounded soldiers in the military hospitals and private homes. Each day, the Diuguid wagons carried the dead to the City Cemetery. One-tenth of the white male population of Lynchburg was in uniform—either in the Silver Grays who assisted in preserving public order or in the regular army. The trickle of Union POWs who had shuffled from one Lynchburg railroad depot to another was about to become a flood.

Chapter 2

The Decline of Richmond

The 1850s was a decade of growth and prosperity for the city of Richmond. The discovery of gold in California in January 1848 had a positive effect on many major urban centers of the United States, including Richmond whose citizens now considered it to be the cultural and economic capital of the Upper South, not just the Commonwealth of Virginia. As the end of the first year of the decade approached, the Richmond elite were more concerned about obtaining tickets to the concert by Jenny Lind on December 20 than unpleasant matters like fugitive slaves, abolitionists, sectional tensions, or potential POWs. Those tribulations were part of Christmases yet to come; in 1850, Richmond's future was as bright as the streetlights outside the Marshall Theater where "The Swedish Nightingale" was to perform.[1]

In the 1850s, Richmond's population grew by 10,430, or an increase of 37.5 percent. There was, however, another side to the flood of gold that fueled the U.S. economy from 1848 to 1857. Signed on July 4, 1848, the Treaty of Guadalupe Hidalgo, which ended the war between the United States and the Republic of Mexico, ceded a vast domain that stretched from the Rio Grande River to the Pacific Ocean, and the question of whether to permit slavery to be introduced into this new territory threatened to tear apart the republic.

The provisions of the first Fugitive Slave Act of 1793 were circumvented in a number of ways or ignored altogether because implementation was delegated to the states. Runaway slaves who crossed into a free state were usually safe and could be absorbed into the free Black population. The revised Fugitive Slave Act, which was a key component of the Compromise of 1850, placed the responsibility for enforcement on the federal government. Then Canada or Mexico became the only safe destinations for slaves who dared to make the perilous journey to freedom. Richmond newspapers regularly ran detailed advertisements offering rewards for the capture and return of escaped slaves. Although

Chapter 2. The Decline of Richmond

the most heavily traveled routes of the Underground Railroad passed through central and western Virginia, many slaves escaping from Tidewater passed through or near Richmond on their way to Cincinnati, Ohio—the "Grand Central Station" of the Underground Railroad. That route was made even more perilous by the bounty hunters who used every means at their disposal to capture every African American they could find. They were aided by spies and informers who were rewarded for their treachery.

During the Virginia Constitutional Convention of 1850–51, the rupture between eastern and western Virginia widened as the slave-owning elite of Tidewater and the Piedmont were able to strip the state of its statutory right to manumit slaves as well as forbidding owners to free their own slaves. Thus, in Virginia, manumission was illegal after 1851. The western counties where slavery was rare were forced by the new constitution to bear a larger part of the state tax burden because, for assessment purposes, slaves were permanently undervalued since the U.S. Constitution counted each slave as only three-fifths of a person. Thomas Jefferson had advocated a system of public education, only to have the concept vetoed by the General Assembly on the excuse of its potential cost. In the 1850s sessions of the General Assembly, it was rebuffed yet again, therefore maintaining a permanent underclass of poor unschooled whites. The use of the secret ballot was also prohibited, leaving voters open to intimidation, if not physical harm. Consequently, the approval of the new constitution in October 1851 by a margin of eight to one was no surprise, nor was the smoldering antipathy between the two Virginias.

Before 1870, education in Virginia was a privilege, not a right. Only those who could afford an education received one, and only a small percentage of those persons—almost entirely white men—attended a college or university.[2] White laborers were dependent on their social superiors for their knowledge of national politics and policies. When they were told that their way of life was under attack, many believed it because they had no other frame of reference. What was actually at risk was the lifestyle of the privileged slave owners who dominated the political establishment of the Old Dominion. The white laboring class also was constantly reminded by their "betters" of the threat that emancipation meant to their livelihood and social status. Already in competition with free Blacks, they were persuaded to risk their lives to defend slavery, which was supposedly ordained by God. Most of the wealthy citizens of Richmond did not concern themselves with squabbles in

Congress or the General Assembly; for them, life was good, and that was all that mattered. The shops of the capital were filled with the best merchandise from home and abroad, Richmond's theaters and concert halls catered to all levels of society, and its excellent rail and canal systems meant the wonders of the wider world could be secured by a ticket. Then, in the fall of 1859, Southern complacency received a shock from which it never recovered.

Late on Sunday, October 16, 1859, rumors began to spread along the valleys of western Virginia that the federal arsenal at Harpers Ferry was under attack. John Brown, an abolitionist from Connecticut who was implicated in the 1856 "Pottawatomie massacre" in Kansas,[3] and 22 heavily armed raiders sought to seize the arms and supplies stored there to support a slave uprising across the South. Only 28 years had passed since Nat Turner and his fellow slaves had spread fire and blood across Southampton County, Virginia, before they were stopped. Many feared that this village at the junction of the Potomac and Shenandoah rivers could be the site of another insurrection. This act of civil disobedience was crushed by October 18. U.S. Marines led by Lieutenant Israel Greene under the command of Colonel Robert E. Lee recaptured the arsenal. In the hard-fought engagement, one Marine was killed and one was wounded. Eight members of the Maryland Militia also were wounded. Ten of the raiders were killed, seven—including Brown—were arrested, and five escaped. Charged with treason, murder, and attempting to incite a slave rebellion, Brown and his fellow raiders were placed under the guard of two West Point graduates, Thomas Jackson and Jeb Stuart, both of whom within two years entered the Confederate Army.

An editorial published in the *Richmond Enquirer* on October 25, 1859, argued that although thwarted, Brown's raid had succeeded in advancing the cause of disunion. The writer laid the blame for this unwarranted attack on Virginia soil on "Black Republican Ossawattomites of the North," and he used the term "Confederacy" three times in his opinion piece.[4] Stirred by such language, men all over Virginia began hastily organizing militia units to counter the next slave rebellion which never occurred. In October 1859, the nation stood at a crossroads, and its fate was, in a sense, in the hands of the governor of Virginia, Henry Alexander Wise. Brown was found guilty on November 2 and sentenced to death. Governor Wise could have commuted Brown's sentence and committed him to an asylum where he would have been lost to history, but instead, he chose to hang him and further divide public opinion. According to Virginia law, a full month was required to elapse

Chapter 2. The Decline of Richmond

before a convicted felon could be executed. Governor Wise ordered that the execution be set for December 2, and on that date, Brown was hanged. The vehement abolitionist whom most Southerners regarded as a monster had now become a martyr to many in the North.

Almost 80 years separated the Battle of Yorktown from the firing on Fort Sumter, and most Americans had forgotten the hardships associated with a protracted conflict. There had been wars and rumors of wars during those eight decades, but they were brief and waged for the most part by professional soldiers and sailors. Few citizens, either North or South, were prepared for the final crisis that led to the Civil War, as it began to accelerate with South Carolina's secession on December 20, 1860. A week later, Fort Moultrie was evacuated, and its garrison moved to the unfinished Fort Sumter in Charleston Harbor. When the first attempt to resupply Fort Sumter failed, President Buchanan's response was to call for a National Day of Prayer and Fasting to be observed on January 4, 1861. South Carolina's secession started a domino effect. Between January 9 and February 1, 1861, Mississippi, Florida, Alabama, Georgia, Louisiana, and Texas left the Union while Virginia hesitated.

Encouraged by the fact Virginians were discussing the possibility of secession in public meetings and in the press, the "Richmond Junto," that powerful alliance of slaveholders from eastern Virginia and the Piedmont, was able to pressure the Virginia General Assembly to call a convention in the New Year to decide whether Virginia should secede from the Union, resolve the question of how the state would be governed in case of an emergency, and fashion a new constitution to replace the one approved only a decade earlier. Most of the delegates from every county and independent city were elected by the beginning of February, and when the statewide results were made public, it was obvious that the majority were Unionists.

Facing the probable defeat of their carefully crafted plan, the secessionist minority quickly fell under the spell of former governor Henry A. Wise who assumed the leadership of their faction. Wise had already organized a counterconvention of young hotheads who were willing to use intimidation to overwhelm the duly elected representatives of the people if they failed to endorse secession.[5] Over the next two months, Wise would lie, use pressure, coercion, and the threat of mob violence, as well as break the same laws that sent John Brown to the scaffold to force Virginia to leave the Union, sure in the knowledge that his successor, Governor John Letcher, would do what he was told to do—even pardoning treason.

Early in the deliberations, three commissioners from the newly formed Confederate Congress arrived in Richmond to address the convention. It is also possible that during their stay in Virginia, they discussed with Wise and the other leaders of the Virginia secessionists the possibility of moving the capital of the Confederacy from Montgomery, Alabama, to Richmond. Wise was a politician and not noted for his altruism. If Virginia were going to risk its future by joining the Confederate States of America, the least its sons could demand that the capital of the new nation be Richmond.

It was not the attack on the unfinished fort in Charleston's harbor but rather President Lincoln's call for 75,000 volunteers to crush the rebellion that led to Virginia's departure from the Union. Governor Letcher refused the president's request for 2,340 soldiers. On April 17, the convention delegates voted 88 to 55 to submit to the voters on Thursday, May 23, a resolution proposing separation from the Union. It was a mere formality; only the western part of Virginia offered any serious opposition. On April 22, a mass meeting held in Clarksburg was followed by the first session of the Wheeling Convention on May 13, 1861, which would lead to the creation of West Virginia on June 20, 1863. The protection of slavery and a false perception that Virginia shared a special kinship with the states of the Lower South had finally ended the agony of indecision.

Despite the fact that Richmond was seriously overcrowded, some Confederate bureaucrats decided that all potential Union POWs would be sent to the capital, to be held there until they could be paroled and exchanged. Because the first battlefield engagements were in Virginia and the city was a railroad hub, initially it seemed a good idea. By 1860, five lines serviced Richmond, which was also the terminal point of the still-unfinished James River–Kanawha Canal. Those in authority also endorsed the widely held belief that one decisive Confederate victory would mean peace and Southern independence. With the conflict at an end and life returned to normal, the few POWs in Confederate custody would be free to return home. In the months between Virginia's secession and the first major battle in July, there were a number of skirmishes in which prisoners were taken and exchanged on the spot—a circumstance that seemed to confirm the assumption that captured enemy soldiers would not pose a challenge for the fledgling republic. When the first Union POWs arrived in Richmond early in July, they were regarded more as a curiosity than a threat.[6] By the end of the month, however, they had become a potential logistical problem, and the man who might

Chapter 2. The Decline of Richmond

have a solution to that difficulty already had arrived in Richmond in June.

Born in 1800, John Henry Winder was the son of Brigadier General William H. Winder, whose failure to stop the British at the Battle of Bladensburg led to the burning of Washington in August 1814. Young Winder entered West Point that same year, but his father's debacle haunted his own mediocre career until its end. Graduating in 1820 as a second lieutenant, Winder learned that promotions were rare in peacetime. He left the army in 1823, but financial problems forced him to reenter it in 1827 at his previous rank. While serving as an instructor in tactics at West Point during the 1827–1828 session, he met two cadets who profoundly influenced his later career—Jefferson Davis and Robert E. Lee. Unfortunately, Winder's bad temper cost him his place at West Point in the summer of 1828, and he was reassigned to the artillery. Finally, by 1842, he earned the rank of captain. During the Mexican-American War, he received two brevet promotions for bravery—major and lieutenant colonel—but at war's end, he reverted to the rank of captain. While on medical leave in January 1861, Winder finally was promoted to the rank of major. Three months later, he resigned from the U.S. Army[7] and applied for a commission from North Carolina where he lived. All he was offered was a colonelcy in an infantry regiment. Insulted, Winder, the artilleryman, headed to Richmond.

After meeting with President Davis on April 20, he received the rank of brigadier general and the next day he was appointed assistant inspector general of the camps of instruction.[8] Winder was a soldier, not a bureaucrat, but this did not stop Davis from assigning him one new job after another, including the supervision of captive Union soldiers. In 1861, the average life expectancy for a white male was 40, and John Winder was a 61-year-old man who had recently recovered from a serious illness—not the feisty young instructor Davis remembered from his student days. This was the moment for which Winder had waited for his entire military career and he did not intend to let ill health and a lack of administrative experience jeopardize this chance to add luster to the Winder name. He relentlessly drove himself to justify Jefferson Davis' faith in him until February 6, 1865, when he suffered a fatal heart attack.

Winder moved swiftly to assemble all the Union soldiers who had been allowed to remain free in Richmond on their own recognizance and placed them under guard in the recently requisitioned Harwood's tobacco factory at the corner of Main and 26th streets. With the arrival of the prisoners taken at the first Battle of Bull Run on July 21, more buildings were secured to house them, including Liggon and Company's tobacco factory at the corner of Main and 25th streets.[9] Among their number were civilians trapped behind Confederate lines in the commotion that followed the battle. Alfred Ely, a Republican member of the U.S. House of Representatives for the 29th New York Congressional District, which included the city of Rochester, was in confinement until December 25, 1861. His journal is the most detailed record of the evolution of the treatment of Union prisoners during the first months of the war.

In the introduction to his memoir, Ely explained how he became embroiled in the battle. The Thirteenth New York Volunteer Infantry Regiment—the Rochester Regiment—had been involved in the skirmish at Blackford's Ford on July 18,[10] and when Ely learned that seven men in that unit had been wounded, he could not resist the temptation to visit them and witness the impending battle that might put an end to the rebellion.[11] Instead, he was taken prisoner in the melee that followed the Union defeat and shipped by train to Richmond with hundreds of captured officers and enlisted men. Their first night was spent in temporary quarters under heavy guard while the Liggon's factory was prepared.

Ely's initial impression of Winder was favorable, after the general visited the prisoners on the following morning, July 24, to assure them that they would be moved to new quarters before the end of the day, as well as promising that the guards were forbidden to fire at anyone going to look out of a window. Winder might vow that the guards were barred from using prisoners for target practice, but nonetheless, it soon became almost routine. Late in the afternoon, imprisoned officers were herded into the first floor of Liggon's factory in the area facing the James River. Although opened, the windows were barred. The rest of the large room was filled with machinery and guards. The remaining two stories held enlisted men. There was no furniture in the room, and therefore, there was nowhere to sleep but on the floor.

Over breakfast the next morning, the officers formed the Richmond Prison Association, organized themselves into messes, and pooled their resources to buy useful items until they were exchanged. In the midst of this activity, another civilian inmate captured after the battle joined them. Calvin Huson, Jr., was a district attorney for the city of Rochester and a friend of Alfred Ely. Both men considered themselves POWs, when in fact they were bargaining chips to effect a possible exchange. After inspecting Liggon's on August 5, Lieutenant David H.

Chapter 2. The Decline of Richmond

Todd,[12] who was the direct overseer of all Union prisoners in Richmond, acting on orders from General Winder, dismissed the enlisted men who were servers at the various officers' messes and informed the remaining inmates to prepare to move again, this time to Howard's warehouse next door.[13]

Here, there were makeshift tables and benches as well as a tin plate and cup for each man. Luckily, the prisoners were able to purchase flatware and bedding. Ely specifically mentioned buying a cot for $5.[14] Using their combined resources, they supplemented their regular rations with milk and other groceries. These purchases were made by one or two officers who gave their word of honor to return. The enlisted men resumed their duties cleaning their officers' quarters and serving their meals. The officers bought Richmond newspapers[15] and were permitted to send and receive letters, which were censored. The major factories and warehouses in Richmond were supplied with gas, water, and urinal troughs, so the prisoners were able to cook on gas burners and bathe.[16] Ely noted in his journal that he bathed more during that summer than he had in his own home over the previous decade[17] because a cake of soap, a rough towel, and a tepid tub provided temporary relief from a hot, humid Richmond summer.

The Richmond Prison Association was formed to combat boredom with every conceivable activity from lectures, discussion groups, physical exercise, games of skill to the mastery of foreign languages. The men developed a routine that filled the day from dawn until all lights were extinguished at nine, but the question that haunted them all was the uncertainty of parole and exchange. As the weeks passed, many men became convinced that the government in Washington had forgotten them. What they did not know was that President Lincoln's advisers felt that negotiating with the representatives of the Confederate States of America over the dilemma of POWs was tantamount to recognizing that government as legitimate. Public pressure eventually forced them to do so but not in the late summer of 1861. Ely constantly discouraged talk of escaping, which might, even if it were successful, put the remaining inmates in jeopardy. Then on September 3, a rumor began to circulate among the guards, slaves, and prisoners that one of the surgeons working in the Union hospital ward had escaped. Colonel Charles A. De Villiers of the Eleventh Ohio Volunteer Infantry was the "doctor" in question, but he was not a surgeon, although he was able to convince the authorities that he was. While on parole in Richmond, he petitioned Jefferson Davis in person, asking that Union POWs be treated humanely.

On September 1, the day his parole expired, he performed his regular medical duties and walked out of the prison, never to be seen again in Richmond.[18] When the De Villiers escape was confirmed, all further shopping expeditions were forbidden as were all newspapers.[19] Ely appealed to General Winder, and access to newspapers was restored the next day, and then, on September 6, a large bundle of newspapers from all over the United States was delivered to Howard's warehouse.[20]

Three days later, shortly after dawn, Captain George C. Gibbs,[21] the officer of the day, accompanied by two armed lieutenants and a police detective with a bowie knife, arrived and began a thorough search of everyone and their personal property looking for weapons. All they found were a few penknives.[22] Within 24 hours, 40 officers and 116 enlisted men were ordered to prepare for departure that afternoon for Castle Pinckney in Charleston Harbor.[23] Winder obviously intended to reverse the initial plan to keep all Union prisoners in Richmond until they were exchanged because space already was at a premium. On September 17, he visited Howard's warehouse and informed the men that a second group would be leaving Richmond shortly for Louisiana. Of greater concern to Ely was the condition of Calvin Huson, Jr., who was quite ill with what appeared to be typhoid fever. The Union surgeons still in captivity were to be released soon, and if Huson could accompany them, he might have a chance to recover with proper care. Winder interviewed him the following day and promised to submit his petition to the surgeon general. The doctors left for Norfolk on September 21 without him, and 250 men were shipped to New Orleans. Each day, Huson grew worse, and by October 5, when he received the surgeon general's rejection of his request for release, he was confined to his cot.

General Winder finally agreed to allow Huson to be moved to a private residence where he could receive constant care. Captain George Gibbs made all the arrangements, and Ely assumed Huson's expenses. On October 10, one month after he fell ill, Huson was moved to the home of Mrs. John Van Lew where he died five days later. Assisted by Gibbs, Ely then made all the arrangements for his friend's graveside service and burial in the Van Lew family plot in Shockoe Hill Cemetery in Richmond. Ely also wrote a detailed account of Huson's life from his capture to his death. Once approved by the censor, it was sent to Mrs. Ely who delivered it to Mrs. Huson. In mid–19th-century America, having a good death surrounded by family or friends was the end of life desired by all. It was to be followed by burial accompanied by the proper rites and words of comfort for the bereaved. For soldiers who died far

Chapter 2. The Decline of Richmond

from home, comrades or officers were expected to write a letter of condolence detailing the last hours of the departed hero. Ely performed this duty for Huson, but most of the Union POWs who followed him to the grave in Richmond were not so blessed. Fortunately, this was not the case in Lynchburg where the Union dead were treated with much the same respect accorded the Confederates.

On October 21, 1861, General Winder was named commander of the Department of Henrico, and true to his promise, Ely remained at Howard's warehouse saying goodbye to old friends and greeting new ones only to see them in turn leave for a prison somewhere in one of the Confederate states. On Christmas, 10 weeks after the death of his fellow hostage, Ely was released and sent home. Enlisting the help of Charles Lanman[24] as his editor, he published his journal in 1862. It is valuable for a number of reasons, not the least being the favorable impression of General Winder who, in February 1862, was named provost marshal of Richmond. The crime wave in Richmond had spiraled almost completely out of control, and with the declaration of martial law in Richmond on March 1—which included the suspension of habeas corpus and civil jurisdiction—Winder became the de facto dictator of the Confederate capital.

As early as July, at Winder's urging, the Confederate War Department began to explore the opening of an auxiliary prison somewhere in North Carolina. In Salisbury, the dilapidated Maxwell Chambers textile mill, which belonged to Davidson College, was available for $15,000. Its rail connection made it a partial solution to a growing problem, and the property was purchased on November 7. Repairing the building began at once, but it was not ready when the first prisoners arrived from Richmond a month later. On January 11, 1862, the War Department ordered newly promoted Major George C. Gibbs to assume command of the Salisbury prison and to raise several companies to provide guards for the facility. By January 30, Gibbs had put the camp in good order and created a new regiment, the Forty-Second North Carolina Volunteer Infantry, for field service. Instead, in June, this new regiment took the train from Salisbury to Petersburg, Virginia, and then changed trains for Lynchburg where they disembarked and marched to the Fair Ground. They were still under the command of newly promoted Colonel Gibbs who was acting on orders from General Winder to prepare a new auxiliary POW camp to receive the first Union captives from General Stonewall Jackson's Valley Campaign. Since the encampment for Confederate soldiers, other than Virginians, was adjacent to the POW camp, the first guards were men trained at Salisbury. Gibbs separated officers from enlisted men, and the former eventually were assigned to a vacated tobacco warehouse in the city, while the latter were held at the Fair Ground. The success of this solution influenced General Winder to commandeer Belle Isle for a similar arrangement in July 1862.

In addition to grappling with the challenge of POWs, General Winder was responsible for military and civilian malefactors. The former were usually guilty of minor offenses, while the latter were arrested for crimes both minor and major, including treason. They soon outgrew the Henrico County Jail on Main Street and were moved to Castle Godwin on Franklin Street. This was not a problem unique to Richmond. When Lynchburg's population, like that of the capital, doubled in 1861, the city jail could not hold all the remanded felons, so escapes became a regular occurrence, and the city authorities were unable to handle the problem. Winder's solution to the overcrowding was to appropriate more commercial buildings. In late October 1861, he had added Mayo's tobacco factory and Taylor's tobacco factory to Howard's warehouse for Union prisoners, but by early 1862, all three were filled to capacity. Members of General Winder's staff began to look for a larger structure in a less congested area, and they found it at the corner of 20th and Cary streets.

In 1845, John Enders, Sr., began building the first of three four-story tobacco warehouses that were to be connected, but in 1852, he was killed in a construction accident. Although the third warehouse finally was finished, the completed structure remained empty until 1854, when Luther Libby rented the entire complex from Enders' heirs. With access to the canal as well as the river, Libby and Son, ship chandlers and grocers, quickly became a thriving business, but on March 24, 1862, Libby was given only 48 hours to remove everything from the premises; two days later, the new prison was ready for its first occupants. Since the rear of Libby Prison fronted on the canal, goods and personnel could be moved without public notice. That end of Cary Street was close to the railway station, and there was less traffic than on Main Street. The three conjoined buildings were designated as East, Middle, and West, and each had a separate entrance. The hospital was located on the first floor of East, the kitchen occupied the first floor of Middle, and offices and the guard room took up the ground floor of West. Eventually, Luther Libby was allowed to operate a small grocery store in West. Initially, officers were housed on the second floor of each building while enlisted men were held on the third floor. Each of the nine rooms allotted to the

Chapter 2. The Decline of Richmond

prisoners was 45' × 105' and had both gas and water. They were unfurnished, and most of the windows, although barred, had no glass. The ceilings on the first and second floors were seven feet high, but the third story was opened up to the pitched roof and therefore better ventilated.[25] Libby Prison was built on a slope allowing for the inclusion of a basement. East building housed a carpenter's shop; Middle contained four cells for prisoners; and West accommodated the slaves who worked in the prison.

Winder's choice of the staff of Libby Prison was evidence of his lack of experience in choosing subordinates: he tended to select young men without any real military experience. Soldiers who preferred to be in the thick of battle rather than managing a prison filled with vermin-infested Yankees did not seek to be included in his pool of candidates. Unfortunately, his dilemma was exacerbated further by the low regard in which he was held by his superiors who denied him access to more qualified candidates.

Lieutenant Thomas Pratt Turner was commandant of Libby Prison; he was 21, short, slender, and acutely aware of what he considered his physical shortcomings. He matriculated at VMI in August 1858 but withdrew on April 10, 1860, to accept an appointment at the U.S. Military Academy at West Point. From July 1, 1860, until April 22, 1861, he was briefly a plebe. Supposedly, he left West Point to join the Confederate Army.[26] He was cold and at times cruel; the prisoners despised but feared him. Private Richard R. Turner (no relation), also briefly at West Point, was second in command. A former overseer who knew how to use a whip, he was designated as the prison jailer. He was large, short-tempered, and enjoyed physically abusing anyone who angered him.[27] The POWs hated him. In his memoir *Eye of the Storm*, Private Robert Knox Sneden offered a further reason for Turner's sadistic pleasure in punishing the captives in Libby Prison: "Years ago, while a cadet at West Point, he forged something, was tried and dismissed [from] the service in disgrace. He now vented his spite on all Union officers who fell in his power."[28] Briefly, Lieutenant George M. Emack was part of the Libby staff, but he transferred to field service to raise a cavalry troop in his native Maryland. As he was also noted for his cruelty, the prisoners did not regret his transfer.[29] They loathed Erasmus Ross, the obese clerk who registered prisoners and inspected their quarters every morning after roll call. He was always fully armed and accompanied by two guards who punished any prisoner who responded aggressively to Ross' verbal abuse.[30]

Doors were cut in the internal walls on the second and third floors to facilitate the guards and the cleaning crews. Thus, it was possible to go from a room in the East building to its counterpart in the West building without using the stairs or going outside the prison. All doors and windows were under 24-hour surveillance. Prisoners could be shot for pausing in a doorway or looking out of a window. In the early months of the war, the guards at Libby were young soldiers who tended to relieve their frustration by abusing the prisoners and, in some cases, using them for target practice. As the war drew to a close, older men, often members of the home guard, were assigned to Libby Prison, and they were more humane.[31] Just as life at Libby Prison settled down to a monotonous routine, the Seven Days Battles flooded Richmond with new captives in July 1862. This forced Winder to rethink completely the deposition of Union prisoners. Colonel Gibbs had produced a workable solution to the problem of overcrowding in Lynchburg, and Winder copied it.

From the upper story of Libby, it was possible to see Belle Isle, whose 54 acres had been a favorite destination before the war for those wishing to escape the summer heat. Situated at the fall line of the James River, it was a perfect place for a picnic. A footbridge connected this retreat from the noise and bustle of Richmond. The Old Dominion Iron and Nail Works owned Belle Isle, but there was no objection to its being requisitioned by the government as a prison for noncommissioned officers and enlisted men as long as the Union prisoners were restricted to the lower sandy beach. In peacetime, this beach, with its views of the Richmond skyline, attracted artists.[32] The rapids at this point were treacherous, and prisoners who tried to escape by swimming drowned. Libby was now exclusively for officers. This was thought to be only temporary because Richmond was filled with rumors that a system of parole and exchange was to be implemented by the fall, solving the POW problem.

On July 12, 1862, Secretary of War Edwin M. Stanton authorized General John A. Dix to meet with Confederate General D.H. Hill to discuss a solution to this growing challenge. The two generals met on July 17 and, using the Anglo-American Cartel of 1812 as a model, had a proposal ready to present to their respective governments the following day. The Dix-Hill Cartel was signed on July 22, and its provisions seemed reasonable and easy to implement. There was a scale for exchanges—rank for rank and a sliding scale using certain numbers of privates to redeem an officer.[33] All prisoners in the eastern theater were to be conveyed to

Chapter 2. The Decline of Richmond

Aiken's Landing on the James River—later to City Point. Vicksburg, Mississippi, was to be the exchange point in the western theater. Each government would appoint two agents to oversee the operation of the cartel. It took six weeks before the system was fully functional, but by mid–September, the exchanges were well under way. The Confederate government was particularly anxious to start the process as soon as possible. It was not merely a question of limited resources but a critical one of manpower. The population base from which Confederate soldiers were recruited was much smaller than that of the North, and therefore, the protocols governing parole and exchange were flagrantly ignored by Confederate officials and commanders. Once a Confederate soldier was freed, he was back with his unit as soon as possible. By 1862, Confederate soldiers were committed to serve as long as the war lasted, while Union soldiers had a set term limit, usually three years. Many reenlisted and received a bounty for doing so, but the federal military hierarchy was concerned that former POWs would complete their three years and then leave the service. In many cases, they were correct. However, what ultimately caused the cartel to collapse was the practice of treating captured Black Union soldiers as fugitive slaves. On July 30, 1863, President Lincoln signed General Order 252, which suspended the Dix-Hill Cartel until the Confederate government agreed to abide by all the regulations. In August, General Grant refused to reinstate the full agreement. However, in July 1862, that crisis lay far in the future, and surely General Winder hoped that the challenge to the plan expressed by President Davis might be solved through negotiation.[34] Yes, Libby was packed and Belle Isle had passed its capacity, but a satisfactory end was in sight.

By the middle of July when Dix and Hill held their first meeting, 3,000 Union soldiers were already on Belle Isle, and within a month, there were 2,000 more.[35] Rows of Sibley tents protected the inmates from the elements, although there were never enough of them to shelter all the internees. The commandant, Captain Norris Montgomery, allowed his charges to bathe in the safe shallows of the river and supplement their meager rations by purchasing food from the sutlers who clustered around the footbridge which was the entrance to the camp. Early in August, the Forty-Second North Carolina Volunteer Infantry under the command of Colonel Gibbs was assigned to the Department of North Carolina and left Lynchburg. Almost immediately, Captain Thomas Pratt Turner was transferred to the Hill City to restore order as provost marshal. Captain Henry Wirz was temporarily put in charge of the Richmond prison network, and he quickly asserted his authority. Wirz removed Captain Montgomery, whom he considered too lenient, and personally assumed command of the prison camp on Belle Isle. Swiftly, he canceled all privileges and ordered the sutlers from the premises. Under his direction, strict military procedures were observed. Luckily for the Union prisoners, by mid–September the Dix-Hill Cartel was emptying prison camps throughout the Confederacy,[36] and on September 23, 1862, Belle Isle was closed. Slaves removed the tents and temporary structures before cleaning and fumigating the areas occupied by the Union prisoners. Replaced in early October by Captain Thomas D. Jeffries, Wirz was sent throughout the South to collect and return Union prisoners to Richmond to be exchanged. When Turner returned to Richmond later that month, Jeffries assumed the role of provost marshal in Lynchburg. Upon his return to Richmond, Wirz rejoined General Winder's advisory staff.

Once the Dix-Hill Cartel agreement was signed, Winder had to face another challenge—where to house the ever-increasing number of runaway slaves, Confederate soldiers accused of crimes, Southerners suspected of disloyalty to the Confederacy, Yankee deserters, Union spies, and women who were for the most part political prisoners. In early August, Winder appropriated a row of three factory buildings on Cary Street to create Castle Thunder. He also ordered that a gallows and a whipping post be installed behind the center building as a constant reminder to the inmates of what might happen if they dared attempt an escape or break any of the prison rules. Palmer's factory held Union deserters and eventually the overflow from Libby. Whitlock's warehouse was reserved for women and Blacks, while Gleanor's tobacco factory housed Confederate deserters and male political prisoners. To supervise this menagerie of the miserable, Winder chose the flamboyant Captain George W. Alexander, poet, playwright, pirate, and sadist. Dressed in black and accompanied by Nero, his huge black Russian boar hound, he prowled the wards looking for prey. Fashionable Richmond referred to Castle Thunder as "Château de Tonnerre,"[37] no doubt a reference to the infamous Château d'If, familiar to readers of Alexander Dumas' popular novel *The Count of Monte Cristo*. Alexander, like the warden of that historic prison, was willing to make life comfortable for those who were able to pay his prices. Castle Thunder was unique in the Confederacy.

From the time the Dix-Hill Cartel was signed in July 1862 until December of that year, there were nine engagements in Virginia—seven Confederate victories and two that were inconclusive. Therefore, the

Chapter 2. The Decline of Richmond

departure of paroled Union soldiers more or less equaled the arrival of new Yankee prisoners, but Winder and his staff were able to manage the process with only minor problems that arose from time to time. Then, without warning, President Davis halted the exchange program just as hundreds of POWs were preparing to go home for Christmas. The suspension lasted until January 7, 1863. Meanwhile, the prisons began to overflow. On January 17, the *Richmond Dispatch* recorded the arrival of 1,600 Union prisoners captured in Tennessee by General Bragg and shipped via Lynchburg to Richmond. In that same issue, it was announced that Belle Isle again was fitted with tents to accommodate the new arrivals.[38] The temporary inmates were soon on their way to City Point escorted by Lieutenant Virginius Bossieux, who ironically would assume another role on Belle Isle when it was permanently reopened in mid–May. The *Richmond Dispatch* reported on May 13 that the several thousand Union soldiers who arrived by train the previous day were already confined to Belle Isle awaiting parole and exchange.[39] This scenario would be repeated over and over again as captives from the western and eastern theaters were shipped to Richmond. Shortly before President Lincoln suspended the cartel in late July, the soldiers captured by Lee's army during his invasion of Union territory began to arrive. Overwhelmed and in failing health when the scheme that he had patterned on Gibbs' Lynchburg system began to collapse, Winder hastily sought an expedient solution to the crisis. His answer was Andersonville, and the man whom he put in charge was Captain Henry Wirz who had served him so efficiently at Belle Isle the previous fall.

Taken prisoner during the Battle of Gettysburg, Lieutenant Colonel Frederick Cavada of the 114th Pennsylvania Volunteer Infantry spent the better part of a year as a prisoner in Libby Prison. His candid and sometimes humorous memoir, *Libby Life: Experiences of a Prisoner of War in Richmond, Virginia, 1863–64*, was published in 1865 and confirmed much that had already appeared in print about the prisons in Richmond. Official government reports and memoirs published later corroborated or supplied further details of life in the Richmond prisons as the system was slowly collapsing from a lack of resources and leadership.

The routine established by Winder and his staff in March 1862 remained unchanged until the last inmates were admitted three years later. All Union prisoners, regardless of rank, were taken first to the clerk's office in the West building where they registered, stripped to the skin,[40] and surrendered everything of value unless they had hidden it so it could not be detected. Once they were permitted to dress, they were escorted to their assigned accommodation.[41] Cavada described the chamber where he was housed as "long, low, dingy, gloomy and suffocating."[42] The 200 officers who shared this tightly packed space had less than five square feet to store their scant belongings and sleep at night. Each morning began with the entry of two slaves. The first—"Old Ben"—tried to maintain his cheerfulness as he woke the officers with news of the day, only to be followed by "The General" who carried a cast iron pot packed with hot tar that filled the room with what he called "good Yankee smoke" to fumigate the air, which was a foul mixture of sweat, dirt, human waste, and rancid food. This was an attempt to lessen the effects of "crowd poisoning." Before the acceptance of Louis Pasteur's germ theory, most members of the medical community believed that many potentially fatal diseases—and not just those of the respiratory system—were caused by breathing air polluted with minute particles produced by living conditions like those found in Libby Prison.[43] Then Old Ben and The General marched through the room, across the hall, and into the next chamber.

Next, the guards carrying trays of pieces of corn bread no bigger than a man's fist called out the numbers of the various messes while they placed "breakfast" on a long table. The man designated to collect the corn bread did so and distributed it to his messmates who washed it down with water from the muddy James River.[44] This corn bread made without bolted meal was now standard fare throughout the Confederate prisons in Virginia, whether it be Richmond, Lynchburg, or Danville. Already rejected for consumption by Confederate soldiers, it contained pieces of corncob, cockroaches, other insects, and at times pieces of mice that had smothered in the meal bins.[45]

After breakfast, there was the first of two daily roll calls at which the prisoners were carefully counted, and those who were sick were separated from the rest and escorted to the infirmary in the East building.[46] Modesty forgotten, the remaining officers stripped, sat on the floor, and began "skirmishing" or hunting for lice, or "graybacks," one garment at a time.[47] Union prisoners did not have extra clothes, so they had to keep the ones they wore every day free of vermin; if they were able to wash a shirt or underwear, they had to do so carefully. The prisoners used the same large tub to bathe themselves, especially during the hot summer, sometimes three or four at a time. The water was drawn through a hydrant mounted above the tub, but its use was forbidden after nine o'clock when all activity ceased in each ward. The man who broke this

Chapter 2. The Decline of Richmond

rule would spend a week in one of the dungeon cells in the Center basement with one piece of corn bread and some water per day.[48]

In 1861, modern medicine was still in its infancy, and the elaborate rituals surrounding ever-present death were strictly observed. All efforts were made to see that the departed were accorded every deference as their mortal remains were laid to rest. In the fall of 1861, Union officers were allowed to pool their resources to see that their comrades were properly buried, but two years later, that was no longer the case. Then there was rarely a good death among the soldiers who died in Libby Prison and their bodies were treated like animal carcasses. It was in the dank subterranean chamber of the West building that the naked bodies were carried to await burial. It was open to the dogs and hogs that roamed the neighborhood looking for food, and rats infested every floor of Libby. Slaves drove the wagons that carried the dead to the burying ground at Oakwood Cemetery.[49] Officers of the U.S. Army were stacked like cordwood in coffins that were reused once their contents had been dumped in unmarked mass graves with only the whispered prayers of the ragged sextons from General Winder's charnel house to mark their passing. By contrast, the Union POWs—regardless of rank—who died in Lynchburg were buried with care and reverence throughout the war.

The inmates of Libby were allowed to receive boxes of food and clothing from relatives and charitable organizations, but like their letters, these gifts were opened and inspected by the guards who took what they wanted to keep or sell. This pillaging took place in plain view of the prisoners who dared peek out of the windows at the canal barges being ransacked.[50] When a Union officer was summoned to collect his box, the jars and cans were opened; he was then required to spread his blanket on the floor, and the contents were dumped together, ruining everything. When this exercise in cruelty was finished, the men were allowed to keep the wooden boxes for fuel or "furniture."[51] Early in February 1862, each prisoner was limited to one letter a week that could not exceed six lines.[52]

For some of the prisoners, the ransacking of the Christmas boxes from home was the catalyst for a well-planned and carefully coordinated escape from Libby. Beginning on December 19, 1863, five three-man crews crept down to the basement each night to work shifts in the darkness with handmade tools fashioning a tunnel that was between 60 and 70 feet long, It was finished on Tuesday, February 8, 1864, and the next night, 109 Union officers crawled through the rat-infested shaft to an exit that the guards could not see because it was concealed in one of the stalls of a shed once used as a stable behind Carr's tobacco warehouse.[53] Two men drowned, 48 were recaptured, and 59 reached Union lines and safety. Those fortunate escapees owed their lives to Elizabeth Van Lew and her network of spies that even penetrated the White House of the Confederacy. Along with her co-conspirators Van Lew provided safe houses, disguises, and a secure means of flight for Union prisoners willing to take the risk of trying to escape and reach their own lines.

Canadian-born Private Robert Knox Sneden left in his journal a detailed account of the night of the escape. A member of the Forty-Eighth New York Volunteer Infantry, he had been taken prisoner at Locust Grove, Orange County, Virginia, on November 27, 1863, and incarcerated in the Crew and Pemberton Prison, which was across Cary Street from the exit of the tunnel. It is probable that the slaves who serviced the prisons on Cary Street disclosed the details of the escape with Union soldiers whom they could trust. After all, they shared a common cause: a Union victory would mean an end to slavery.

Sneden included a map with his account of the successful breakout that led to draconian measures within the Richmond prisons and throughout the entire Confederate penal system. Colonel Thomas E. Rose and Major Andrew G. Hamilton, the masterminds of the escape, were the first men to crawl to safety, followed by the 15 members of the excavation crew; then it was every man for himself.[54] Sneden recorded the free-for-all as it was told to him: "The rush to escape by the Tunnel—everyone wanted to be first. In order to get down the chimney as well as along the tunnel it was necessary to strip naked—wrap their clothes in a bundle, and push this on before them. Each man was able to cobble together civilian dress from gifts from home or fellow prisoners.[55] As soon as it was seen that only a few could set out before daylight, all rushed for the mouth of the tunnel who could—each man being determined to get out first. The room was now so crowded that there was the danger of suffocation for some while all were struggling to get in the hole. The strongest men forced their way to the front while the weak ones were roughly pushed aside and jammed against the walls."[56]

Major Thomas Pratt Turner's first order after he learned of the escape was to arrest the officer of the guard and the sentries on duty that night and imprison them in Castle Thunder, but they were quickly cleared of any involvement in the escape and released.[57] The inmates who had not attempted to escape were subjected to guard patrols every two hours, roll calls at random, and repeated inspections of their living

Chapter 2. The Decline of Richmond

quarters. The captured fugitives were packed into the cells in the basement of the Middle building and fed a daily meal of bread and water.[58] On February 28, less than three weeks after the successful tunnel escape, there was a second effort to liberate the Union officers. This time, the rescue was attempted by two Union cavalry columns led by General Judson Kilpatrick and Colonel Ulrich Dahlgren. Rumors of the ill-conceived raid provoked Winder to order that barrels filled with gunpowder be placed under each one of the Libby buildings to be detonated if Kilpatrick's force breached the Richmond defenses, a pitiless plan threatening the lives of over 1,000 officers.[59] Whereas Kilpatrick withdrew at the first sign of resistance, Dahlgren, who was unaware of his superior's retreat until it was too late to do likewise, tried to complete his mission. The debacle ended with his death and the capture of more Union soldiers to house in the already overcrowded Richmond prisons.

Although living conditions in Libby Prison were substandard at best, they were almost sumptuous when compared to those on Belle Isle after the suspension of the cartel on July 30, 1863. It had been reactivated as a prison camp on May 13, 1863,[60] on the same three sandy acres of the eastern end of the island, but with the collapse of the exchange program, it eventually expanded to six acres. Belle Isle is one mile long and a quarter mile wide, or roughly 54 acres with the highest elevation of 55 feet. Bossieux, the new commandant, was confronted with the task of preparing Belle Isle for an influx of prisoners who faced an incarceration that might last for months. In the summer of 1862, he had escorted prisoners to City Point. Now he had to feed, house, and guard 3,000 of them—perhaps three or four times that number before the cartel was reactivated. His reputation among the prisoners was for the most part positive; he left the punishment of malefactors to his two sadistic assistants, known only as Sergeant Hite and Sergeant Marks. Under the supervision of the guards, slaves and prisoners labored to surround the entire perimeter with a ditch three feet wide and eight feet deep; this was the inner "deadline." Using the soil from the ditches, five-foot-high earthworks were constructed at 40-foot intervals and each one was manned by an armed guard. The entrance to the prison was a massive gate that opened onto a 20-foot walkway that ended at the river's edge. It was flanked on either side by an eight-foot-high wooden fence. The gate was bolted at nightfall and opened early in the morning.[61]

The James River flowing west to east was divided into three segments. The upper segment of 10 feet was reserved for drinking water, the next 30 feet for bathing, and just beyond the entrance, 150 feet for the latrine. During fine weather, prisoners were allowed to bathe in the river in squads of 75, which, as the numbers increased week by week, meant a bath every six months.[62] The camp was arranged along a long corridor bisecting 60 alleys lined with Sibley tents in various stages of disrepair. These provided shelter for some of the inmates, but there were never enough accommodations for all of the prisoners. Some men dug burrows in the sandy soil, while others were forced to sleep in the open regardless of the weather. Periodically, Bossieux was able to provide straw for bedding. The Union soldiers were divided into squads of 20 with a member designated to collect all supplies for his company.

The standard daily ration per soldier was two ounces of bacon or four ounces of beef, half a pound of corn bread, and a small cup of beans or rice—all of inferior quality. They were slowly being starved to death.[63] The meals that were distributed at 9:00 a.m. and 3:00 p.m. were prepared in the cookhouse which was outside the compound. From time to time, the Confederate mess sergeant drafted a dozen Union soldiers to work in the kitchen, a prized position for those who obeyed the rules and caused no trouble. Prisoners were permitted to purchase food from outside the prison, but money was in short supply, so some talented artists turned to counterfeiting U.S. "greenbacks" which were preferred to the inflated Confederate currency. Since these notes did not appear in circulation in the North until March 10, 1862, most Southerners were unfamiliar with them and willingly accepted the colorful bogus bills. Rather than eat the often tainted meat, some men resorted to catching rats that abounded on Belle Isle and cooking them. There are a number of conflicting stories that dealt with the capture, killing, and eating of Bossieux's pet dog.[64] Union prisoners committing such "crimes" were sometimes punished by being gagged, their hands tied behind them, and mounted on a narrow sawhorse about eight feet off the ground. Ropes were then tied to their ankles and their legs, being stretched as far as possible, were secured to pegs hammered into the ground. They were then left to fall off their perch or die trying.[65] During the winter, Private Josephus Hopwood and some of his comrades were discovered trying to tunnel out of the prison; they were reprimanded but not punished.[66]

In addition to the cookhouse, there was an office for the commandant, quarters for the guards, and a hospital that was really just an infirmary. Serious cases were transferred to a hospital in Richmond. There was a cemetery in plain view from every part of the camp and a battery of cannons all along the ridge above the camp. In case of a mutiny among the prisoners, the artillery company could put an end to the

Chapter 2. The Decline of Richmond

revolt with several volleys of canister. Although the James River was deep and swift around Belle Isle,[67] the prison staff appeared obsessed with the possibility of attempted escapes via the river, so the latrines or sinks could not be used after dark. Since diarrhea was chronic among the majority of inmates, the alleys and the main corridor had to be cleaned every morning. The stench was unbearable in the spring, summer, and fall and almost as bad in the winter. The collected human waste was thrown in the pit that surrounded the camp and lightly covered with dirt.

Every morning, hundreds joined the line seeking help at the infirmary. Many stood for hours picking the lice from their clothing, only to be told to return the next day. When those who were seriously ill were finally sent to one of the hospitals in the city, many never returned. In November 1863, 181 ill Union soldiers whose condition was critical were returned to federal authorities for treatment. Upon their arrival at the military hospital in Annapolis, Maryland, Assistant Surgeon Samuel J. Radcliffe noted in his initial report, "Every case wore upon it the visage of hunger, the expression of despair, and exhibited the ravages of some preying disease within.... Their hair was disheveled, their beards long and matted with dirt, their skin blackened and caked with the most loathsome filth, and their bodies and clothing covered with vermin."[68] This was only the vanguard of the regiments of misery that made their way to Maryland in 1864.

In December 1863, there was an outbreak of smallpox on Belle Isle. Union general Benjamin Butler, who was in command of the Department of Virginia and North Carolina, which was composed of the parts of those states controlled by the federal government, sent enough vaccine to Richmond to successfully stop the spread of the disease. He also exchanged 520 Confederate soldiers for an equal number of Union prisoners. Once he learned of this impromptu transaction, President Davis forbade his staff to have any further contact with Butler whom he considered an outlaw with a price on his head. Exasperated by the almost continuous abuse of Union soldiers by a number of women in New Orleans, Butler had issued an order on May 15, 1862, that any female engaging in such activities was arrested as a prostitute.[69] The spitting at Union soldiers and the insults ceased. For Davis, questions of etiquette and the strident demands by the citizens of Richmond that POWs be removed from the Confederate capital at once took precedence over the looming crisis in the military penal system.

Josephus Hopwood was 19 years old when he mustered into L

Company of the Seventh Illinois Volunteer Cavalry on September 1, 1861. A year later, on September 13, he was taken prisoner at Iuka, Mississippi, when his saddle girth broke and he was thrown from his horse. After 10 days in Vicksburg, he was paroled for exchange. Except for a short furlough with his family, he was stationed at the Jefferson Barracks in Saint Louis, Missouri, until he was formally exchanged in March 1863. He rejoined his regiment near Memphis, Tennessee, and a game of "cat and mouse" began between the Seventh Illinois Cavalry and General Nathaniel Bedford Forrest that lasted until October 11, when near Collierville, Tennessee, Hopwood was captured again. This time, he gave his mount to a wounded comrade and tried unsuccessfully to rejoin his unit on foot. Forrest was infamous for stripping his captives of everything except the bare essentials, but somehow, Hopwood managed to secret his blanket, which "helped save the lives of a least two other boys"[70] during the bitterly cold winter of 1863–1864. Almost 70 years passed before he dictated his memoir to his wife, and time had softened the horror of those five months on Belle Isle. He did not complain about the quality of the rations, only their paucity—he weighed only 115 pounds when he was released. He did not regret selling his coat to buy bread, but he could not forget the daily toll of deaths from starvation or the bitter cold. In March 1864, an exchange was arranged, and the quota was filled starting with Company One. So many men had died during the winter that the ranks of all companies were depleted. Hopwood was in Company Sixty-Three, and like many of his comrades, he simply stepped into the place of a soldier who had died and gained his freedom.[71]

Sergeant Jacob Osborn Coburn was not so lucky. Coburn was 30 when he enlisted in Company I of the Sixth Michigan Volunteer Cavalry on September 8, 1862, and before he was taken prisoner at Charles Town, West Virginia, on October 18, 1863, he had already survived a serious bout of diarrhea and recovered from a potentially dangerous wound. Coburn kept a diary from the day he was captured until six days before his death on March 8, 1864. Time did not temper his memory; the hunger, lice, rats, filth, inhumanity of soldiers on both sides, and his slow, agonizing death permeated each page of his journal. Because he was a sergeant, Coburn was put in charge of a company on Belle Isle. Within the camp, there was a group of prisoners—the Raiders—who preyed on their comrades in arms stealing food, clothing, shelter, and anything else of value to ensure their survival.[72] When he was robbed by these men as he carried the daily rations to his company, Coburn gave

Chapter 2. The Decline of Richmond

his portion to one of his men. His old "camp complaint," the chronic diarrhea that eventually killed him, returned. In November, through the efforts of Brigadier General Neal Dow of the Thirteenth Maine Volunteer Infantry, who was a prisoner at Libby, the federal government sent boxes of uniforms, warm clothing, and blankets to the prisoners on Belle Isle. Although they were grateful for Dow's efforts on their behalf, most of the men sold these items to their guards for money with which to buy food. Ultimately, Coburn was sent to a hospital in Richmond where he received adequate care and a diet to mitigate the symptoms of his disease, but it was too late. Captured during the twilight of the Confederacy, Coburn was condemned to endure the weeks from late October to early March slowly dying of starvation and diarrhea. He never ceased to hope to be exchanged, but even now, he lies buried in Richmond, far from home.

As Coburn lay dying, General Winder announced the final solution to the POW problem: in groups of 400, inmates from Belle Isle were sent to Camp Sumter near Andersonville, Georgia. The transfers began on February 7, 1864.[73] At the same time, officers were sent to Camp Oglethorpe near Macon, Georgia. Tragically, the successful approach to the conundrum of POWs developed in Lynchburg in the summer of 1862 failed to become the pattern for the military penal system that was evolving throughout the South, but Henry Wirz was no George Gibbs—far from it.

CHAPTER 3

The Lynchburg System

The first in-depth newspaper article mentioning Union POWs arriving in the Hill City appeared on November 15, 1861, in the *Lynchburg Daily Virginian*. There was no mention of the number of prisoners, only that they were escorted from the headquarters of Brigadier General John B. Floyd[1] at Cotton Hill, Fayette County, (West) Virginia, by soldiers from Kentucky. The prisoners marched approximately 125 miles from Cotton Hill to Dublin, Pulaski County, Virginia, where they boarded the Virginia and Tennessee Railway for Lynchburg. What was deemed newsworthy was the information that once the Confederate officer from Kentucky delivered his charges to the city jail on Wednesday afternoon, he fell in the James River–Kanawha Canal while crossing an unfinished bridge closed to pedestrian traffic. Although he appears to have ignored the warning signs, he was able to swim, so he was unharmed.[2] The fact that the story was not on page one, that there was neither mention made of the number of Union soldiers nor the size of their Confederate escort, implied that shipping POWs from Lynchburg to the capital via the Southside Railroad to Petersburg and then transferring them to the Richmond and Petersburg Railroad was an established routine.

A week later, Lynchburg was briefly involved in an event that was anything but routine when 94 Union prisoners from General Floyd's headquarters arrived at the Virginia and Tennessee depot, guarded by 24 Confederate soldiers under the command of Captain H. Clay Pate of the Petersburg Rangers. The reporter who covered the story wrote exactly what he knew his readers expected: "The prisoners were, and had the appearance of being a very ignorant set. They are principally from Ohio, Kentucky, Illinois, and Western Virginia, and were captured at Guyandotte, Va., in the late fight at that place, by the cavalry attached to Gen. Floyd's Brigade. They were marched from Guyandotte to Dublin Depot on the Va. & Tenn. R.R., a distance of two hundred miles, and

Chapter 3. The Lynchburg System

after a few hours delay here in changing cars, were sent 'On to Richmond.'"[3] The November 23 edition of the *Lynchburg Daily Virginian* carried a terse article, "The Reported Burning of Guyandotte Contradicted." The officers accompanying the Union prisoners dismissed the rumors that Union troops had destroyed the pro-secessionist town on the banks of the Ohio River.[4]

Located in Cabell County, (West) Virginia, "Guyandotte," according to the *Daily Intelligencer* of Wheeling, (West) Virginia, "has always had the reputation of being the 'orneriest' place on the Ohio River. It was at 'Guyan' where counterfeiters, horsethieves, and murderers did most congregate." The author further maintained that it was the first town on the Ohio River to display the secessionist flag.[5] In October, the Union Army opened a recruiting camp in Guyandotte over the protests of some of the pro-secessionist citizens, but within a month 150 men had joined the Ninth (West) Virginia Volunteer Infantry and had begun their training. From his headquarters at Cotton Hill, General Floyd ordered Colonel John Clarkson and Colonel Albert G. Jenkins to proceed with a force of 1,200 cavalrymen to Guyandotte with orders to destroy Camp Paxton and kill or capture the recruits as well as any local Unionists they could catch. By sundown on November 10, they were close to their objective. Jenkins was familiar with the area and he knew exactly which secessionists his scouts were to notify. With the pale light of a waxing gibbous moon, the cavalry move into place and remounted. They struck just as Sunday evening church services were ending. Some of the villagers had already retired for the night and the streets were more or less deserted. Grabbing their weapons, Union soldiers rushed to meet the enemy, but they were quickly overwhelmed. Three Confederates were killed and 10 were wounded while 10 Union soldiers were killed and 20 wounded. Although the town was surrounded, some Union soldiers slipped through the Confederate lines and headed to the Union garrison at Ceredo, which was seven miles downriver.

A detachment of Union soldiers from the Fifth (West) Virginia Volunteer Infantry arrived by steamboat from Ceredo early the following morning, but the Confederates had already left Guyandotte. Before Colonel John Zeigler could stop them, some of his soldiers began torching the homes and businesses of known secessionists. Tensions between the two river towns had been building for months, and the destruction of Fort Paxton and the capture of its garrison whipped the soldiers into a frenzy. By the time they were brought under control, two-thirds of the buildings in the town were damaged. Guyandotte was rebuilt, and a restored Camp Paxton continued to serve as a recruiting center for the Ninth (West) Virginia Volunteer Infantry, which was one of the units engaged in the Battle of Lynchburg in June 1864.

While the arrival in Richmond of the Union prisoners taken at Guyandotte raised the problem of overcrowding in the Richmond prisons to a crisis level, it also reminded General Winder and his staff that Lynchburg might prove an ideal location for an auxiliary camp because it was an established transportation hub before the outbreak of the war. The Virginia and Tennessee Railroad gave access to the western theater, the Orange and Alexandria Railroad serviced the Piedmont, the upper Shenandoah region, and northern Virginia, while the Southside Railroad linked Lynchburg to Petersburg, which had direct access to Richmond. The James River–Kanawha Canal also offered a connection between Lynchburg and Richmond, which might prove useful when any of the railroads were threatened or damaged by the enemy. The Hill City was already a major supply depot as well as a garrison city for the Confederate Army. Soldiers from Virginia were stationed at Camp Davis near the center of Lynchburg. Units from Confederate states other than Virginia were stationed just outside the city limits on the approximately 30.5 acre Fair Ground, which formed a scalene triangle. Its longest side, which was 2,100 feet, served as the main entrance of the property and was part of the Lynchburg-Salem Turnpike.[6] Its shortest side, which fronted on Forest Road, was approximately 1,580 feet and eventually crossed Blackwater Creek, while an almost impenetrable primal hardwood forest formed the third side measuring 1,800 feet.[7] With Confederate soldiers in close proximity, it was an ideal location for a POW camp.[8] Occasionally, civilians performed guard duty at each of the POW camps in the Confederacy, but guards with military training were better able to maintain order in such a facility because they were not easily intimidated, reducing the possibility of escapes. In 1863, the Fair Ground also was chosen as the location of one of the four quartermaster's depots for horses,[9] thus providing another level of security. There were natural springs on the property[10] as well as stables and stalls[11] used in peacetime for livestock, which could be shared among the military personnel, both Union and Confederate.

The system of prisons in Richmond, which seemed to never stop expanding, was very unpopular with the citizens of the capital who resented the consumption of vital supplies by enemies who might escape at any moment and imperil their city. The citizens of Lynchburg who read the newspapers were aware of the situation in Richmond, but

Chapter 3. The Lynchburg System

they were assured that the Lynchburg facility was to be a transit camp without a stockade. It was to be a "line camp"; any prisoner approaching the clearly marked deadline was warned, and if he did not stop, he was shot. All supplies used by the prisoners were shipped from Richmond. A camp was to be established in Lynchburg; General Winder had already decided that, but the final decision on where to locate the facility lay with the members of the city council. In November 1861, their greatest concern was the crime wave that the local police force could not control, and besides, the outcome of General Winder's "experiment" in Salisbury, North Carolina, was still in the planning stage. Ostensibly the most important matters on the agendas of regular as well as called meetings of the Lynchburg City Council were lawbreaking and exemptions from military service for prominent citizens as well as important government functionaries. The proposed POW camp was not a topic of serious discussion. Finally, on March 8, 1862, one of the members moved that the council request that President Davis declare martial law in Lynchburg so the army under orders of a duly appointed provost marshal could stem the crime wave. One of the duties of a provost marshal was the deposition of POWs. Unfortunately, voting on the motion was postponed on a technicality.[12] General Thomas "Stonewall" Jackson's campaign in the lower Shenandoah Valley, which began two weeks later, forced the city fathers to decide quickly where, how, and when Lynchburg's auxiliary POW camp was to be ready to receive its first inmates.

Although General Winder obviously was impressed with the ease with which the authorities in the Hill City handled the prisoners from Guyandotte in November, he clearly was concerned with the apparent lack of preparations six months later to establish a facility in Lynchburg. On June 1, 1862, the newly promoted Colonel George C. Gibbs and the Forty-Second North Carolina Volunteer Infantry left Salisbury, North Carolina, for Petersburg, Virginia, where they changed trains for Lynchburg. Upon arrival, they disembarked, marched out to the Fair Ground, and occupied their assigned quarters. The men of the Forty-Second had been trained to guard prisoners and secure the perimeter, but there was neither a prison camp nor inmates. Colonel Gibbs was in Lynchburg to correct that oversight, but when he sought to accomplish his mission, he encountered an administrative anomaly in the person of Captain John Galt, assistant commissary of subsistence, who claimed to be the commander of the post.[13] This confusion lasted for days until General Winder finally resolved the bureaucratic tangle in Gibbs' favor. On June 6, the *Lynchburg Daily Virginian* printed a notice that the first

Union prisoners taken during Jackson's Valley Campaign would be sent to Salisbury,[14] and the following Tuesday, June 10, 37 Union officers arrived at the Orange and Alexandria station. They left for North Carolina the following morning on the Southside Railroad,[15] but later that afternoon, a horde of hungry and thirsty Union soldiers that seemed to number in the thousands arrived in Lynchburg. Greeted by a cannonade and a brass band playing "Dixie," they marched under guard down Main Street and up the 5th Street hill that led to the Fair Ground.[16] They bivouacked in a field outside the area designated for the POW camp[17] surrounded by soldiers trained by Colonel Gibbs who took control of the situation and began to bring order out of chaos while ignoring the protests of Captain Galt.

Charles Button, editor of the *Lynchburg Daily Virginian*, described the arrival of the Union prisoners as they marched through downtown Lynchburg on their way to the Fair Ground: "The poor devils looked jaded and dirty, whilst some of them were actually bare-footed. Perhaps they made as good an appearance as the same number of our own men would have made under similar circumstances.—although they came

Lynchburg's Market House where Union POWs assembled before marching to their respective prisons (author's collection).

Chapter 3. The Lynchburg System

into our country upon a hostile mission and deserved death on the battle field, there was much in their woebegone appearance to excite our sympathy."[18] The following day, Button visited the Fair Ground and interviewed several of the prisoners; this time, he was less disposed to be charitable toward the enemies of the Confederacy. "The prisoners of whom we spoke yesterday are encamped near the Fair Ground; and will, we understand, remain here for several days. We indulged in conversation with a number of them yesterday and found them exceedingly insolent. They seem to presume upon their condition as prisoners to offer insult to those who would reason with them calmly about the folly and wickedness of their invasion of our territory, and the war in which they are engaged. They say that they are fighting for the flag and the Union, and that every man in the North is pledged to restore the Union."[19] If Button had taken the opportunity to interview the Union soldiers with more care, he might have discovered the details of their arduous journey, which began for some of them on the morning of May 24 and ended 18 days later with their arrival in Lynchburg.

Private Charles Blinn of A Company, First Vermont Volunteer Cavalry, Private Ziba Roberts of D Company, Twenty-Eighth New York Volunteer Infantry, and Corporal Michael Henry VanBuskirk of F Company, Twenty-Seventh Indiana Volunteer Infantry, were among the first inmates of the Lynchburg POW camp, and each kept a journal providing details of their capture and the exhausting journey that brought them to the field outside at the Fair Ground on June 11, 1862. They remained in Lynchburg for two months before being transferred to Belle Isle in Richmond, and during their time in the Hill City, they recorded the details of Colonel George Gibbs' creation of an efficient and humane system for retaining POWs, which might have been a model for other camps had it not been for the elitist attitude of some of his colleagues and superiors. Gibbs was from Florida, not Virginia, a fact that eventually cost him the command of the Forty-Second North Carolina Volunteer Infantry. The majority of the members of the regiment wanted to be commanded by a North Carolinian.[20]

Charlie Blinn was a native of Burlington, Chittenden County, Vermont. Born on January 27, 1843, he was the third child of Chauncey and Edith Blinn. He had an older brother and sister as well as two younger brothers and two younger sisters. His father was a turner, which was a skilled craft. Like his siblings, Charlie was educated in the public schools of Burlington, and when the war began in April 1861, already he had been accepted by the University of Vermont. Instead of beginning his college career, he joined the First Vermont Cavalry on September 21, 1861, and mustered into A Company on November 18, 1861. His first taste of battle was the Shenandoah Valley Campaign of 1862, which began in March and ended in June. On May 24, A Company was trapped by a deliberately set fire and raked by grapeshot when they tried to break through the Confederate line at Middletown, Virginia. Whereas his mount was killed instantly, Blinn was not wounded but badly bruised. Relieved of his military equipment but not his personal possessions, Blinn and his fellow prisoners began the march from Middletown to Newtown, Virginia, where they were quartered for the night in a deserted house but received no rations.[21]

Born on July 31, 1840, Ziba Roberts was the youngest of the four sons of Ziba and Susan Roberts of Shelby, Orleans County, New York. He, his brothers, and a younger sister had grown up on the family farm. He did not attend school beyond the sixth grade because his diary lacks the polish and analysis of the Blinn and VanBuskirk journals, but the data he recorded were nonetheless valuable. On November 8, 1861, he enlisted in the Twenty-Eighth New York Volunteer Infantry as a private at Medina, Orleans County, New York, and mustered into D Company that same day.[22] The Shenandoah Valley Campaign was also the Twenty-Eighth New York's baptism by fire. On the morning of June 25, while Charlie Blinn and his comrades were preparing to march from Newtown to Winchester, Ziba Roberts and his fellow soldiers in D Company were about to be captured at Bunker Hill, Virginia, by soldiers of the battle-seasoned Seventh Virginia Cavalry under the command of General Turner Ashby. Relieved of their weapons and leathers, they waited under guard for orders from General Jackson as to their next destination.

Meanwhile, the men of the Twenty-Seventh Indiana Volunteer Infantry were trying to hold the city of Winchester, even though they were outnumbered. Like the men of the First Vermont Cavalry and the Twenty-Eighth New York Infantry, it was their first real engagement, but they fought street by street and forced the enemy to pay a heavy price for their victory. By late afternoon, the five VanBuskirk cousins had surrendered their weapons and equipment. Under guard, they rested and waited. Corporal Michael Henry VanBuskirk, born in 1840 in Monroe County, Indiana, was the only son of Isaac and Elizabeth VanBuskirk. With his three younger sisters he grew up on the family farm and was working for his father when he enlisted in the Twenty-Seventh Indiana at Indianapolis on September 12, 1861, and mustered into F Company.

Chapter 3. The Lynchburg System

Well written, his diary is filled with data that complemented those of Blinn and Roberts.

The men of the First Vermont Cavalry reached Winchester on May 25 and were housed in the courthouse which, until recently, had been used as a Union hospital. The overflow was quartered in the railway station while captured officers had liberty on parole of honor and were able to move freely about Winchester.[23] The following day, Ziba Roberts and the prisoners from the Twenty-Eighth New York Infantry reached Winchester. Unlike the men from Vermont, their captors fed the New Yorkers—bread for breakfast and beef soup for supper.[24] The prisoners from the Twenty-Seventh Indiana were detailed to bury their dead comrades; it was an emotionally demanding task that took days to complete, but the Confederate soldiers who supervised the process treated their enemies kindly.[25] Roberts was very interested in food, and most of his diary entries contain notes on grub. Through all the chaos, the women of Winchester provided food for the Union captives, and the gratitude of the men was duly recorded. Mike VanBuskirk summed up the feelings of his men when he wrote, "They have no supplies here & we would have suffered had it not been for the ladies of the place. God bless them."[26] Charlie Blinn echoed his sentiments on May 28: "Their kindness will ever be held in grateful remembrance by a hungry people."[27]

For three days, the prisoners waited at various locations in Winchester for something to happen, dependent on the generosity of the women of Winchester and the kindness of their captors. From morning until night, the streets were filled with Confederate units on their way to somewhere—and there were dozens of supposed answers to that question. On May 29, rations arrived from the kitchens of Winchester and Frederick County, but there was nothing on May 30 other than rumors. Some believed that the POW units were to leave that afternoon, but it was not until the following morning that the order to vacate the courthouse was given. At noon, the men of the First Vermont Cavalry left for Woodstock, Virginia. The combination of no food for two days and blistering heat meant that they covered only 15 miles before they had to stop for the night. They were guarded by soldiers from the Twenty-First Virginia Volunteer Infantry, most of whom were from Southside Virginia. Charlie Blinn described them as "the most God forsaken regt [sic] in the Southern Confederacy.... They are with few exceptions a poor, ignorant set of men in every sense of the word." They slept that night in a newly plowed field. After sunset, it started raining, and by morning, they were standing in knee-deep mud.[28]

The Twenty-Seventh Indiana headed to Woodstock that same afternoon,[29] but the Twenty-Eighth New York, bound for the same destination, did not leave Winchester until the next day in the pouring rain.[30] Upon arriving at Woodstock, all three units headed south to Mount Jackson as the rain intensified. When they reached the Confederate general hospital in that village, they were finally under a roof, but they did not receive anything to eat until the following morning.[31] With a small piece of half-baked corn bread and a couple of bites of fat bacon, the Union prisoners headed toward their next objective—Harrisonburg. It rained all day and night. According to their guards, the reason for the scant rations was that General John C. Fremont was "pressing" General Jackson.[32] This intelligence sparked a rumor that spread through the ranks—Fremont was attempting to free all the captives before they reached their ultimate destination.[33]

The Twenty-Eighth New York covered only nine miles before they were ordered to bivouac in an open field where they remained until the next day, June 4, when in the pouring rain they completed the final 16 miles to Harrisonburg where they were lodged in the garret of the courthouse and received their first real rations since May 29.[34] The men of the Twenty-Seventh Indiana drew their first regular provisions that same night.[35] On the morning of June 5, Ziba Roberts and his fellow soldiers headed for Waynesboro, marching 17 miles "over one of the worst roads in Virginia," and spent the last hours of daylight and the entire night in an open field. He slept well because although he was hungry, he was exhausted.[36]

Waynesboro, like Lynchburg, owed its origin to a safe ford in a major river. In this case, it was located where the trail from Staunton to the Rockfish Gap crossed the South River, which was the southern fork of the Shenandoah. In the mid–18th century, Joseph Teas established a tavern there for travelers passing through the upper Shenandoah Valley. By 1862, Teasville had become Waynesborough or Waynesboro, a main stop on the Virginia Central Railway.[37] There is no official document detailing why the Union soldiers who were bivouacked next to the tracks were not transported on one of the trains that passed through Waynesboro bound for Charlottesville, their final stop before Lynchburg. It is ironic that Confederate general Jubal Early saved the Hill City from the ravages of Union general Hunter during the Battle of Lynchburg in June 1864, only to lose to Union general Philip Sheridan in the Battle of Waynesboro in March 1865. Early's victory against Hunter prolonged the war, while his loss

Chapter 3. The Lynchburg System

to Sheridan set in motion the events that led to the war's end a month later.

The rumor about General Fremont attempting to free the captured Union soldiers may well have been true because Mike VanBuskirk related a strange incident that occurred on June 5: "This morning while they were giving us rations they seemed scared. They began to throw the bread over the fence at us by the wagon loads, just like feeding hogs. Soon they rushed us out & all began to skidaddle." The Union prisoners then covered 20 miles on very bad roads. That night, they slept in an open field and were heavily guarded.[38] The prisoners from the First Vermont Cavalry were trying to sleep under equally unpleasant conditions. All three diarists had the same rendezvous point—Waynesboro, just east of Staunton—but they arrived there by different routes and at staggered times.

On the morning of June 6, the prisoners from the Twenty-Eighth New York Infantry marched 11 miles from the field where they had spent the night at Waynesboro. There, they waited all day near a bridge belonging to the Virginia Central Railway hoping that they might board a train for their ultimate destination—wherever that might be—but they were disappointed yet again. At nine that evening, they received some food and then bedded down for the night in the rain. Meanwhile, Charlie Blinn and his fellow cavalrymen marched into Harrisonburg in a downpour, but they were soon herded into the courthouse and fed. In the morning, they left Harrisonburg and marched 20 miles toward Waynesboro but by a circuitous route that took most of the day because the road was knee deep in mud. At sundown, they reached Weyers Cave where they camped for the night. There were no rations, but local farmers gladly sold them bread at $2–$3 per loaf.[39]

Roberts reported that they had crackers for breakfast, and then around noon, a light rain began to fall. In the early afternoon of June 7, more prisoners arrived, including Mike VanBuskirk and his Hoosiers, who, having been counted, thought they were going to board the cars at the Waynesboro depot. Instead, they spent yet another night in the open.[40] Very late in the afternoon of June 8, the prisoners from Vermont arrived in Waynesboro also expecting to board a train for Charlottesville. Instead, they were able to rest only briefly before they prepared to cross the crest of the Blue Ridge Mountains. The group of which Ziba Roberts was a member left Waynesboro at half past four. He had a "very lame foot" which made the 12-mile hike very difficult.[41] Blinn and his fellow prisoners followed at five o'clock, accomplishing the journey in four hours. In his journal, he made special note of the famous railway tunnel that recently had been cut through the heart of Afton Mountain.[42] Once they reached the valley, the men were allowed to bivouac in an open field beside the road that led to Charlottesville.

As rations were being drawn, the Union captives were informed that they were a day's journey from North Garden depot, which lay south of Charlottesville on the Orange and Alexandria Railway; it was there that they boarded the cars for their journey's end—the POW camp outside the city of Lynchburg. By nightfall, they reached their destination in the pouring rain. Each soldier had received a quarter pound of bread and a quarter pound of bacon that morning and, at midnight, another eighth pound of bacon and a pint of flour. They slept in the woods, and during the night, one soldier escaped.[43]

The rain began again at dawn on June 10, and by evening, the mud was six inches deep in places. It was impossible to find a dry spot to sleep that night.[44] The showers stopped by the morning of June 11, and after a quick breakfast, the men began to board the cars at nine o'clock. It took two hours to load the train, so it did not leave the North Garden depot until 11. Because of the load that the engine had to pull as well as the state of the rails, the first soldiers did not step off the train in Lynchburg until four in the afternoon, and the guards were still unloading prisoners at half past five. Forming in orderly ranks, over 2,230 American soldiers in torn and mud-spattered uniforms of Union blue marched up Main Street to the jeers and catcalls of the riffraff who had been waiting for hours to "greet" them to the Hill City. Some, like Ziba Roberts, were too sick to care, while the rest just wanted to find somewhere to rest.[45] The POW camp was not ready, so they spent six days in a field outside the Fair Ground. The onlookers along Main Street were hostile, but the peddlers who swarmed all over the field—like the lice the soldiers picked from their clothing and each other every day—were friendly and ready to sell food items as well as tobacco products at exorbitant prices.[46] They took coins, U.S. currency, and Confederate bills. By nightfall, they were gone, and the "Boys in Blue" were asleep under the almost full moon.

Although Colonel Gibbs considered the Fair Ground "entirely unsuited to the purpose,"[47] he had no choice but to work with the space, especially when the assistant quartermaster, Captain Edward McCormick, assured him that no other site was available.[48] It is reasonable to assume that Colonel Gibbs chose the wooded side of the Fair Ground for the POW camp because it provided a modicum of security.

Chapter 3. The Lynchburg System

Charlie Blinn twice mentioned in his journal the birds singing in the oak grove,[49] which provides supporting evidence of this being the site of the POW camp. With the noises associated with a military camp, hearing birdsong in any other part of the Fair Ground was impossible. The presence of Confederate soldiers in the adjacent portion of the Fair Ground also provided some security against escape attempts, but that was small comfort when the other problems facing Gibbs were considered. Although under guard, 2,230 noncommissioned officers and privates were crowded into a field without food or water in mid–June. Some of the men were wounded; others were suffering from fatigue, hunger, thirst, and heat exhaustion. Fresh spring water was available, but there were no buckets to carry it to the prisoners. Surely, Captains Galt and McCormick were aware that General Jackson's captives were on their way to Lynchburg—the telegraph lines were undamaged—but nothing was done to prepare for "OUR YANKEE GUESTS," as Charles Button described them.[50]

The large field outside the Fair Ground was crowded with peddlers as soon as dawn broke on June 12—described by Ziba Roberts as "a very fine day and a very warm day." He bought a local newspaper for 25 cents, which he soon considered a waste of money because it was "filled with lies," so he spent most of his day sleeping.[51] Mike VanBuskirk spent his morning buying "plenty of rations,"[52] while Charlie Blinn continued his description of Lynchburg. He bought a brown paper copy of the *Lynchburg Republican* from a local boy for 25 cents, commented on the fact that the city was filled with sick and wounded soldiers, and made special mention of the College Hospital, which was relatively close to the Fair Ground.[53] The following day, June 13, the *Lynchburg Daily Virginian* carried an exposé on counterfeit Confederate currency and how to identify it and claimed the supposed source of these spurious notes were the Yankee prisoners who had arrived in the Hill City on Wednesday.[54] Twenty-four hours later, the quantity of peddlers in the temporary camp dropped significantly, while the number of prisoners increased. With the addition of 500 men captured at Port Republic, the total of Union soldiers under guard approached 2,800, and rumors began to spread that everybody was going to be shipped to North Carolina in the morning.[55]

Slaves continued to work from dawn to dusk preparing the acres designated for the POW camp. There was neither time nor material to build a stockade, so it was indeed a "line camp," clearly marked so there was no question about areas that were off-limits to prisoners. Saturday,

June 14, was the end of the workweek, and even the enslaved were given Sunday as a day of rest. None of the Union soldiers camping outside the Fair Ground was sent to Salisbury, North Carolina, that sultry Saturday; in fact, more prisoners arrived that afternoon. Rations of any kind were in short supply, and Charlie Blinn began to complain about the "salt horse" that was offered to the men, but he was more concerned about the prisoners who appeared to be close to death.[56] Sunday was quiet except for a few civilians who came to harass the Yankees from a safe distance.[57] The men had enjoyed a couple of days to dry their clothes and remove most of the mud that still clung to their boots and trousers. Then in the afternoon, there was another violent storm, and they were soaked again. There was no wood with which to build fires to dry their clothes, cook their food, or provide warmth.[58] Obviously, there was a hailstorm close to Lynchburg because the temperature fell quickly, and it "was very cold through the night."[59] That same day, June 15, Colonel Gibbs sent General Winder a telegram briefly describing the situation at the Fair Ground with the promise of a detailed report after he fully assessed the situation.[60] Two days later, 30 Union officers arrived at the temporary camp, bringing the total to 2,830. This number did not include two freemen and one slave who were captured during the Valley Campaign and shipped to Lynchburg on the same train. These unfortunate men were taken to one of the dealers in slaves in central Lynchburg to be sold.

It was obvious on June 16 that something was about to happen. The men of the Twenty-First Virginia Volunteer Infantry were called into proper formation, as were the soldiers of the Forty-Second North Carolina Volunteer Infantry who formally assumed full responsibility of guarding the Union POWs, while the Virginians marched down the Lynchburg-Salem Turnpike to return to field service. Charlie Blinn considered the North Carolinians as "the finest looking body of men I have seen in the Confederacy."[61] With the changing of the guard, the men began to assemble their belongings as even more prisoners arrived at the makeshift camp. It was a perfect summer day—sunny and mild—a perfect day to pack and wait, and that is exactly what Ziba Roberts recorded in his diary.[62]

At noon on June 17, 1862, the first inmates of the Lynchburg POW camp crossed the deadline and began occupying their assigned places.[63] The rules instituted in the Richmond prisons were followed in Lynchburg as circumstances permitted. Whenever possible, each prisoner was assigned to a squad not to exceed 20 men from his own unit. Tasks were

Chapter 3. The Lynchburg System

rotated unless one member, like Ziba Roberts, preferred a particular job. Roberts enjoyed cooking for his mates, and his culinary adventures were well recorded in his diary. There were two meals a day, breakfast at 9:00 a.m. and supper at 3:00 p.m. Some of the men commandeered the available stables and sheds, but Charlie Blinn favored the field where he had slept since June 11. In any case, he preferred the open air. He also grumbled that there was only one spring, no place to bathe, and nowhere to wash clothes.[64] VanBuskirk also complained about the water supply as well as the lack of wood for cooking fires.[65] Within a week, Colonel Gibbs supervised the alleviation of these deficiencies.

According to Ziba Roberts, there were no rations distributed until the evening of June 18—and then only flour and bacon. However, he was busy on behalf of his mess. He sold his revolver for $7 to another Union prisoner and used a dollar to buy bread while saving the remaining six for the next emergency.[66] While Roberts was conducting business, Colonel Gibbs submitted his report to General Winder. After repeating his concern about the lack of security at the Fair Ground, Gibbs turned his attention to the conditions that the prisoners had been forced to endure since their arrival: they had no shelter, adequate water, or food. Men either were sleeping in livestock stalls or under tents made from their blankets or oil cloths. There was no lumber available to repair the stalls, fences, or gates. Captains Galt and McCormick blamed each other for the absence of food and fuel on-site as well as buckets to draw water from the springs. There was neither a hospital tent nor any medical personnel present to treat the sick or wounded. Gibbs refused to acknowledge Galt's assertion that he was in charge and assumed command of the post, forbidding anyone to enter the camp without his permission.[67]

General Winder's reply to Colonel Gibbs was immediate. Secretary of War George W. Randolph sent a telegram to Galt and McCormick informing them that if they wished to retain their positions, rations identical to those issued to Confederate soldiers were to be delivered at once to the POW camp under the command of Colonel Gibbs. They were also to requisition tents to house the men. After these orders were executed, they were to submit a detailed report on why they had not anticipated the needs of the prisoners who had been in transit for weeks.[68] Acting on further orders from the secretary of war, Lieutenant Colonel John Withers, assistant adjutant general, issued Special Orders No. 145, which ordered Captain Galt to halt the shipment of supplies from Lynchburg and requisition what was required by the POWs and their guards, paying the owners in certificates of impressment or at market prices with currency.[69]

There was rain early on June 18, but around noon, the skies cleared and there was a rainbow. At that same hour, Colonel Gibbs issued an order allowing the prisoners to write a letter home and he promised to personally forward them. Charlie Blinn noted all this in his diary beginning with "Col. Gibbs commanding the 42nd is a gentleman."[70] The following day, the long-promised improved rations arrived, and Ziba Roberts included the menus for his mess in his diary. In the morning, he made pancakes, using the flour he had drawn the previous evening and cooking them in the bacon grease that resulted from frying the quarter pound allotted to each man. At supper, the men of Roberts' mess feasted on pork chops, beans, and bread.[71] However, the absence of fresh fruits and vegetables in the diet of many soldiers left them vulnerable to scurvy.

In his letter to General Winder on June 18, Colonel Gibbs mentioned that although there were prisoners who were sick, none had died since he took command. Poignantly, the next day, the first death occurred. Nineteen years old at the time of his enlistment,[72] Private Patrick Dowling and his wife, Mary, were residents of Lawrence County, Ohio.[73] He joined the First (West) Virginia Volunteer Light Artillery on October 31, 1861, at Ceredo, Wayne County, (West) Virginia, just 15 miles from his home on the other side of the Ohio River. That same day at Ceredo, he mustered into B Battery.[74] Although he was stationed at Ceredo at the time of the raid on Guyandotte, it is unlikely that he participated in that attack since he was in the artillery, not the cavalry. Private Dowling was captured at Strasburg, Virginia, in May 1862.[75] Therefore, he was one of the first Union soldiers to enter the Lynchburg POW camp, and he was the first to die there, of heat exhaustion and dehydration. He was buried at the City Cemetery the day he died, in grave number 6 in the fifth line of lot 172 in a wooden coffin 72 by 18 inches.[76] Because West Virginia did not become a state until July 1863, it was ironic that the first casualty at the Lynchburg camp was a member of a Virginia unit loyal to the Union.

Charlie Blinn's entry in his journal for June 20 referred to Private Dowling when he wrote, "Nearby lies a man dying. He was sun stroked and is groaning in great agony."[77] The death of another Union soldier did not occur until June 24.[78] Blinn also mentioned that a prisoners' cemetery had been established near the Fair Ground, and "4 to 7 bodies are carried hence to their final resting place."[79] Located two miles from

Chapter 3. The Lynchburg System

the Fair Ground, the City Cemetery opened in 1806. A gift from John Lynch, founder of Lynchburg and a devout Quaker, the City Cemetery was the resting place for all races, the enslaved and the free, patricians and paupers, residents and strangers, and it was here that Union and Confederate soldiers were buried in a section reserved for the war dead. Most of the POWs were interred in the "Yankee Square," but when it was full, Union soldiers were laid to rest in other parts of the cemetery.

George A. Diuguid had assumed the management of the family business in 1856, after the death of his father, Samson Diuguid. They were skilled cabinetmakers who had specialized in federal-style furniture since 1817, but they also fashioned wooden coffins for those who could not afford the more expensive iron ones. During the Civil War, the creation of fine furniture was replaced by the seemingly endless task of making caskets for soldiers from both sides. Diuguid's workers fashioned them in several sizes from any wood available.[80] Their names, ranks, companies, regiments, death dates, and exact place of interment were carefully recorded by a member of Diuguid's office staff.

The care and respect accorded the Union dead by the staff of the hospitals in Lynchburg, the employees of Diuguid, and the slaves who oversaw every step in their final journey was not the norm during the Civil War, and thus it sets the Lynchburg POW camp apart from all the other internment camps in the Confederacy. The ministers and priests of Lynchburg took turns conducting the funeral services that occurred almost daily.[81] This adherence to the proper care of the departed continued until the last Union soldier died in a Lynchburg military hospital in June 1865. By the end of the war, a shroud was all that was available for some burials. When embalming became impossible because of a lack of proper supplies, bodies were packed in charcoal to be shipped to grieving families both above and below the Mason-Dixon line.

Charlie Blinn was concerned that the daily average number of deaths was around six,[82] including both Confederate and Union soldiers. During June 1862, seven Union soldiers died in the Lynchburg POW camp. In July, the number rose to 57; by August 15, there were 12 Union deaths at the Fair Ground before the original inmates were transferred to Belle Isle. In mid–September, they were paroled for exchange and shipped to Annapolis, Maryland.[83] All but two of the Union soldiers who died in the POW camp by mid–August were buried by Diuguid. The two soldiers who were not taken to the City Cemetery were laid to rest on the far edge of the Fair Ground, and there is no mention in any extant records of why this occurred. Burials took place every day of the week at the City Cemetery, and victims of serious diseases like smallpox and typhoid fever were buried next to persons who died of natural causes or from wounds. Before the POW camp was abandoned in April 1865, there were several more graves on the far side of the Fair Ground, and most of them were suicide victims. Depression haunted the lives of soldiers and sailors from both sides during the Civil War, and all three diarists—Blinn, Roberts, and VanBuskirk—expressed feelings of despair during their brief incarceration, and yet they survived imprisonment and the war.[84] In the 19th century, suicide was regarded by many as a spiritual crime, and burial in consecrated ground was denied to those who took their own lives. Their remains were interred in an area outside a cemetery and often in unmarked graves.

The first day of summer—June 21, 1862—was sunny and very hot, but there was good news to report. Each soldier received a small cake of soap so they could wash for the first time since late May, and slaves erected wall tents to house the sick and wounded.[85] This temporary hospital was staffed by a physician assisted by slaves who performed custodial tasks and nursing duties. With the opening in August of auxiliary hospitals in requisitioned tobacco factories in Lynchburg, the field hospital at the POW camp became an infirmary, while the seriously ill or wounded Union soldiers were assimilated into existing medical facilities.

Whereas lice could be kept under control by the daily, meticulous ritual of removing them from every item of clothing, scurvy was another matter. Medical authorities attributed the disease to a lack of fresh vegetables in the diet.[86] The British navy solved the problem of scurvy by introducing citrus fruits, especially limes, which, when properly stored, can last for months. Citrus fruits were unavailable in central Virginia in 1862, but for sale in the city market were vegetables like cabbage, turnip greens, collards, mustard greens, sweet potatoes, tomatoes, and white potatoes, as well as fruits including strawberries, blueberries, watermelon, and raspberries—all of which are rich in vitamin C.

Captains Galt and McCormick obviously heeded General Winder's threat because Ziba Roberts noted in his diary that he added fresh meat, sugar, beans, vinegar, and salt to his larder, and to mark the first day of summer, he served his mess a pudding.[87] As they became available, Roberts added some of those fruits and vegetables so necessary for good health from local vendors. Army life slowly was getting back to normal as evidenced by a droll remark of Mike VanBuskirk: "The boys are

Chapter 3. The Lynchburg System

just now getting reduced to fighting weight. They will fight over wood, bread, anything."[88]

The first week of summer saw a number of welcomed changes at the Lynchburg POW camp. Tents of every size, condition, and description arrived and were distributed to the inmates who erected them in an orderly manner, or as Charlie Blinn expressed it, giving the camp a "Yankee appearance." Colonel Gibbs permitted the men to post pro-Union signs on their tents.[89] Mike VanBuskirk described his tent as "a poor thing," but at least it gave him some protection from the sun and rain.[90] Starting on June 23, the men were permitted under guard to wash their clothes and themselves in the brooks that flowed through the woods near their camp.[91] Roberts was able to buy items like baking soda from local vendors who visited the camp on an almost daily basis selling to the Confederate soldiers as well as the Union prisoners. Thus, Ziba was able to start making soda bread instead of having to buy it.[92]

There were, however, daily reminders that they were still prisoners—the random roll calls, the never-ending struggle against lice, the enforced idleness, the lack of intellectual stimulation, the guards who responded with alacrity and efficiency to every potential crisis, and the ever-present deadline. Policing the camp and keeping it neat provided the inmates with some physical exercise but not enough. Because the facility in Lynchburg was supposedly a transit camp, creating a prisoners' association—like the one at Libby—among 3,000 inmates was next to impossible. On orders from Richmond, the prisoners were forbidden to obtain newspapers and the possession of one was punishable with a $25 fine;[93] however, for an extra 25 cents, local vendors wrapped your purchase in a cleverly disguised newspaper.[94]

In the middle of the night on June 30, a member of the Second Massachusetts Volunteer Infantry was caught stealing money from one of his comrades. As soon as the commotion began, the guards were on-site and took the already beaten thief into custody. They found that he had $200 when they searched him before locking him in the temporary jail. In the morning, he was returned to camp where his squad was waiting at the deadline, and as soon as he crossed it, the brawl began. Armed with swords, the guards stopped the fight but not before the pickpocket's fellow inmates gave him another thorough beating.[95] When requested, firewood was brought to the deadline, and Union soldiers were allowed to collect it there from the guards. Ziba Roberts enjoyed chopping firewood and making kindling. He even earned a drink of whiskey when he performed that task for the quartermaster.[96]

Sketch of the Fair Ground POW camp based on diary entries of prisoners (original sketch by Edmund D. Potter).

As soon as the hospital tents were erected on June 21, the sick and wounded Union prisoners were in line when the doctor opened his surgery every morning. Charlie Blinn mentioned in his journal that five men from his regiment were admitted to the hospital on June 23.[97] Four days in a row beginning on June 26, Ziba Roberts went to see the doctor for his injured foot, which was still painful, and for diarrhea. Finally, on June 30, he was admitted to the hospital. The next day, he was released with pills for his diarrhea, and over the next several days, his condition improved.[98]

Many doctors considered the camp diet to be the main cause of this common complaint among soldiers of both armies.[99] One of the standard treatments for diarrhea was calomel pills, aka mercurous chloride. Their frequent use could cause mercury poisoning. It is highly unlikely that the doctors in the Lynchburg hospitals had access to calomel because of the Union blockade. However, a skilled apothecary could make pills from the leaves of blackberries, blueberries, or red raspberries, all of which were rich in tannins that were proven to relieve the symptoms of diarrhea without side effects. Under the circumstances, it is reasonable to assume that these were the pills dispensed in the temporary POW hospital. Ziba Roberts was not a solitary sufferer. Mike VanBuskirk wrote in his diary on July 2, "We are all sick, one is not able

Chapter 3. The Lynchburg System

to give the other a drink of water. About a quarter of a mile to water." On July 4, VanBuskirk was admitted to the hospital with a serious case of diarrhea and he was not released until July 12.[100]

The final entry in volume 1 of Blinn's journal was dated July 4, when he celebrated the 86th anniversary of Independence Day.[101] There was a flurry of patriotic activity among the inmates, but when wagonloads of provisions arrived at the Fair Ground that afternoon, there was even more reason to celebrate. Because it was a working day and not a holiday in the Confederacy, the supplies were unloaded at the Southside Railroad depot and delivered to Captain Rodgers. The consignment included 12,000 pounds of bacon, 137 barrels of flour, 1,440 pounds of rice, 24 bushels of beans, 25 bushels of salt, and 60 candles for the hospital. Regular deliveries of rations were made to the Lynchburg POW camp, and from time to time, extra items like vinegar, coffee, sugar, fresh beef, fresh mutton, soap, and whiskey were included. Those few supplies not consumed by the time the Dix-Hill Cartel was in full operation were returned to Richmond.[102] Colonel Gibbs had kept his word about securing adequate provisions, but by mid–July, even the arrival of the long-promised supplies did not relieve the depression suffered by many of the prisoners.

Corporal VanBuskirk was a man of strong faith, and his thoughts written on July 19, 1862, were filled with hope for his eventual deliverance: "When I think of my lonely condition shut out from the outside world, deprived of communication with my friends at home & while confined on all sides by a strong guard line, under all these afflictions it is a source of joy to me that I have one friend who is ever with me & and in whom is all my trust. Through his goodness & tender mercy I still hope to enjoy the company of my friends & relatives once more."[103] Then tragedy struck.

Relations between the inmates and the guards had been unusually good since the camp opened, but on the evening of July 21, one of the guards shot and killed Private Marquis Bower of Company E, Sixty-Sixth Ohio Volunteer Infantry. The circumstances that led to this tragedy are unknown, but the effect on the prisoners was immediate. Mike VanBuskirk recorded the event that night and expanded on it the following day: "Last night one of the guards shot a prisoner. He fell against our tent & soon expired. His blood is on our tent. That will wash out, but the blood that rests upon the murderer's hands will not."[104] Since the POW camp opened, 31 men had died of disease or their wounds; two were from Private Bower's regiment, while three more of his comrades lay close to death in the hospital.[105] He was not near the deadline because he fell against a tent, but somehow, his behavior provoked a guard to fire with deadly results. Private Bower's death was doubly poignant because the day he was buried at the City Cemetery, the Dix-Hill Cartel was signed. Parole for the inmates of the Lynchburg POW camp was no longer a dream; it was soon to become a reality. On July 28, Mike VanBuskirk noted the good news in his journal: "It appears we are all going to be exchanged in a short time. O joy in camp."[106] Private VanBuskirk was among the first inmates to leave Lynchburg on August 8, 1862.

That morning, the prisoners marched from the Fair Ground to the Southside Railroad depot and boarded the cars for Petersburg. There, they transferred to the train that brought them to Richmond at about nine o'clock that night. Their final destination was Belle Isle where they stayed until mid–September.[107] The following morning, Private Roberts and the remaining internees captured during Jackson's Valley Campaign boarded the cars around noon and headed to the Confederate capital. The march from the Richmond depot to Belle Isle was one and a half miles. Roberts noted in his diary on August 10 that he was now able to wash clothes and go swimming. VanBuskirk also noted the chance to swim.[108] On September 13, 16 weeks after the first Union soldiers were captured by General Jackson's forces, the original inmates of the Lynchburg POW camp marched to Aiken's Landing just below Dutch Gap on the James River and were paroled into Union custody—free men at last.

As the Union prisoners who were well enough to travel were packing their few possessions for the long journey to Richmond, the men of the Forty-Second North Carolina Volunteer Infantry were preparing to make that same trip. Colonel Gibbs had received orders from General Lee that his regiment was to enter field service.[109] With Colonel Gibbs out of the way at last, Captain John Galt assumed command of the Lynchburg POW camp, but his tenure was short lived. In the August 20, 1862, edition of the *Richmond Dispatch*, there was a brief article announcing the appointment of Lieutenant Thomas Platt Turner, commandant of Libby Prison, as the provost marshal of the city of Lynchburg. Not only was the Hill City to be under martial law, but Turner was also in charge of the POW camp. His appointment was intended not only as the first step to ending the crime wave that had gripped the city since April 1861 but also as a solution to the problem of deserters from the Confederate armed forces. Far from the fields of battle, Lynchburg had become a rendezvous point for defectors. While Turner was

Chapter 3. The Lynchburg System

on assignment in Lynchburg, Lieutenant William H. Allison of Elliott's City Battalion was in charge of Libby Prison under the command of Captain Henry Wirz.[110]

Before he left for Lynchburg, General Winder promised that Lieutenant Turner was to be promoted to captain as soon as possible, the rank held by most provost marshals, but the approval of his advancement in rank stalled in a Senate committee. Turner thus was faced with dealing with officers like Galt who outranked him. Frustrated at every turn by one crisis after another, Turner appealed to George W. Randolph, secretary of war.[111] His carefully worded petition proved successful. Captain Turner was able to check the crime wave, deal with the deserter problem using both persuasion and the noose, and leave the Union POW camp in good order before he was replaced as provost marshal by Captain Thomas D. Jeffries. At the end of October, he returned to Richmond to assume his duties as commandant of Belle Isle.[112]

During the year that the Dix-Hill Cartel was enforced, the Lynchburg POW camp functioned smoothly as an auxiliary transit camp. Wounded or ill Union soldiers were triaged at the depot or in the infirmary at the camp and assigned to a hospital inside the city where they remained until they were fit to travel. If they died, they were buried by Diuguid in the City Cemetery. The duration of stay of the sick and wounded who survived might be a few days, weeks, or months, while their comrades might wait at the camp for a few days or a couple of weeks at most. They then traveled to Richmond via Petersburg and either marched or took the cars to Aiken's Landing or later to City Point to be paroled.

However, without warning on December 24, 1862, President Jefferson Davis issued General Orders 111, which suspended the parole of Union officers in retaliation for General Benjamin F. Butler's ordering the execution of William B. Mumford for treason on June 7, 1862. Mumford was convicted of desecrating the U.S. flag that he removed from the New Orleans Mint on May 26. According to Davis' order, if apprehended, Butler was to be hanged at once, and all officers serving under him were worthy of the same punishment. Enlisted men and noncommissioned officers continued to be treated as POWs and thus eligible to be paroled and exchanged, but Black Union soldiers were to be returned to their owners by their respective state governments.[113] Davis' mandate was both ill-timed and ill-advised because the cartel was more advantageous to the Confederacy than the U.S. government. By the end of 1862, when a man joined the Confederate Army or Navy, it was for the duration of the war with no term limits. Men who volunteered for service in a Union unit did so for a set period, usually three years, so there was a concern that paroled Union POWs were more likely to choose not to reenlist.[114] This possibility was soon confirmed.

On December 28, 1862, Lieutenant Colonel William H. Ludlow, who was the agent for exchange of prisoners at Fort Monroe, Virginia, wired Secretary of War Edwin M. Stanton asking for instructions concerning the provisions of General Orders 111. Stanton replied at once that no Confederate officers who were POWs were to be paroled until further instructions were issued by his office. Two days later, Union general in chief H.W. Halleck notified all the major generals in the field that Confederate officers were to be detained until further notice.[115] Private soldiers and noncommissioned officers continued to be paroled for exchange.

After the Union victory at the Battle of Stone's River in early January 1863, the western front was quiet until early March when the first signs of spring were evident in mid–Tennessee. Thus, when orders arrived from Major General Rosecrans' headquarters that the 30-mile area between Franklin and Columbia be reconnoitered, Brigadier General Charles C. Gilbert might have sent a small scouting party to probe the area looking for the enemy, but instead, on March 4 on Gilbert's orders, Colonel John Coburn of the Thirty-Third Indiana Volunteer Infantry—a force of 2,837 men encumbered by an extensive baggage train—began the journey from Franklin to Columbia. They had advanced barely 13 miles when, long before they reached Thompson's Station, they encountered a Confederate force five times larger.[116] Surrounded by the enemy, Coburn's men fought until they were forced to surrender. The dead numbered 48, the wounded 247, and POWs 1,151. Confederate casualties numbered 300.[117] Colonel Coburn's men were not allowed to bury their dead or tend the wounded. They were ordered to begin immediately a 75-mile march to the depot at Tullahoma, Tennessee, where they boarded the first train of many that brought them to Lynchburg.[118]

On March 17, 1863, the Lynchburg camp was faced with an unexpected challenge when at least 1,000 prisoners captured at the Battle of Thompson's Station arrived at the Virginia and Tennessee depot. They began the approximately 560-mile journey from Tullahoma, Tennessee, on March 5, and when they arrived in the Hill City, many were near death from untended wounds or exposure. They had marched through days of constant rain, forded waist-deep streams, been stripped

Chapter 3. The Lynchburg System

of everything but their uniforms, and during their 500-mile rail journey, they rode on flat cars. Those who died of their wounds or exposure were buried in unmarked graves along the route. The last food they had was provided by residents of Shelbyville, Tennessee, on March 7.[119] The most serious cases were evaluated at the depot and taken by ambulances to hospitals throughout the city. Those enlisted men and noncommissioned officers who were able to walk marched out to the Fair Ground, while the officers were assigned to one of the tobacco warehouses. Among the hundreds who were treated in the city's hospitals, only eight died.[120] It was a testament to the quality of medical care available in Lynchburg to all in need. The officers and enlisted men who were ambulatory left for Richmond on March 16.[121] On April 1, the first 400 prisoners from the debacle at Thompson's Station were paroled at City Point, Virginia, and two weeks later, the remainder joined them.[122]

Then on June 30, 1863, President Lincoln issued General Order 252, which suspended the cartel over the question of the treatment of Black Union soldiers by Confederate commanders in the field as well as the official policy of the Confederate government toward armed Black soldiers and their white officers. Black Union soldiers who were former slaves were to be returned to their owners. Those who were free by birth or manumission were likely to be sold as slaves, and white officers who commanded Black soldiers could be shot for inciting a slave rebellion. The implementation of these penalties devolved on the individual Confederate states. Despite this interruption, exchanges still occurred on a limited basis.

In November 1863, Major General Benjamin Butler was appointed commander of the Department of Virginia and North Carolina, and once he began acting as a special agent for exchange, he was able to facilitate one-for-one exchanges for the following nine months. Although Butler was considered an outlaw by the Confederate government and subject to immediate execution if captured, Colonel Robert Ould, the Confederate agent of exchange, was permitted by the Davis administration to negotiate with Major John E. Mulford, Butler's assistant agent for exchange.[123] Even as Butler was taking up his command in Norfolk, Captain Sidney Winder, General Winder's son, was on his way to Georgia to find a suitable location for a camp to hold all the Union soldiers and noncommissioned officers. Fort Sumter near Andersonville, under the command of Captain Wirz, admitted its first prisoners on February 24, 1864. The Lynchburg auxiliary camp remained in operation until the end of the war, but its inmates were no longer sent to Richmond;

instead, they headed south to Danville, Salisbury, and eventually, to Andersonville.

Along with hundreds of Union soldiers, Corporal Charles Smedley and Private John Northrop[124] were captured on May 5, 1864, during the Battle of the Wilderness. Their first destination was Orange County Court House which was approximately 20 miles from where they were taken prisoner. From there, they were marched to Gordonsville where they boarded the train for Lynchburg. Northrop's train arrived at the Orange and Alexandria depot in Lynchburg at three in the afternoon on May 9, and the prisoners marched up Main Street to 5th Street and the remaining miles to the camp. The 600 soldiers[125] were greeted by the usual assembly of locals whom Northrop described as "some of the dirtiest objects found in the filthiest portions of the cities," and he described Lynchburg as "dirty, dilapidated, cluttered with businesses."[126]

When Northrop reached the camp, all the shelters were occupied. Successive provost marshals had not replaced the tents returned to Richmond in the late summer of 1862, and therefore, there was nowhere to sleep but in a hollow by one of the streams that flowed near the Fair Ground. The Union prisoners were guarded by boys too young to be drafted and old men—the Silver Grays. Among the men also under guard were Union sympathizers who were on parole from the local jail. Lynchburg residents still came to sell produce while others just gawked at the Yankees. Others came for more serious purposes, some to bring a cart loaded with free home-baked bread, some to apologize for the treatment of the captives, and one to denounce the Confederate government. Heedless of warnings from a guard, one citizen turned to Private Northrop and said so all could hear, "We would be glad to see you out of here; we are sorry that men have to be so treated for this worthless government." He tore up some Confederate money and threw a roll of it to the Union soldiers. The man ignored the guard's threat to shoot him. However, when several more guards were summoned, he did not resist arrest. After that encounter, contact between prisoners and nonmilitary personnel was forbidden, including civilian sentries.[127]

The train in which Corporal Smedley traveled to Lynchburg left Gordonsville shortly before midnight and arrived in Lynchburg at 10 in the morning of May 10. Upon reaching the POW camp, he and his fellow Pennsylvanians were placed in the same deep gully with Smedley and the New Yorkers, just as rations—hardtack and bacon—were being issued.[128] Both Northrop and Smedley mentioned the presence of several cannons on the hill above them,[129] a precautionary feature also

Chapter 3. The Lynchburg System

very much in evidence on Belle Isle. After four nights of sleeping in the open—including three in pouring rain—Private Northrop and his fellow mess members boarded a train headed south on May 13.[130] On May 17, Charles Smedley wrote a final letter to his father, and the following morning he began that same journey. He died on November 16, 1864, still a prisoner. John Northrop, resident of Los Angeles, California, died September 22, 1923.

In the months following the Battle of Lynchburg, Union POWs, primarily from the western theater, continued to arrive in Lynchburg where they were held at the Fair Ground camp before being shipped south. Those who were wounded or seriously ill were treated in the military hospitals in the city, where 108 Union soldiers died between June and December 1864. They were buried in the City Cemetery by Diuguid.[131]

On October 1, 1864, Corporal Charles A. Coward of G Company, Tenth New Jersey Volunteer Infantry, was the second and last prisoner shot by a guard at the POW camp. He was taken to Massie's tobacco factory for treatment, but the wound was mortal.[132] Toward the end of January 1865, the renewal of a regular prisoner exchange began with the endorsement of General Ulysses S. Grant.[133] Initially, preference was given to the "walking wounded" and those who were not critically ill, but soon, all prisoners were eligible for parole and exchange. The last Union soldier to die in Lynchburg was Private Sidney Acker of M Company, Eleventh Michigan Cavalry. On June 3, 1865, like all his fallen comrades, he was buried in the City Cemetery by Diuguid.[134]

Chapter 4

Vermin and Vespers

In his communiqué to General John H. Winder dated June 18, 1862, Colonel George C. Gibbs mentioned that 30 Union officers were admitted to the newly opened POW camp but that they "are in a different part of the grounds from their men."[1] In some cases, officers were separated from the other prisoners for their own safety. Many of the officers in volunteer units owed their commissions to wealth, connections, or both, and often they were not popular or respected by the men under their command. In any case, there was little danger that they could rally the enlisted men and take control of the Fair Ground. Many of the officers in the Union and Confederate Armies had no military training before the war. Most men in the lower ranks tolerated their posturing and incompetence, while some like Frank Wilkeson openly despised them. At the age of 18, Wilkeson enlisted as a private in the New York Eleventh Volunteer Light Artillery on March 29, 1864, and he left the service when he resigned his commission as a first lieutenant on March 14, 1866. He earned his rank because he was a first-class soldier and a natural leader whom the soldiers under his command esteemed.

Wilkeson had nothing but contempt for officers twice his age who, in his opinion, were not fit to tie the bootlaces of the common soldiers under their command. His disdain was also leveled at men like Major General Joseph Hooker, Brigadier General Ambrose E. Burnside, Brigadier George G. Meade, and Brigadier John Pope who only wasted lives. He also had no respect for most of the graduates of West Point. Wilkeson laid some of the blame for the tremendous loss of life during the Civil War on the fact that they were trained to be commanders, not soldiers.[2] His memoir, first published in 1886 under the title *Recollections of a Private Soldier in the Army of the Potomac*, was unlike many similar works because G.C. Putnam's Sons, a major publishing house, issued it. This is not surprising because Wilkeson was the son of Samuel Wilkeson, a journalist, and Catherine Cady, the sister of Elizabeth

Chapter 4. Vermin and Vespers

Cady Stanton, one of the leaders of the women's suffrage movement. His father was a war correspondent for the *New York Times*, and after the war, Wilkeson also wrote for said newspaper and *Harper's Weekly*. The riveting eleventh chapter of his memoir, "How Men Die in Battle," sets his work apart from most of the other memoirs of the Civil War.

During the Battle of the Wilderness, May 5–7, 1864, Wilkeson experienced an epiphany. Because of the nature of the terrain, which was heavily wooded, the light artillery was ordered to go into reserve just outside the forest and wait to engage the enemy. The cacophony of rifle fire seemed endless. Amid the din, almost soundlessly, a hospital was created to the rear of the cannon; it included a fleet of ambulances and wagons filled with medical supplies. No sooner were the surgeons' tents erected than the first casualties came staggering out of the undergrowth. As the morning progressed, the sun rose higher in the sky only to be obscured by a haze of rifle fire. By noon, Wilkeson could resist the lure of battle no longer. Knowing that it was easier to ask forgiveness than permission, he slipped away from his post and headed down the narrow road that led to the front lines. Almost immediately, he saw the wounded, the dying, and the dead in the shade of trees just coming into full leaf. Soon, he encountered armed guards patrolling access to the rear, and when Wilkeson asked why there was a picket line behind the army, he received a quick reply from one taciturn guard: "Sending stragglers back to the front.... No enlisted man can go past me to the rear unless he can show blood."[3]

Despite the guard's advice to return to his battery, Wilkeson pressed onward until he was 40 yards from the battle line. Retrieving the cartridge belt and rifle from a fallen Union soldier, he joined a squad and began firing into the thick cloud of gunpowder smoke. Early in the afternoon, there was a lull in the fighting, and Wilkeson was disappointed that no attempt was made to take advantage of this opportunity. "We did not advance. Indeed I saw no general officer on the battle-line to take advantage of any opportunity that the battle's tide might expose a man of military talent. I had seen some general officers near the reserves, but none on the front line."[4] Quick action on the part of an officer like Brigadier General George H. Thomas might well have prevented what happened next. Troops under the command of Confederate lieutenant General A.P. Hill attempted to turn the Union left flank, opening a wedge between the Second and Fifth Corps. Luckily, the Union forces were able to regroup and thwart this maneuver. Wilkeson fought until nightfall brought a temporary halt to the battle.

Somehow in the dark, he found the Fortieth New York Volunteer Infantry and bedded down among friends. In the morning, he tried to return to his battery, but he was not allowed to pass the picket because he was not wounded and still was outfitted like an infantryman. He fought on the front line another full day, but the next morning, May 7, having discarded his leathers and rifle, he was able to slip past the guards because he was escorting an ambulance. Wilkeson was reprimanded for being absent without leave, but the boy who left his post to experience battle returned to his unit a man. Twenty-two years passed before he shared how those three days had taught him the full meaning of bravery and sacrifice. In 1895, nine years after Wilkeson published his memoir, Stephen Crane's masterpiece, *The Red Badge of Courage*, appeared. Henry Fleming, its hero, and Frank Wilkeson could well have been comrades in arms.

Cowards and bounty jumpers[5] earned Wilkeson's contempt, but the men who faced death every day with fear and the resolve to do their duty won his respect, if not reverence. On the second day of the Battle of the Wilderness, Wilkeson, who was rattled by the bullets flying all around him, fell in with an older soldier who taught the artilleryman how to fight as an infantry soldier. All day long they skirmished as a team until the older man took a bullet in his "bowels," which knocked him to the ground. Retrieving his rifle, he refused all help, choosing to die fighting.[6] If death came instantly, it might be described as "good," but too many soldiers suffered an agonizing death and none more so than those trapped by the fires that erupted in the dry underbrush that was everywhere. Badly wounded soldiers, catching whiffs of the acrid smoke on the wind that swept through the forest, lay with their cocked rifles ready to commit suicide rather than be burned alive.[7] Near the fighting around Spotsylvania Court House, Wilkeson encountered a large group of wounded men lying quietly in the shade of a grove of large oaks waiting for death to claim them. One was even filling his pipe for one last smoke before the end.[8] Later Wilkeson noted, "Long before the campaign was over I concluded that dying soldiers seldom called on those who were dearest to them, seldom conjured their Northern or Southern homes, until they became delirious."[9] Many of the letters from commanding officers or friends to grieving family members describing the "good death" their loved one had experienced were carefully crafted half-truths meant to spare them the agony of knowing what really happened. When it came to informing the public about the plight of POWs, there was no such restraint. Some of the most graphic descriptions of

Chapter 4. Vermin and Vespers

the Confederate camps appeared before the war ended, and they were often accompanied by graphic photographs taken once the prisoners were paroled into Union custody.

Once the Confederate government in Richmond began to rent or requisition permanent structures for hospitals and other purposes, the captured Union officers in Lynchburg were moved to more secure quarters. Unfortunately, it is not known whether Colonel Gibbs or Captain Turner moved the 30 officers from the Fair Ground camp to one of the tobacco factories, probably Wade's tobacco factory on Lynch Street,[10] but they were certainly established there when the Union soldiers captured at the Battle of the Wilderness arrived in Lynchburg in May 1864. The descriptions of the ramshackle quarters where officers were housed indicated that numerous men had been confined there in circumstances not unlike those at Libby Prison.

While trying to rally all the men under his command, Major Charles Mattocks of A Company, Seventeenth Maine Volunteer Infantry, was captured on May 5, 1864, just as the slaughter at the Battle of the Wilderness was accelerating.[11] By nightfall, with 9 other officers and 150 men, Mattocks was under guard at Parker's store near the Old Orange Plank Road, the site of a cavalry skirmish earlier in the day. The following morning, they began a 20-mile march to the Orange County Court House, which they reached at nightfall. Exhausted, after spreading their rubber blankets, they slept on the ground wrapped in their woolen blankets. Boarding a train on May 7, they arrived in Gordonsville where they were marched to a nearby field, searched, and stripped of everything of value. The prisoners of all ranks were housed in a tobacco factory near the station to await transport to Lynchburg. Finally, at two o'clock the following afternoon, they boarded the train to the Hill City.[12]

Major Mattocks remarked in his journal, "We have had a great time on the cars today." As their train slowed to pass through Charlottesville, it was mobbed by students from the Albemarle Female Institute[13] who thought they were greeting Confederate soldiers. When, to their disgust, they discovered cars full of Yankee prisoners, the girls fled. "Such screeches and such skaling [sic] of fences I never saw, and such skedaddling back. They surpassed the Rocky Mountain Sheep."[14] Three miles outside Charlottesville, the train lost power, so the last cars were left on a side track. Thus, Major Mattocks was among those who did not reach Lynchburg until the following dawn. The officers were housed on the second floor of Wade's tobacco factory on the upper end of Lynch Street, while the enlisted men and noncommissioned officers were marched to the Fair Ground.

On May 12, Mattocks recorded the arrival of an officer from the Third Michigan Volunteer Cavalry, bringing the total number of incarcerated officers to 111. This was not unusual save for the fact that he had been a prisoner at Libby Prison for seven months and was emaciated. He had been on his way south to Danville when he slipped off the train, but he was so weak that he was unable to make good his escape.[15] His presence seemed to confirm the rumors that the Confederate authorities were systematically starving Union prisoners. On May 15, Mattocks began to describe life in what he designated "Hotel de Yanks."

Each day while in Lynchburg, they received a tiny piece of pork and a small loaf of corn bread, the starvation diet that was routinely issued daily to the inmates in the Richmond prisons. The windows could not be opened, so there was no circulation of fresh air save through one partially boarded window. The men passed their time talking, playing cards, or reading if the slaves that serviced their prison could smuggle in a book or newspaper. The latter were read aloud and subjected to lengthy discussions, particularly those dealing with political and military subjects. By the spring of 1864, most dailies in the Confederacy had been reduced from four pages to two because of a critical shortage of newsprint paper. The guards, however, were veritable repositories of rumors and gossip, which they readily shared with their charges hoping to undermine their morale. Prisoners were allowed to write notes to family members and friends, but they were confined to the front of one-half of a standard sheet of paper. These brief notes were then carefully censored, a practice that began when the first Union prisoners were jailed in Richmond in 1861.[16]

The men were organized into 10 messes; each week, a new member of the mess collected the daily rations and distributed them to his messmates. Major Mattocks and his fellow officers exchanged their U.S. "greenbacks" for Confederate script, at a rate of five to one. For instance, a poor-quality woolen blanket that cost $5 in U.S. dollars cost $25 in Confederate script.[17] With Confederate money, they also were able to supplement their daily rations because once their regular chores were done, the slaves who worked in the prison were allowed to shop for the Yankees at the city market, which was only a few blocks from their prison.

Mattocks survived his ordeal as a POW in part because he was in good physical condition and he also never lost his sense of humor. In his

Chapter 4. Vermin and Vespers

diary, he included a sketch of "The only article of Furniture in the 'Hotel de Yanks' at Lynchburg, Va. May, 1864," a potbelly stove.[18] The men were forced to sleep on the floor, and Mattocks used his boots as a pillow—which he also sketched in his "Journal."[19] He began his first entry on May 17 by speculating on the possibility of parole and exchange, never realizing that before nightfall, he and his 110 fellow officers were to leave "Hotel de Yanks," march to the Southside Railroad depot, and board the prison train headed South.[20] Mattocks eventually escaped from Columbia, South Carolina, rejoined his unit, and received the Medal of Honor for his actions during the Battle of Sailor's Creek on April 6, 1865.

First Lieutenant John V. Hadley of B Company, Seventh Indiana Volunteer Infantry, was captured on May 5, 1864—the opening day of the Battle of the Wilderness—but he found his stay in Lynchburg hardly amusing and the quarters he shared with Charles Mattocks anything but adequate. Hadley left Butler University and entered the service as a corporal on September 13, 1861. He was severely wounded on August 30, 1862, during the second Battle of Bull Run but recovered quickly. On October 1, 1862, he was promoted to first lieutenant and assigned to the staff of Brigadier General of Volunteers James Clay Rice who commanded the Second Brigade, Fourth Division, Fifth Corps. Rice's subordinates referred to him behind his back as "Old Crazy." Five days after Hadley was captured, General Rice was killed during the Battle of Spotsylvania Court House. Hadley rose through the ranks and earned his promotions—he was the kind of officer of whom Frank Wilkeson approved.

Hadley was one of 500 prisoners escorted to General Lee's headquarters before beginning their day-and-a-half trek to Gordonsville. Mattocks and his men had been hastily searched in an open field. By contrast, Hadley and his men were taken one by one into a small office under the guard of two soldiers with fixed bayonets. There, they were strip-searched by order of the provost marshal who confiscated everything of value as well as any item that interested him, including one soldier's used ivory-handle toothbrush. Once they were dressed in what was left of their uniform, each prisoner was told to bivouac under guard in a nearby field until their daily rations arrived. Finally, at nine o'clock that night, each man was given two ounces of bacon and a pint of cornmeal, but they had neither wood to build a fire nor utensils with which to prepare a meal.[21] Around noon the next day, the 500 men were loaded on open cars and began the long, tedious journey to Lynchburg over tracks badly in need of repair.

Hadley's remarks upon his arrival in the Hill City only served to reinforce the fact that it was the only major urban area in Virginia untouched by the war. He was struck first by the beauty of the place nestled at the foot of the Blue Ridge, the gently flowing James River, streets that climbed the hills, and handsome buildings from another era unscarred by war. "From the signs of freedom and comfort all about, it was hard to believe that we were prisoners."[22] When the enlisted men, who were bound for the Fair Ground, were separated from the 14 officers, Hadley's illusions were shattered. They were locked in a poorly ventilated, vermin-infested chamber that was 700 square feet of filth. The inmates—16 criminals and 14 Union officers—were not allowed to leave the room. Overcrowding due to the influx of prisoners from the Battle of the Wilderness was likely the reason for placing Union officers in the same room as criminals. At the end of their "cell," all the human waste was deposited in two leaky barrels. When these makeshift chamber pots were filled, slaves assigned to the prison emptied the contents in the prison yard behind the building and returned them. With every breath he took, Hadley was reminded of the accepted belief among most of the members of the medical community that malodorous air could fatally infect those who breathed it. Because of the stench that permeated everything in his prison cell, he believed those in authority were trying to shorten the lives of their captive foes.[23]

The only comfort that Hadley seemed to have derived from his three-day ordeal was finding the names of a number of missing comrades scratched on the wall near one of the small windows. "I well-nigh shouted for joy when I saw them, and thought that I was upon the same road, and would meet them within a few days."[24] His wish was granted on May 17 when all the Union officers from Wade's tobacco factory and the men from the Fair Ground boarded the train at the Southside depot and headed to Danville.

Second Lieutenant Joseph Ferguson of E Company, First New Jersey Volunteer Infantry, was taken prisoner on May 12, 1864, during the Battle of Spotsylvania Court House. After being stripped of his personal possessions, he and his fellow captives immediately were forced to march the approximately 40 miles to Gordonsville to prevent the possibility of their being rescued by the ever-shifting line of battle. There, the same provost marshal who had interviewed Lieutenant Hadley confiscated everything else of any value, including tents and blankets, and consigned his prisoners to a dank cellar where they spent the night with only a handful of cornmeal for food.[25] No fresh air in an open field for

Chapter 4. Vermin and Vespers

them and no rancid bacon either. The next morning, Ferguson and his fellow prisoners were released from their dungeon to begin the long journey to Libby Prison in Richmond.

Ferguson was not in Richmond very long, but nonetheless, he experienced all the horrors of the place that were already familiar to readers in the North. His fellow prisoners below the rank of second lieutenant were assigned to Belle Isle, which by the spring of 1864 was tantamount to a death sentence. Union prisoners were being shifted to camps farther south, so Ferguson was soon on his way to Lynchburg packed in a cattle car. With him was a 17-year-old boy who had been shot in the shoulder, but when Ferguson tried to get some water to wash the soldier's wound, their guard refused.[26] The young private was not mentioned again, so perhaps on arrival in Lynchburg, he was assigned to one of the hospitals where he received proper treatment.

When the cars were unloaded at the Southside depot, all Union captives not ill or wounded were put in charge of one of the local militia units which Ferguson described as "the most tyrannical tools who had charge of us while in Virginia."[27] When they trudged up 9th Street hill to Main Street, they were greeted by the usual surly crowd that had gathered to harass the latest group of Yankee prisoners. While waiting to advance, Ferguson asked a bystander, who appeared sympathetic, if he might have a drink of water, and the man complied. The Good Samaritan immediately was arrested for giving comfort to an enemy combatant and supporting the Union cause. Walking those four blocks from 9th Street to 5th Street—where the officers were separated from the noncommissioned officers and the enlisted men—amounted to running a gauntlet of verbal abuse, but on the day that Ferguson came to Lynchburg, the "Boys in Blue" fought the profanity with a song. Suddenly, one of the officers began singing "The Battle Cry of Freedom," and soon, every Union voice joined the choir, drowning out the catcalls. Then they marched in step as if on parade, leaving the "welcoming committee" far behind them. Only the slaves followed these tired, bedraggled soldiers who were the champions of their freedom. One of their number already had been beaten by local hooligans when he offered a prisoner some tobacco.[28]

The POWs, whether at Wade's tobacco factory or the Fair Ground, received no food that night because they had sung a "Yankee hymn" on Main Street.[29] Sleeping was almost impossible because the third floor was occupied by the overflow from the city jail and their noise never ceased day or night. From the window at the far end of the room where the Union officers were confined, Ferguson could watch slaves at work in the enclosed yard where the privy was located. Each prisoner was allowed to make only one visit per day and only under guard. No exceptions were made for this rule, even for those suffering from diarrhea. Ferguson also watched what appeared to be the death of a Black soldier from New Jersey who had served as the cook for an officer in his regiment. The soldier who had received a chest wound when he was captured was now bayonetted in the side.[30] During the week Ferguson spent in Lynchburg, his daily ration consisted of a small piece of partially cooked corn bread and an even smaller piece of pork. Finally, the Union inmates of Wade's tobacco factory were marched down to the Southside depot and packed in filthy cattle cars—80–90 per car with no ventilation—and headed to Danville, Virginia, the next stop on the way to Macon and Andersonville, Georgia.[31]

On July 4, 1863, shortly after he graduated from Harvard Divinity School, Charles Alfred Humphreys enlisted in the Union Army. On August 21, he mustered into S Company of the Second Massachusetts Volunteer Cavalry with an officer's commission as a chaplain. While on reconnaissance near Aldie, Virginia, on Wednesday, July 6, 1864, Humphreys and his comrades encountered a group of Mosby's Rangers.[32] In the ensuing skirmish, a number of men were killed or wounded. Humphreys was captured the next day by the ranger who had stolen his horse, and with his fellow captives, the chaplain began the 70-mile journey on foot to Orange Court House, which they reached on Sunday. After a meager meal, they were put in dirty cattle cars and began their journey to Gordonsville. That night, they slept in a cattle yard near the railroad tracks. On the morning of July 11, they were reloaded in the same cars for the seven-hour journey to Lynchburg, their next destination.[33]

Humphreys was imprisoned in a tobacco factory[34] very close to the College Hospital where preference was given to Confederate soldiers from Virginia and Union soldiers from West Virginia because the Confederate government did not recognize the secession of the western counties from the Old Dominion in July 1863. By the summer of 1864, most of the tobacco factories in Lynchburg were filled either with wounded soldiers from both sides or with Union prisoners. Barely three weeks had passed since the Battle of Lynchburg and some captives from the POW camp at the Fair Ground and those soldiers captured during the battle were crowded into every available space while they awaited shipment to facilities farther south—Macon, Georgia, for

Chapter 4. Vermin and Vespers

officers and Andersonville for noncommissioned officers and enlisted men.

The factory where Chaplain Humphreys was kept had three stories, but the upper floor was an attic, which was too hot to use in the daytime because of its tin roof. Two hundred of the 650 Union soldiers packed into the warehouse were wounded, but when Humphreys arrived, they had not received any medical attention. The officers were temporarily housed in a room 12 feet square. Because he was a clergyman, Humphreys was allowed to tend the wounded. With permission from the prison commandant, he sent a written request for medical supplies to the chief steward at the nearby College Hospital. The slave who delivered the note returned with a verbal reply: "You shall have nothing. We must get rid of the Yankees in one way or another."[35] Thus, the only bandages available were rags smuggled into the prison by the slaves who worked there, and the only antiseptic was water.

In his later account, Humphreys implied that the mortality rate was extremely high during the time he was in Lynchburg,[36] but he obviously was unaware that after Richmond, Lynchburg was the largest hospital center in the Upper South.[37] The carts that passed by Humphreys' prison contained Confederate as well as Union dead on their way to the City Cemetery to be buried by Diuguid. During the nine days Humphreys was in Lynchburg, data for 17 Union soldiers were entered in "Diuguid Soldiers Book"; 14 died at Crumpton's tobacco factory, two at the College Hospital, and one at Camp Davis.[38]

In addition to his complaints about the close confinement, the filthy bare floors on which they were forced to sleep, and the misinformation the guards shared with the prisoners hoping to shatter their morale, Humphreys was concerned about the food. He ate the half pound of corn cake he received daily and discarded the rotten pork, but he worried about the health of one of his messmates, Lieutenant Charles Walter Amory,[39] who had been wounded and was losing strength because he could not eat the food. Humphreys exchanged his cavalry boots with one of the guards for a pair of shoes and $250 in Confederate script. With it, he bought palatable food for Amory, especially white bread.[40] With permission from the commandant, slaves purchased most of these extra food items from the city market.

Humphreys quickly earned the reputation of being a sincere man of faith, and a delegation from all the floors in the prison asked him to conduct a service on Sunday, July 17. He received permission from the officer in charge to hold the meeting, and at three o'clock in the afternoon, despite the heat, the third floor was packed. Humphreys selected Psalm 137 as his text because the hardships he had suffered over the last 10 days emboldened him to speak his mind. The words so familiar to many broke the silence: "By the rivers of Babylon, there we sat down, yea we wept, when we remembered Zion." He then continued through verse 5, "If I forget thee, O Jerusalem, let my right hand forget her cunning," before pausing to remind his comrades to remember their country's cause, endure their present suffering, and have faith that the Union would triumph. They finished the service by standing and singing "America." On the edge of his audience was the officer of the guard and several of his subordinates, so Humphreys perhaps was not surprised when he was arrested shortly after he had lain down to sleep that night. He was taken on orders of the provost marshal, Captain Van R. Otey, to the guardhouse.[41] Many Southerners were well versed in scripture and knew how Humphrey's psalm of choice ended. Verse 8 echoed the provocative words of Humphrey's sermon: "O daughter of Babylon, who art to be destroyed; happy shall he be, that rewardeth thee as thou hast served us." It was, however, the following and final verse that sent him to a cell fouler than the one he left: "Happy shall he be, that taketh and dashed thy little ones against the stones."[42]

Humphreys spent three nights in the crowded guardhouse, which was located in the attic of a two-story building in the center of Lynchburg. The room was 12 feet by 30 feet with two small windows overlooking a small yard surrounded by a high fence. Under the glassless windows was a barrel that served as the privy. The room was so full that it was impossible to lie down on the floor to sleep. Humphreys was reunited with his comrades from the tobacco warehouse on the morning of July 20, and together, they marched to the train that carried them to Danville. However, Humphreys' final destination was to be Castle Pinkney in Charleston Harbor. There, he joined other Union officers whose behavior while prisoners had offended the Confederate authorities to the point that they were now subjected to friendly fire. Finally, in early September, he was paroled for exchange. On September 17, he arrived home. By October 13, he had returned to his regiment.[43]

John Springer Heald was 23 when he joined the Ohio 116th Volunteer Infantry on August 8, 1862. On September 9, he mustered into C Company as a sergeant. Severely wounded on June 5, 1864, during the Battle of Piedmont, he was placed in a hospital in Staunton, Virginia. When Union brigadier general of volunteers David Hunter left Augusta County, that facility came under Confederate control. On June

Chapter 4. Vermin and Vespers

28, wounded Union prisoners were loaded on a train four miles outside Staunton—64 men per car—and shipped to Lynchburg. The journey took a full day; when they reached the city, they were offloaded and marched to the commandant's headquarters.[44] Here, they were deprived of their crutches and walking sticks lest they use them as weapons. Some, like Heald, could not walk unassisted, but they were beaten into line and marched to a slave pen in the rear of the building. A mob followed them, cheering the guards who physically and verbally abused them for moving too slowly. Barely 10 days had passed since General Hunter's failure to take the city, and the rabble was in a foul mood.[45] Heald was unaware that nine of his comrades had been killed and 29 wounded during Hunter's abortive attempt to take Lynchburg. It was ironic that those men from his regiment who still lived were being treated with care at the overcrowded College Hospital while Heald was unable to obtain clean water to wash his own wound which had only begun to heal.

Before they were locked inside the enclosure, the prisoners were given a small piece of bread and some fat pork, the first food they had eaten in days. In the morning, they were taken to the POW camp at the Fair Ground because in the aftermath of the Battle of Lynchburg, there was no space available in the officers' prison or any of the hospitals. Heald's description of the ravine and the brook where he and the other wounded men could clean their wounds and bathe is the same area in the POW camp described in the narratives of several enlisted men who were detained there. They all remained there for two days under constant guard.[46] On July 1, those prisoners from Staunton who could walk and 1,200 recently captured Union soldiers began a 70-mile march from Lynchburg to Danville. Normally, this journey was made by train, but the rails were still under repair. Without food or water, the journey was made on foot in the midst of a summer heat wave. Heald survived the death march, but many did not.[47] The system that had evolved for two years and had worked with such efficiency until the summer of 1864 was overwhelmed by the influx of too many prisoners, a critical lack of supplies and equipment, and a dwindling supply of qualified personnel to administer it.

The spring of 1861 seemed far in the past, but many remembered how the first crisis dealing with Union prisoners began in 1862 and Colonel George Gibbs' successful response to it. The presence of so many men from remote rural areas living in close quarters led to the outbreak of several epidemics including measles and smallpox—both of which

Abandoned in May 1861, Lynchburg College became the first Confederate military hospital in Lynchburg. During Reconstruction, it was a barracks for Union soldiers (author's collection).

were potentially fatal in young adults. The response of the medical community was immediate, and such cases were isolated in the Pest House Hospital, which stood just outside the Lynchburg city limits; other diseases and injuries were treated in private homes until, with support from the city council, the doctors opened the Hill City's first hospital in the deserted buildings of the first Lynchburg College.[48]

When the faculty and student body from Lynchburg College marched off to war, the empty campus was transformed into the College Hospital, the first military infirmary in the city. Its conversion to a general hospital, which accepted sick and wounded military personnel regardless of unit, rank, or branch of service, was relatively easy, and the first measles-related death of a Confederate soldier was recorded there on May 20, 1861. Its capacity was established at 500, which was unrealistic; many more beds were needed, particularly facilities closer to the railway depots where triage was performed. After that preliminary examination, wounded or seriously ill soldiers were sent to the College Hospital or a private home somewhere in the city based on the nature and severity of their condition. Most of these patients had

Chapter 4. Vermin and Vespers

already received preliminary treatment at a field hospital that served the needs of one particular unit. Luckily, solutions to the lack of hospital beds were found on Main Street.

Among the numerous hotels in Lynchburg that accommodated travelers and businessmen in the 1850s, two of them saw service as hospitals during the war. The Union Hotel—known as the Ladies Relief Hospital during the war—stood at 600 Main Street and was open from 1861 until shortly after the war ended. With a capacity of 100 beds, the Warwick House Hotel at 1003 Main Street was in use from August 1861 until the opening of the "tobacco hospitals" a year later.[49] The first Union casualty recorded in Lynchburg was Private Wallace Smith of the Sixtieth New York Volunteer Infantry, who died at the Warwick House Hospital on April 24, 1862, and was buried by Diuguid at the City Cemetery that same day.[50]

Before the war ended, 32 structures in Lynchburg had served as general hospitals, but the Ladies Relief Hospital was the most celebrated, and its indomitable founder, Lucy Wilhelmina Norvell Otey, became a Virginia legend. Despite the work of Florence Nightingale during the Crimean War (1853–1855), Americans still considered nursing an occupation inappropriate for women. As the war progressed, hospital authorities everywhere, overwhelmed by the enormity of the task of caring for thousands of casualties, reluctantly permitted married women, widows, and Catholic nuns to assist in the hospitals as nurses. However, unmarried women, regardless of age, were allowed to perform only the most limited tasks. They might write or read letters, bring flowers, read the Bible or other appropriate books, or wipe a fevered brow, but they could not perform nursing duties lest they inadvertently view a man's genitalia.

Mrs. Otey believed that this was utter nonsense and she said so to anyone who listened. When she offered her services, and those of some of her close friends, as nurses, she was rebuffed by Dr. William Otway Owen, the chief surgeon, who said he wanted neither flies nor women in his hospital.[51] Mrs. Otey refused to take no for an answer; instead, she took the train to Richmond and requested an appointment with President Jefferson Davis. What she said to Davis is not recorded, but when the formidable Mrs. Otey boarded the train for home, she had permission to open the Ladies Relief Hospital and a captain's commission as well. In a letter dated August 30, 1936, William Walker Hurt, who became a field-worker for the Historical Inventory, Works Progress Administration of Virginia, wrote to Anne Norvell Otey Scott, a granddaughter of Mrs. Otey, that recently he had forwarded a copy of Lucy Mina Otey's commission as a captain to Dr. H.J. Eckenrode, the state historian. Unfortunately, the current location of that copy of her commission is unknown.[52]

With her army of 500 women, regardless of race or creed, she declared war on dirt, disease, and death. Of the other hospitals in Lynchburg during the war, none had the record of survival or the reputation of the Ladies Relief Hospital because of Mrs. Otey's emphasis on cleanliness as well as the devotion of her nurses to the welfare of their patients.[53]

The Confederate Congress passed a joint resolution in March 1862 encouraging farmers to plant foodstuffs instead of tobacco. This provided Surgeon General Samuel Preston Moore with the justification he needed to appropriate 19 tobacco factories in Lynchburg to be used as hospitals. The owners had two choices—they could allow the government to requisition their tobacco factory or they could let it on a lease to be terminated at the end of the war. Surely, the latter option was preferred because the owner received modest rent for his property,[54] and although it did not equal his prewar annual income, it was better than nothing. Male and female slaves of all ages, who were leased before the war by their owners to the proprietors of the various tobacco factories, had manufactured and packaged the tobacco products on which Lynchburg's wealth was based. Lest their owners lose a significant part of their annual income, these same slaves toiled in the hospitals performing all the labor-intensive tasks that provided a modicum of care for the patients, both Confederate and Union. The men collected the wounded and sick and delivered them by wagon or ambulance to their proper destination, carried them on stretchers to their assigned cot, and acted as their nurses. The women cooked, cleaned, laundered, and nursed. White women volunteered as nurses in only three hospitals—the College Hospital, Ladies Relief Hospital, and Pest House Hospital. The same law that allowed the Confederate government to appropriate a tobacco factory for a hospital was used to commandeer empty factories as prisons for Union officers. The sequestered factories housed casualties and prisoners until the end of the war because in March 1863 and again in February 1864, the Virginia General Assembly passed measures that continued the restrictions against the cultivation of tobacco. By 1865, it was so rare in Virginia that a "plug" was more negotiable than Confederate currency.

Between April and August 1862, 14 of the tobacco factories secured

Chapter 4. Vermin and Vespers

Miller's Tobacco Factory on the right and Knight's Tobacco Factory on the left served as military hospitals from August 1862 until April 1865 (courtesy Lynchburg Museum System).

by the Confederate government were opened as hospitals. They retained that status until April 1865, while, during that same period, five other factories were used for the same purpose on a temporary basis. The permanent tobacco hospitals were Booker's, Burton's, Candler's, Christian's, Claytor's, Crumpton's, Ferguson's, Ford's, Knight's, Langhorne's, Miller's, Reid's, Taliaferro's, and Saunders'. The temporary tobacco hospitals were Chambers', Massie's, Planters', Sheau's, and Wade's.[55] These brick structures rested on solid stone foundations and were several stories high with tin roofs. Their framing and flooring were designed to sustain heavy loads. Although spartan, with only the bare necessities, they were perfect buildings to adapt for hospital use. Their floors and walls muffled sounds. Temporary walls were installed easily to create offices and surgeries. However, they were filthy and everything was covered with tobacco dust, especially the windows. The slaves who had worked in these factories were given the herculean task of cleaning them once the equipment was removed. Pratt Hospital was also a permanent hospital located near Camp Davis, where Virginia soldiers were housed, but there were also temporary hospitals at Camp Nicholls, Dudley Hall, and the Odd Fellows Hall.[56] During the war, at least 50 private dwellings also served as temporary hospitals and convalescent homes.[57]

Lynchburg was remote from the major contested areas of the Upper South, but it was accessible by rail, although the journey grew longer as the war progressed because the tracks and equipment steadily deteriorated. During the first two years of the war, wounded and ill soldiers were simply left on the platforms of the various Lynchburg depots to be evaluated and collected by the slaves assigned to the various general hospitals. As the daily totals of sick and wounded arriving in the city increased, it was necessary to reorganize the original hospital system in the name of compassion and efficiency. In August 1863, the Wayside Hospital was created as a triage and assignment center. It was located originally at the corner of Franklin and 9th streets,[58] but within a month it was moved to the block on Jefferson Street between 6th and 7th streets, which was within walking distance of the three railroad depots.[59]

After triage, Confederate soldiers in need of special nursing were sent to the Ladies Relief Hospital. Those who needed immediate surgical attention were transported to the Odd Fellows Hall on 12th Street between Main and Church streets.[60] Those suffering from serious communicable diseases like measles, typhoid fever, and smallpox were sent to the Pest House at 315 Wise Street.[61] Soldiers with minor wounds and other ailments were assigned to one of the general hospitals. The staff at the Wayside Hospital received regular reports from all of the hospitals, and thus, the staff knew which beds were available. After surgery, patients were transferred to one of the general hospitals. Confederate soldiers who were well enough to resume limited duties were then sent to Camp Nicholls, which was next to Camp Davis, whereas recovering Union soldiers were transferred to the POW camp at the Fair Ground or the tobacco warehouse designated for officers.

With this well-ordered modus operandi in place and functioning by 1863, Dr. Owen and his medical staff sought to make the system more efficient and economical. By the beginning of 1864, the supervisors of the three specialty hospitals—Wayside Hospital, Ladies Relief Hospital, and Pratt Hospital—reported directly to Dr. Owen and therefore were not supervised by the same authority that oversaw the general hospitals. There were three general hospitals in Lynchburg, each one composed of several divisions. General Hospital Number One consisted of three divisions and was organized as follows: Division One—Read's tobacco factory and Booker's tobacco factory; Division Two—Langhorne's tobacco factory; and Division Three—Burton's tobacco factory and Candler's tobacco factory. Likewise, General Hospital Number Two was composed of three divisions and was organized as follows: Division One—Chamber's tobacco factory, Christian's tobacco factory,

Chapter 4. Vermin and Vespers

and Sheau's tobacco factory; Division Two—Ford's tobacco factory and Crumpton's tobacco factory; and Division Three—Miller's tobacco factory and Knight's tobacco factory. General Hospital Number Three included two divisions, each with a single factory: Division One—the College Hospital; and Division Two—Ferguson's tobacco factory. Each of the general hospital divisions as well as the three specialty hospitals was supervised by a surgeon. The Pest House was in a category all by itself.[62]

When the system developed in Lynchburg, which afforded Union POWs several levels of care, is compared to facilities available in Richmond, it truly deserves the appellation "prototype." In his exposé *The Prisoner of War, and How Treated*, which was published shortly after the end of the war, Second Lieutenant Alva C. Roach of the Fifty-First Indians Volunteer Infantry included a chilling description of the "care" Union prisoners received in the Richmond hospitals during the last two years of the fighting. The infirmary in Libby Prison did not have enough bunks, so most of the patients were forced to lie on the floor without any covering. The men brought from Belle Isle to the hospital for Union prisoners often died shortly after they were admitted. As prisoners from Belle Isle were shipped South early in 1864, they were sent first to the prison in Danville, which was trying to cope with an epidemic of smallpox. This was a death sentence for most half-starved Union soldiers from Belle Isle who were not vaccinated against the variola virus. While dozens of men were dying from smallpox in Danville,[63] the medical authorities in Lynchburg were about to take a radical step that saved potential victims from it.

Although vaccination against smallpox had been practiced since the late 18th century and both George Washington and Napoleon I had required their soldiers to be protected against it, most Americans at the time of the Civil War were not vaccinated. Vaccination against smallpox was more common among the literate and urban dwellers, but the majority of enlisted men in both the Union and Confederate armies came from rural backgrounds, and unless they had survived cowpox—a milder form of the disease—they had no immunity to the often fatal form of *variola major*. It was possible to recover from smallpox, but the skin on the patient's face, arms, and legs was often horribly scarred. The death rate among the smallpox patients who were sent to the Pest House between April 1861 and June 1863 was 50 percent, which was 15–20 points above the national average. That was unacceptable to Lynchburg physician Dr. John Jay Terrell who volunteered in the late summer of

1863 to become the doctor in charge of the Pest House Hospital. Dr. Owen readily accepted his offer. Dr. Terrell then made three demands of his superior: first, that he report directly to Dr. Owen on all matters relating to the operation of the Pest House Hospital; second, that he might select three male nurses to perform specific tasks—a painter, a master carpenter, and a druggist; and third, that he be supplied with vegetables, milk, and whiskey as needed. Whiskey, when combined by a druggist with a number of easily obtained pieces of bark from certain trees and shrubs, produced "bitters," which were considered essential to the healing process from smallpox. Dr. Owen agreed to all of Dr. Terrell's conditions, and the latter immediately assumed his new assignment.

Because the Pest House was overcrowded, a barn on the property was commandeered, cleaned and repaired, the exterior painted yellow and the interior painted black, and disinfected with slaked lime. Slaked lime was a 19th-century remedy for spaces where unpleasant odors might accumulate; it also stopped decomposition. Once the lime had reduced the stench in the barn and the Pest House, it was replaced with noncaustic white sand to absorb odors.[64] The barn was then equipped with cots and fresh linens. After some of the patients from the Pest House proper were bathed and given clean clothes, they were moved to the barn while the main building underwent the same renovation, room by room. Initially, Dr. Terrell had a serious problem with the soldiers assigned as nurses to the Pest House Hospital. They could not withstand the stench produced by excretions from the smallpox lesions and threatened to ask for transfers to field duty. They were somewhat mollified by the quickly executed reforms and renovations, and Dr. Terrell's lurid tales of life on the front lines ultimately convinced them to stay.[65] Another solution to the need for skilled, competent nurses came from the Roman Catholic Church. Father Louis-Hippolyte Gache, chaplain at the College Hospital, was the only local clergyman to visit the Pest House Hospital regularly, and he was able to gain permission for some of the Sisters of Charity to assist Dr. Terrell. The members of this order were trained nurses who worked in both Union and Confederate hospitals during the war. Like Father Gache, they were inoculated against smallpox. Slowly, the death rate from the disease dropped from 50 percent to 5 percent. Patients were not released from Dr. Terrell's care until they were fully recovered—Union soldiers to the POW camp or the officers' prison and Confederate soldiers to Camp Nicholls or a private residence that served as a convalescent home.

Chapter 4. Vermin and Vespers

On May 5, 1864, during the first day of the Battle of the Wilderness, Captain George W. Watson of Company H, Ninetieth Pennsylvania Volunteer Infantry, was hit twice as he led a charge on a Confederate battery. The first bullet fractured his right thigh; the second hit his sheathed sword bending it while badly bruising the already shattered limb. The ground around him was littered with the wounded, dead, and dying men from his unit. It was not until May 7 that he was found and taken to a Confederate aid station where his right leg was amputated up to his thigh. He awoke to find his cap, haversack, and his left boot stolen. He later saw his right boot still on his severed right leg being carried to a burial pit. Using his last bit of money, he paid a Confederate soldier to fashion him a crude cot. Watson was one of 800 wounded men lying in that wooded area in sunshine and rain. As the days and weeks passed, the number dwindled as death harvested the victims of the Battle of the Wilderness, but Watson survived on his meager daily rations, the occasional cup of water, and a periodic change of the dressing on his wound, which miraculously did not become infected. Finally, on June 5, a full month after he was wounded, Watson was loaded in an ambulance and carried to the Orange Court House railroad. The following day, along with the wounded, both Union and Confederate, he was put on a train to Gordonsville and then to Lynchburg where he was assigned to a ward for officers in one of the tobacco hospitals,[66] probably Crumpton's tobacco factory. Captured during Hunter's retreat after the Battle of Lynchburg, Frank Reader made a similar reference to the building where he was held from July 3, 1864, until July 19, when 500 prisoners were put on a train bound for Andersonville.[67]

Watson spent most of his days picking "graybacks" from his clothes and his bedding. One day while killing lice, he remembered that a boyhood companion, George Gamble, a coppersmith by trade, lived in Lynchburg. The link between Philadelphia and Lynchburg was long-standing—dating back to the first Quaker settlers. The slaves who serviced Watson's ward were forbidden to speak with the prisoners. Breaking this rule could result in a severe beating, but one young man whom Watson had befriended was willing to take that chance. Several nights later when the ward was dark, he crept up to Watson's cot and whispered that he had found Gamble who promised to call on him as soon as he was able. It took several days to gain permission to visit a Yankee prisoner, but eventually, Gamble was escorted to Watson's bed. Because of his expertise with copper, Gamble was not in the Confederate Army but was assigned to the Lynchburg locomotive works. He brought Watson $200 in Confederate money that afternoon and, on his subsequent visit, an equal amount.[68]

With the money borrowed from Gamble, Watson was able to buy a pair of crutches and some more palatable food for himself and his comrades on his ward. Despite the possible personal risk, a slave woman who had access to the hospital purchased these items for him. He began to master walking with one leg, and as his skill improved, he was able to help care for the officer in the cot next to him. On September 5, Captain Henry C. Kenner of the Fourth United States Cavalry was admitted to Watson's ward with a mortal chest wound. With an attendant's assistance, Watson tried to make Kenner as comfortable as possible. Before he died on September 8, Kenner told Watson that he had a large amount of money sewn in the waistband of his drawers. He wanted it to be used to care for his fellow officers on that ward. An attendant removed the money after his death, only to have it appropriated by the Confederate surgeon on duty. Shortly after that incident, Watson was transferred to the College Hospital where most of the attendants were white.[69] Finally, in October 1864, Watson was paroled for exchange. After an arduous journey, he was able to convalesce in the military hospital in Annapolis, Maryland, until he was well enough to return home to Philadelphia.[70] Thanks to his strong constitution and the care he received in Lynchburg, Watson survived to live to the age of 86 when the life expectancy for a white male was 40.

It appears the experiences of the Reverend Humphreys and Captain Watson were exceptions rather than the rule in the Lynchburg hospital complex where the majority of physicians were true to their Hippocratic Oath. Dr. Edward A. Craighill was an excellent example of a doctor dedicated to his profession. He was the assistant surgeon at the College Hospital from the late spring of 1863 until the early fall of 1864 when he took charge of the hospital located in Ferguson's tobacco factory.[71] Toward the end of his tenure at the College Hospital, Craighill was responsible for the care of the wounded Union soldiers left at Sandusky by General David Hunter when he made his hasty retreat by moonlight after losing the Battle of Lynchburg on June 18, 1864. Three-quarters of the 117 severely wounded men survived, and they were paroled for exchange when they were well enough to travel.[72] The following year, soon after the end of the war, Dr. Craighill chanced to meet several of his former patients who were part of the Union occupying force. They offered to help him in any way they could. He thanked them for their kindness but accepted only their good wishes,

Chapter 4. Vermin and Vespers

which had lifted his spirits more than any material help they might supply.[73]

By the time Craighill met his former patients in downtown Lynchburg, the College Hospital had become a barracks for the occupying Union forces.[74] The Fair Ground was about to be repurposed as the revitalized city began to expand toward the west, the refurbished hotels were ready to cater to a new clientele, and the tobacco hospitals reverted to their regular function. A completely free labor force was cleaning the last while reinstalling the overhauled machinery. The clandestine tobacco harvest of 1865 was much smaller than those of former years because of the Confederate government's repeated prohibition against growing it, but 1866 was a bumper year. The College Hospital became a barracks until the end of Reconstruction and the Ladies Relief Hospital was again a hotel, but there was still continuity—the Pest House never lacked patients.

Chapter 5

The Lynchburg Campaign

On March 9, 1864, President Lincoln promoted Ulysses S. Grant to the rank of lieutenant general and appointed him general in chief of the Union Army. Immediately, Grant set to work on a strategy called the "Overland Campaign," which was designed to end the war by attacking the Confederacy on several fronts simultaneously.[1] The Shenandoah Valley was still the "breadbasket" of the Army of Northern Virginia, and during the Valley Campaign of 1862, General Stonewall Jackson had conducted a brilliant operation that denied the Union that prize. To reverse that setback, the man Grant chose to open the Valley Campaign of 1864 was Major General Franz Sigel. Honest and straightforward almost to a fault, Grant was a soldier, not a politician; therefore, he was unaware of the reason that led Secretary of War Edwin Stanton to recommend his friend Sigel for this important command.[2] A German refugee from the Grand Duchy of Baden where he was involved in the Revolution of 1848, Sigel owed his rapid advancement in the Union Army to his ability to recruit soldiers from the German immigrant community. Although "I Goes to Fight mit Sigel" was a popular ditty, the Battle of New Market on May 15, 1864, blighted the already lackluster career of Franz Sigel. Former vice president of the United States, Confederate major general John C. Breckinridge, quickly assembled a smaller force, which included cadets from VMI, and momentarily dealt a severe blow to Grant's grand design.

After Sigel was abruptly relieved of his responsibilities, Stanton recommended that he be replaced by another of his protégés, a member of the West Point class of 1822, Major General David Hunter. Grant quickly agreed, and on May 21, Hunter assumed command of the Army of the Shenandoah and the Department of West Virginia. Hunter actually rode to Sigel's headquarters in Middletown in Frederick County to inform him of the change of command,[3] which showed a sensitivity not usually associated with the man known on both sides as "Black Dave."

Chapter 5. The Lynchburg Campaign

Once the requirements of military etiquette were satisfied, Hunter turned his attention to making sure that the soldiers in the Army of the Shenandoah were properly equipped for the campaign that lay ahead of them. One thousand men were without arms and 2,000 were shoeless.[4] While these deficiencies were being remedied, Hunter issued General Order No. 29 on May 22 from his temporary headquarters near Cedar Creek, which was just south of Middletown. In a tersely written introduction and six detailed paragraphs, he outlined the responsibilities of all the soldiers under his command.[5] The precise tone of the document gave encouragement to the soldiers and officers who were still recovering from the debacle at New Market—that they now had a general who understood his business. They knew that Staunton was still their current destination, but this time, they had a West Point graduate to command them. On May 28, the Army of the Shenandoah was on the march. The following day, while the Union Army waited for a bridge over Narrow Passage Creek, burned during their retreat from New Market, to be replaced, reconnaissance showed that the enemy was within striking distance. Therefore, General Hunter did not stop at Mount Jackson but pressed on to Rude's Hill where Confederate troops had been sighted. However, by the time the advanced guard reached the Rude farm, the Confederates had retreated toward Harrisonburg.[6] The Union Army bivouacked at Rude's Hill the night of May 29.

Long before they reached the site of the Battle of New Market, the Army of the Shenandoah was aware of its proximity. The wind carried the smell of rotting flesh, both human and animal, for miles. As the men approached the location of the Union calamity, the roadside was littered with the carefully skinned carcasses of dead, shoeless horses,[7] but it was the partially buried decaying bodies of their comrades that both sickened and infuriated the survivors of New Market. Stripped of everything but their shirts, they had not been buried but only lightly covered with loose dirt, which had been turned into mud by recent rains.[8] The Confederates had buried their dead, including four VMI cadets, in a nearby churchyard with 30 graves properly marked and 8 unknown.[9] The Union Army remained in the New Market area for four days, burying the soldiers who had fallen on May 15 and burning the carcasses of the dead horses.[10]

The primary destination of the first phase of General Grant's Valley Campaign remained Staunton, and on June 2, the Army of the Shenandoah left New Market and headed south to Augusta County by way of Harrisonburg and Port Republic. There was constant skirmishing all along the line of march because the Confederates could not afford to lose either Staunton's supplies or its rail connection. Having beaten the Yankees at New Market, they prepared to do it again at the Battle of Piedmont on June 5, but Brigadier William E. "Grumble" Jones was no John Breckenridge. Despite the support of Brigadier General John D. Imboden, Jones was killed and his hastily assembled force was routed. Hunter had the chance to pursue Imboden and trap him in Waynesboro but chose not to do so.[11] This was perhaps the first in a series of mistakes Hunter made in his Valley Campaign, but that was not initially apparent. On June 6, the victorious Union Army marched into Staunton to martial music. The town that Sigel had failed to take was now at the mercy of "Black Dave" Hunter.

Almost immediately, a committee including the mayor, prominent citizens, and officials—both elected and appointed—appeared at General Hunter's headquarters in the Virginia Hotel. They sought his promise that the city was safe from being torched. He assured them that private property was exempt from destruction, but this guarantee did not apply to military installations or supplies. The Virginia Central Railroad was also marked for destruction. Between their arrival on Monday and their departure on Friday, various units of the Army of the Shenandoah carried out their general's orders. By Wednesday, whole areas of Staunton were smoldering ruins. The smoke was so thick that Hunter moved his headquarters from the hotel to a tent in an apple orchard outside the town.[12] The problem that confronted Hunter was not so much leaving a great deal of his first objective in ashes but rather how to reach Lynchburg and repeat the process. He had two alternatives. The first, which he personally favored, was to march from Staunton to Charlottesville, lay waste the town dear to Thomas Jefferson's heart, and then proceed to Lynchburg. This was the route that Grant outlined in his letter sent from Cold Harbor, Virginia, on June 6, 1864—a letter that Hunter unfortunately never received.[13] However, Charlottesville was deemed too close to Richmond, and there was no reliable information on the status of the Virginia Central Railroad leading to the capital. General Lee might be able to send troops to impede Hunter's planned rendezvous with Major General Phillip H. Sheridan. The second course of action was to reach the Hill City by way of Lexington, Buchanan, and the Blue Ridge Mountains and enter from the west, but a course that took the army over the mountains demanded adherence to a precise timetable. Ultimately, on the advice of his staff, Hunter chose the latter route and left the details to one of his officers, Brigadier General William W. Averell.[14]

Chapter 5. The Lynchburg Campaign

Among the Union wounded at the Battle of Piedmont was Major General Julius Stahel who had commanded the cavalry. Although severely injured in the shoulder, Stahel continued to lead his men until he was no longer able to do so. He recovered, but his field career was over. Like Stigel, he had been involved in the Revolution of 1848, but unlike the congenial but inept German, Hungarian-born Stahel was a competent soldier and commander. Major General Henry Halleck replaced this Medal of Honor recipient with an ebullient Frenchman, Brigadier General Alfred N. Duffié. Hunter appealed to Halleck to send him anyone except Duffié, but Halleck refused, stating that the Parisian was next in line for a command. From the moment they met, Duffié and Averell were enemies. A member of the West Point class of 1855, Averell never missed an opportunity to belittle Duffié to his fellow alumnus, and Hunter was more than willing to listen.[15] Averell's plan for the seizure of Lynchburg assigned a key role to Duffié's cavalry, but it appears that he also intended to make sure that his hated rival failed.

At seven in the morning on June 10,[16] the Army of the Shenandoah left Staunton on four parallel roads and headed south toward Lexington. General Averell's cavalry division took the western road on the extreme right, and the infantry division under General Jeremiah C. Sullivan was on the left of the main force, taking the valley road, which passed through Greenville to Fairfield where they bivouacked. General Duffié, in command of a second cavalry division, headed due east on the road that ran along the Blue Ridge Mountains toward Amherst Court House, while General George B. Crook's infantry division took the main road heading toward Brownsburg, which was located just north of Lexington.[17] Because supplies were quite low and there was no time to forage, Crook's men were put on half rations.[18] General Hunter was with Crook, and he soon ordered a 13-mile detour to Summerdean, where he arrested David Stuart Creigh.[19] The previous year, Creigh had been accused of killing a Union soldier who had attempted to plunder his home and then hiding the body. That night, Crook's division bivouacked at Midway (Steeles Tavern), barely 18 miles from Staunton. Early the following morning, a 10-mile detour to Brownsburg was made; there, Creigh was tried and hanged.[20] Meanwhile, despite limited resources, Brigadier General John McCausland was able to slow the Federal advance by constant skirmishing and using sharpshooters; thus, after the first day, Union forces had only reached a point within 10 miles of Lexington.

Reveille was sounded at four in the morning on June 11. Within an hour, General Sullivan's troops were headed for their rendezvous with General Hunter. The previous afternoon, a 250-wagon supply train from Martinsburg, West Virginia, had encountered Sullivan's force, and now his men had full rations and mail from home. As they approached Lexington, artillery fire was heard. Crook's units had already reached the north fork of the James River—now the Maury River—and were exchanging fire with McCausland's retreating forces, which had tried to destroy the bridge over the stream. Sullivan's men remained on the north side of the river and did not enter Lexington until the following day, June 12.[21] Meanwhile, the Confederate troops positioned on the wooded crown of a perpendicular cliff that rose above the south bank of the river began firing at Crook's troops. Immediately behind the thicket were buildings that formed part of VMI campus,[22] and cadets soon joined the attack. Hunter, who avoided bombarding civilian targets if possible, sent a brigade under the command of General Averell, which forded the river above the place of engagement in an attempt to outflank their opponents.[23] It was difficult to conceal Averell's force from the sentinels on the promontory, so by the time he reached his objective, the enemy had fled.[24] General Crook ordered Colonel C.B. White to execute a similar maneuver from another direction, which also failed to achieve its target.[25] The Confederate regulars retreated to Buchanan while the 250 cadets under the command of Professor Colonel Francis H. Smith, the superintendent of VMI, took the Balcony Falls Road to Lynchburg where they joined the hastily organized defense of the city.[26]

As McCausland's soldiers had retreated to the VMI Post—the name by which that campus is known—they had set fire to the bridge. But although it was badly damaged, the structure was quickly repaired, permitting General Hunter, his staff, and the units under General Crook's command to enter Lexington. By the time they reached The Post, Union soldiers, slaves, and some locals already were plundering VMI barracks. Before Hunter commandeered the superintendent's home as his headquarters, he stopped by the house of Major William Gilham and informed Mrs. Cordelia Gilham that her house was to be burned in the morning because her husband was a rebel officer. She had until then to remove all her family's belongings.[27] Immediately, several officers, including Captains Henry DuPont and William McKinley,[28] helped Mrs. Gilham and her children remove their possessions from the house. Other officers found her shelter in the town and food for her family.[29]

According to Averell's plan, General Alfred Duffié was to cross the James River after destroying the military stores at Amherst Court

Chapter 5. The Lynchburg Campaign

House and dismantle enough of the Orange and Alexandria Railroad to prevent it from being used to reinforce Lynchburg. General Hunter had a reputation for destroying everything in his path, and a rumor sweeping through central Virginia claimed that he had burned all of Lexington. It was assumed that Duffié was doing likewise as his cavalry rode toward the Hill City. Therefore, residents of Amherst County began to seek shelter in Lynchburg.

Averell had no way of knowing that Duffié had almost successfully completed his mission when he convinced Hunter that Duffié was lost. Distracted by his obsession that McCausland and his ragtag regiment continued to occupy parts of Lexington, Hunter granted Averell permission to send 200 cavalrymen to follow Duffié's route, duplicate the same objectives, and rejoin the main force at Liberty in Bedford County, Duffié's original point of rendezvous.[30] Even as Duffié was close to completing his objective, Hunter, at Averell's urging, recalled him to Lexington on June 11. Later that morning, Hunter, consumed by the crisis on the banks of the river, forgot that he had recalled Duffié because he sent him a second order that contained instructions on how to find Amherst Court House where he was to destroy a bridge and do other damage before joining the army in Buchanan. When the courier reached Duffié the following day, June 12, the Frenchman had no choice but to obey orders; however, it took him over 24 hours to rejoin his commander. The limited destruction Duffié had done to the railroad was easily repaired. In the aftermath of the Lynchburg debacle, General Averell blamed Duffié for the failure to take the city when, in fact, the ultimate responsibility lay with Hunter. His remaining in Lexington until June 14, when he should have left for Lynchburg at least a day earlier, saved the Hill City. Hunter claimed he was waiting for another supply wagon train. Ironically, Duffié, while heading to Lexington, intercepted and burned a supply wagon train meant for the Confederate forces that had just reoccupied Staunton.[31]

Ensconced in his headquarters in the home of the VMI's superintendent, Hunter spent a fair amount of time discussing what should be done with the buildings that comprised The Post. The majority of his staff felt that the barracks should be torched because the cadets and sharpshooters had used it as a fort from which to attack the Union soldiers who were trying to occupy Lexington. Furthermore, it was the property of the state of Virginia, which was in rebellion against the United States, and it contained an arsenal that must be destroyed. There were conflicting views. Colonel David H. Strother, Hunter's chief of staff, considered it a seat of sedition where youth from all over the South were schooled in treason,[32] while Colonel Charles G. Halpine, Hunter's adjutant, viewed VMI as a seat of learning, which, after the war, might play a vital role in repairing the fractured union.[33] Unfortunately, those who favored destruction prevailed, and Hunter gave the order that every building except the superintendent's home was to be burned. It was spared because it was Hunter's headquarters and a baby had just been born there with the mother still recovering.[34]

The destruction of the VMI buildings began early on the morning of June 12 while the barracks were being looted. The professors' homes burned quickly, but the fire in the barracks took hours to destroy most of the building. Even the explosion of the arsenal around two in the afternoon did little to hasten its collapse.[35] In addition to the buildings on The Post, several mills, numerous warehouses with their contents, the gasworks, and the town magazine were razed.[36] Coming off picket, Private Charles H. Lynch of the Eighteenth Connecticut Volunteer Infantry described the scene that greeted him upon returning to his billet: "It was a grand and awful sight to see so many buildings burning at the same time."[37] While Hunter enjoyed watching the general conflagration from a hill near VMI, an officer brought him a copy of half a typeset manuscript of a proclamation written by the former governor of Virginia, John Letcher, who was a resident of Lexington. Letcher called on the citizens of Rockbridge County, in which Lexington was located, to "arise and slay the foul Yankee invader."[38] Hunter was furious. Upon entering Lexington the previous day and learning that the former governor had fled, Hunter stationed two officers with the Letcher family and placed a guard around the house in case there might be an attempt to loot it or harm any members of the family. But now Lexington's leading citizen had attempted to incite guerrilla warfare.[39] Hunter ordered that the Letcher mansion and all its contents be burned immediately. The family was given only 10 minutes to vacate the premises.[40] Seventeen-year-old Elizabeth Letcher begged to be allowed to remove some household goods, but her request was denied.[41] As the house began to burn, she attempted to escape with a bundle of clothing, but that too was set on fire. Although other homes were damaged during the exchange of cannon fire between the Confederate and Union batteries on June 11, as well as the brief occupation of Lexington by Federal troops, the Letcher mansion with its dependencies was the only private property destroyed on General Hunter's orders. Former governor Letcher's mother's house was next door, but

Chapter 5. The Lynchburg Campaign

Union soldiers prevented her home from burning by using a bucket brigade.[42]

Washington College was not demolished by fire, but it was vandalized by both Confederate and Union soldiers. Before their retreat on June 11, General McCausland's troops were quartered at Washington College, and they did a fair amount of damage to the campus, especially the library. In his history of the Eighteenth Regiment, Connecticut Volunteer Infantry, Chaplain William Walker remarked, "That the books of the library were scattered over the floor of the building, and the injury done was very great. This was not all the work of Yankees—the rebels did their full share."[43]

On the afternoon of June 12, a trustee of Washington College sought a meeting with Colonel Strother to seek an end to the ransacking of the college. Strother immediately placed a guard around the perimeter and assured the gentleman that Washington College was not to suffer the fate of VMI.[44] However, Strother did not know that a number of books and valuable pieces of equipment from VMI had been moved and stored on the campus of Washington College.[45] The trustee did not share that information with Strother lest General Hunter learn of it and feel compelled to punish the faculty of Washington College for its collusion by burning their college too. Generals Averell, Crook, and Sullivan had already protested to General Hunter concerning "wanton vandalism" against Washington College.[46] While Hunter quickly approved Strother's measures to protect the college, he was more concerned with properly securing his own trophy from the VMI fire—a bronze copy of Jean-Antoine Houdon's marble sculpture of George Washington, which still stands in the rotunda of the state capitol in Richmond, Virginia. The bronze was carefully packed and loaded in a wagon usually designated for the weary and the wounded. It was hauled up the Shenandoah Valley and across the Blue Ridge Mountains to the outskirts of Liberty, Virginia. It was then sent under guard to West Virginia where it was placed in front of the Linsly Military Institute in Wheeling, West Virginia.[47] In 1866, during Reconstruction, Strother was briefly adjutant general of the state of Virginia and thus an ex officio member of the board of visitors of VMI. Using the authority of his office, he ordered the statue returned to The Post in Lexington.[48]

While belittling Duffié, Averell also secured orders from Hunter to depart at two o'clock in the morning on June 13 for Buchanan,[49] the terminus of the James River and Kanawha Canal. He was to command a cavalry force large enough to entrap McCausland there and secure the route by which the army could safely cross the Blue Ridge Mountains. Shortly before the Union cavalry arrived, McCausland ordered the bridge over the James River burned, and the conflagration spread to 11 private dwellings.[50] McCausland and his men then made their escape over the mountains. Arriving amid the chaos, the Union cavalry formed a fire brigade and tried to save as many dwellings as possible because the inhabitants of Buchanan had offered no resistance to the Union troops. In the chaos, they failed to capture McCausland. Averell's men occupied what was left of the town and prepared to wait for the rest of the army to arrive the next day. At least Averell did not have to face Duffié when the Frenchman discovered his duplicity. The constant tension between his two cavalry commanders continued to distract Hunter from his main objective—the seizure of Lynchburg.

Meanwhile, June 13 dawned clear and hot in Lexington. It became a day of relaxation after all the activity on the 12th. Chaplain William C. Walker of the Eighteenth Connecticut stated, "The men needed a rest." The chief pastime among the members of his flock was making rings and other trinkets from the black walnut boards taken from Stonewall Jackson's grave.[51] Some soldiers washed their clothes, bathed, and enjoyed a day of swimming,[52] while others requisitioned supplies from the shops and stores in Lexington.[53] Porte Crayon, Colonel David Hunter Strother's nom de plume, returned to what was left of VMI and spent a pleasant morning sketching the still-smoldering ruins.[54] The printing press on which John Letcher's proclamation calling for guerrilla warfare was to have been printed was found in the woods and destroyed. It was the property of the editor of the *Rockbridge Gazette* who was arrested, interrogated, and released because he produced an 1861 document that indicated he was a Union man.[55]

Shortly before noon, the long-awaited wagon train of supplies arrived with everything but the ammunition Hunter desperately needed. A separate wagon train had been prepared for that, but General Grant was unaware that Hunter had not received his letter of June 6 with his orders for the raid on Lynchburg had been lost or intercepted. By June 13, the Union Army should have been in Charlottesville, not Lexington. Hunter was heading to Lynchburg but by the wrong route. Proper and timely reconnaissance would have determined that the railroad between Richmond and Charlottesville was not operational, permitting Hunter's troops to destroy the Orange and Alexandria Railroad mile by mile as they moved southwest from North Garden to Lynchburg. Since Hunter's exact location was unknown, Grant's cancellation

Chapter 5. The Lynchburg Campaign

of the shipment of ammunition was prudent. If that wagon train had departed on the appointed day and headed up the Shenandoah Valley, General Jubal Early, who was marching down the valley, would have captured it.[56] General Duffié rode into Lexington early in the afternoon, "all sunburned and dusty"[57] and totally unaware of what had transpired during his absence.

When, at 10 o'clock on the morning of June 12, General Duffié had received the order to return to Lexington and rejoin the main army, he had spent barely a day completing the first phase of his mission. He was close to Amherst Court House when he was obliged to join Hunter in Lexington. Duffié had made one serious mistake the previous day. He sent 10 men under the command of a sergeant northeast to Arrington to destroy the railroad there, but they encountered Captain Henry C. Douthat's Battery of the Botetourt Artillery on a train bound for Charlottesville and were killed. If Duffié's entire cavalry regiment—instead of just 10 men—had ridden the 26 miles from the Tye River Gap to Arrington, they may have beaten Douthat's battery and then begun destroying the railroad as they moved south to Amherst Court House. Hunter then could have occupied Lynchburg before Early even reached Charlottesville.[58] The only thing Duffié accomplished was capturing a number of Confederate supply wagons which he ordered burned. He took the guards as prisoners and commandeered the horses. One of the couriers traveling with Duffié delivered a dispatch to General Hunter advising him of this encounter, but it arrived only shortly before Duffié himself rode into Lexington.[59]

General Hunter's chief of staff, Colonel David Strother, received General Duffié's verbal report of his exploits. From the interview, he learned that Duffié's first stop was Waynesboro, which was just a few miles from Staunton. There, he drove the Confederate pickets into the town limits. Turning southward, he prevented the reinforcement of General Imboden, and then passing through the Tye River Gap, he supervised the demolition of five miles of the tracks of the Orange and Alexandria Railroad. He captured 70 prisoners, 700 horses, and 300 wagons. A parcel containing several million dollars in Confederate bills was the dramatic denouement of his interview. Strother checked the facts with several of the men under Duffié's command, and the various numbers were reduced, but nobody could explain the money.[60] Duffié obviously shared his exploits with more than Strother because Lieutenant Colonel William S. Lincoln of the Thirty-Fourth Massachusetts Volunteer Infantry recorded in his 1879 history of the regiment, "Gen.

Duffee [sic], of Crook's command, joined [us] to-day. He has scouted within seven miles of Lynchburg; has cut the Charlottesville Railroad in several places; ... blown up several locks on the James River Canal, and destroyed a number of boats, some of them laden with ammunition."[61] Unlike Lieutenant Colonel Lincoln, General Hunter was not impressed by Duffié or his exploits but instead gave him another unpleasant task.

When the Union troops had entered Lexington on June 11, Colonel Strother noted in his journal that there was a great deal of smoke in the mountains to the east of the town. When questioned, slaves did not hesitate to reveal that upon learning of the approach of a large Union force led by "Black Dave" Hunter, a number of Lexington's residents loaded their possessions and supplies into wagons and took refuge in the nearby hills.[62] Duffié was now given the chore of finding these citizens' camps, requisitioning their horses and livestock, seizing their weapons, destroying their wagons laden with food, clothing, and personal possessions, and then escorting them back to Lexington.[63] Duffié executed Hunter's orders with alacrity and, upon his return to headquarters, learned that the army was to leave for Buchanan at seven o'clock the next morning.[64] General Hunter had spent two days pillaging Lexington when he should have left for Lynchburg on June 12. There was no need to recall Duffié and then wait for him—that veteran of the Crimean War was capable of completing his mission and finding his way to Liberty, which was near Lynchburg. The wagon train laden with supplies could have found the army encamped at Buchanan as well as Lexington. Hunter, the victor of the Battle of Piedmont, was lurching toward defeat, but even though his success was in jeopardy, there was still time to save his mission and occupy Lynchburg.

The morning of June 14 was clear and sultry, a typical summer day in central Virginia. The road was dusty, rough, and rutted in places as the Army of the Shenandoah made its way to Buchanan. Reveille was sounded at dawn, the army left Lexington at seven, and as the sun was setting, their 25-mile trek came to an end. On the morning of June 15, many of the soldiers bathed in the river before beginning the long climb over the mountains.[65] The road was very narrow and twisting, and the ascent was made more difficult because McCausland's retreating troops had cut down trees to slow the Union soldiers' advance. Clearing the path took time, and some wagons slid down into ravines and gullies because their drivers could not navigate the sharp turns. By nightfall, the roughly 18 miles between Buchanan and the Peaks of Otter had

Chapter 5. The Lynchburg Campaign

been traversed, and the army bedded down for the night on the Bedford County side of the Blue Ridge Mountains.[66]

As Hunter headed south, Confederate lieutenant general Jubal A. Early and his hastily assembled force marched toward Charlottesville from Richmond because the Virginia Central Railroad was badly damaged. General John C. Breckinridge, still suffering from an injury received at Cold Harbor in early June, rushed toward Lynchburg, reaching it on June 15. There, he collapsed and was placed under medical observation. Fifteen miles from the Peaks of Otter lay the small town of Liberty—renamed Bedford after the war. Here, on June 16, Hunter made the final blunder that cost him a victory at Lynchburg. Despite the protests of many on his staff, precious hours were wasted burning buildings along the route of march, tearing up portions of the Virginia and Tennessee Railroad, and plundering Liberty.[67] In the midst of this chaos, General Averell shared with Colonel Strother a credible report that Lynchburg was not strongly fortified. After receiving this information, General Hunter finally ordered all units to form ranks and move toward Lynchburg.[68] On June 13, Confederate brigadier general Francis T. Nicholls, who was in charge of Lynchburg's earthworks, had written to General Braxton Bragg that he had been forced to abandon a number of strong defensive positions for lack of personnel.[69] This seemed to confirm Averell's intelligence that Lynchburg was defended only by the sick, wounded, old men, boys, and Confederate soldiers released from the local jail. The Union prisoners in Lynchburg—whether at the Fair Ground or in an empty warehouse downtown—must have hoped that the fear that gripped the city was a sign that deliverance was near. By nightfall, 20 miles lay between the Hill City and the Army of the Shenandoah.

After the Union soldiers filled their haversacks with provisions for the forthcoming battle, the 200 wagons laden with supplies that had reached Lexington on June 13 were returned to West Virginia via Lewisburg and Charleston—along with the bronze statue of George Washington—guarded by Colonel Putnam's regiment of Ohio 100-day soldiers.[70] Hunter simply assumed that all the supplies needed by the Army of the Shenandoah were waiting in Lynchburg. That night, some soldiers slept in a cornfield, while others slept on the banks of the Little Otter or the Big Otter Rivers, but it is probable that General Hunter slept very little. At two in the morning, he roused Colonel Strother,[71] reveille was sounded at half past three,[72] and the army was marching before dawn.

There had been continual skirmishes since Hunter left Staunton, as McCausland tried to slow the Union Army's progress, and on June 17, every mile in the heavily wooded area through which the Army of the Shenandoah passed was vigorously contested. McCausland's troop had been reinforced by Imboden who made good his promise to come to Lynchburg's rescue.[73] Those precious hours wasted in Lexington and Liberty should have haunted Hunter, as he waited four hours while a damaged bridge over the Big Otter River was repaired.[74] By the time the army was trudging down the pike toward Lynchburg, the advantage of starting toward Lynchburg before dawn was lost. The heat and humidity were intense, but Hunter could not resist the urge to halt and burn yet another dwelling because he was convinced someone in the house had fired on his troops.[75] When the Union forces reached New London, Hunter finally called a halt so the soldiers could fill their canteens from the alum spring there,[76] tend the wounded, and bury their dead. Slowly pressing the enemy forward, they reached the ruins of the Quaker South River Meeting House on the Salem Turnpike as the afternoon was waning. Here, the Confederate soldiers made yet another desperate stand before they were overwhelmed by superior numbers and retreated to their earthworks that slaves were completing about two miles west of Spring Hill Cemetery.

When Colonel William H. Powell, who commanded the Third Brigade in Averell's Second Cavalry Division, probed Lynchburg's defenses on the western edge of the city, he discovered that they were barely manned.[77] Upon returning to the Union lines, he requested permission from General Hunter to make a sortie. Hunter refused despite the fact that it was barely dusk and the moon was almost full. During the Lynchburg Campaign, Edward S. Wilson was a second lieutenant in Company H of the Ninety-First Ohio Volunteer Infantry, and in 1893, he delivered a lecture on his experiences under Hunter. Wilson confirmed what Powell had suspected: "I was told by Captain Hart, a Confederate officer at Lynchburg at the time, that they were quite overpowered by the first hour's conflict, and that anything like a general attack would have captured Lynchburg and dealt a fatal blow to the Southern Confederacy, for the loss of stores would have hurt Lee worse than many battles."[78] Seemingly more interested in establishing his headquarters and getting a good dinner than endorsing Powell's urgent request, Hunter lost his last best chance to take the city of Lynchburg.

Half a mile from the ruins of the Quaker Meeting House and cemetery was Sandusky House, the home of retired U.S. Army paymaster Major George C. Hutter, a man whom Hunter knew.[79] Major Hutter had

Chapter 5. The Lynchburg Campaign

Brigadier General David Hunter used retired major George C. Hutter's home, Sandusky, as his headquarters on the eve of the Battle of Lynchburg (courtesy Historic Sandusky Foundation).

served in the Seminole Wars, Black Hawk War, and Mexican-American War, and before his retirement in April 1861, he was stationed at Fort Sumter in Charleston, South Carolina. On June 17, 1864, Harriet Hutter was a polite but uneasy hostess to Hunter, a noted artist "Porte Crayon" (Colonel David Hunter Strother), a popular author "Miles O'Reilly" (Colonel Charles G. Halpine), and two future presidents of the United States, Colonel Rutherford B. Hayes and Captain William McKinley. Soldiers from the Signal Corps had already made a hole in her roof to establish a position from which they could keep in contact with all the Union commanders in the field. The possible destruction of her house as a result of the forthcoming battle was surely on Mrs. Hutter's mind as well as the liberation of the family slaves because Hunter was an ardent abolitionist.

Among the most popular Lynchburg legends passed from one generation to another is how Early used an empty train to trick Hunter and his subordinates into believing that Confederate troops by the thousands were arriving in the city during the night of June 17. Using this elaborate ruse, "Old Jube" supposedly saved the city from being torched by "Black Dave," who then fled under cover of darkness on June 18 to the safety of West Virginia. However, in his *Memoir of the Last Year of the War for Independence, in the Confederate States of America*, Early made no reference to using an engine and two cars to fool the enemy. He did mention that most of his force was still in Charlottesville waiting for transportation or marching the 60 miles from North Garden to Lynchburg. It took him almost seven hours to make the trip, thanks to the poor condition of the tracks and a dilapidated engine. He arrived at one o'clock in the afternoon on June 17, when Union forces were already within sight of the city.[80]

The first account of Early using trains to reinforce the garrison at Lynchburg was found in Hunter's report dated August 9, 1864, which was eventually published in 1891 in *The War of the Rebellion: A Compilation of the Official Records of the Union and Confederate Armies*. Trying to mitigate his poor performance at Lynchburg, Hunter's description of the evening events of June 17 made some later renditions modest by comparison: "During the night the trains on different railroads were heard running without intermission, while repeated cheers and the beating of drums indicated the arrival of large bodies of troops in the town, yet up to the morning of the 18th I had no positive information as to whether General Lee had detached any considerable force for the relief of Lynchburg."[81]

In the decades following the end of the war, histories of Union regiments and memoirs of Union soldiers began to appear, and of particular interest are those that concern soldiers and units that were with Hunter during the Shenandoah Valley Campaign of 1864 because many contain variations on Early's use of trains to turn the tide of battle. In 1879, Lieutenant Colonel W.S. Lincoln recalled hearing "at intervals during the afternoon the screeching of locomotives and the rumbling of cars as they were rolled into the city." Lincoln was obviously referring to the arrival of General Early on the Orange and Alexandria Railroad from Charlottesville.[82] First Lieutenant George E. Pond of the Forty-Fifth Massachusetts Volunteer Infantry added drums and cheering in his 1883 work, *The Shenandoah Valley in 1864*, but he reminded the reader that Hunter was still sure of success as long as the reinforcements were not from Richmond.[83] The following year, Lieutenant Colonel Thomas F. Wildes was the first author to mention an exact time for the "arrival" of the first train filled with reinforcements—10 o'clock on the night of June 17—and he added bands playing as the troops disembarked.[84] By

Chapter 5. The Lynchburg Campaign

the last quarter of the 19th century, students of Hunter's 1864 campaign in the Shenandoah Valley had accepted the train stories as fact and took no issue with what Private Charles J. Rawling meant in 1887, when they read his ominous sentence, "The trains on the railroad could be heard arriving from the direction of Richmond, and there could be no question as to the meaning of this."[85] Lee's most seasoned troops from Richmond supposedly arrived in Lynchburg on the Southside Railroad via Petersburg. Actually, Early's troops arrived on the Orange and Alexandria Railroad by way of Charlottesville. Edward S. Wilson's paper "The Lynchburg Campaign," read on February 1, 1893, to the Ohio Commandery of MOLLUS,[86] added the active participation of the local populace.[87] William Walker of the Eighteenth Connecticut added even more detail, noting that Hunter decided to retreat around four o'clock in the afternoon when the rest of Early's force began to arrive from Charlottesville. The sound of drums and cheering was only an echo when the Army of the Shenandoah headed west just as dusk was fading into twilight.[88]

At the request of the Garland-Rodes Camp of Confederate Veterans of Lynchburg, Virginia, Colonel Charles Minor Blackford, himself a Confederate veteran, was asked to read a paper on June 18, 1901, to mark the 35th anniversary of the Battle of Lynchburg. Subsequently published that same year, Blackford includes what was considered the first detailed printed version of Early's ploy: "During the night of the 17th a yard engine, with box cars attached, was run up and down the Southside Railroad, making as much noise as possible and thus induced Hunter to believe and to report that Early was rapidly being reinforced."[89]

By the late 20th century, there was one final twist to the legend that had taken on a life of its own. Two local histories published in the mid–1980s noted that according to Hill City folklore, General Early chose a particular spot for the empty train to run back and forth during the night of June 17. The tracks of the Southside Railroad passed over the old Tin Bridge. Built of wood, it was covered with metal to protect it from rotting. The residents in the immediate vicinity considered it a public nuisance. Every time a train crossed it, the sound produced supposedly could wake a man from a deep sleep. Combined with shouting and the constant blowing of the train's whistle, Hunter was convinced that General Lee intended to defend Lynchburg no matter what the human and material cost.[90] Surely, this cacophony could be heard at Sandusky; however, Colonel David Strother recorded in his journal at the time it was supposedly happening, "A good supper and slept profoundly."[91]

By the morning of June 18, about 10,000 Confederates faced 19,000 Federals as some anxious citizens milled about the streets listening to the sounds of battle drifting like distant thunder from the west. Many had even packed their valuables intending to flee across the river if the Union Army breached Lynchburg's inner defenses. Convinced that Hunter intended to sack and then burn the city, some merchants pitched what was left of their dwindling stock into the streets and urged passersby to help themselves before the Yankees stole everything that they did not burn. By afternoon, however, more Confederate reinforcements under Generals Robert E. Rodes and John D. Gordon arrived from Charlottesville, tipping the balance against the Union forces. Hunter quickly resolved to cut his losses and retreat to West Virginia, beaten by time and his own incompetence. Before the occupiers left Sandusky, Major Hutter, his wife, and their daughter, Ada, were locked in closets lest they warn the Confederate forces of Hunter's escape. When it was safe to do so, some of their slaves freed them. Hunter was determined to retreat to Liberty by morning. So, by late afternoon, Sandusky had been ransacked, his headquarters emptied, the wounded and dying left outside Hutter's barn, and the Union dead left unburied where they had fallen. Despite knowing that he was exposing the entire Eighteenth Connecticut Volunteer Infantry to potential capture, he ordered them to cover his retreat. They held their position, randomly firing in the direction of the enemy until about midnight when all grew quiet along the skirmish line, and then they slipped into the darkness with only moonlight to guide them. Some fell by the wayside from exhaustion and were later captured, but most of the Eighteenth Connecticut reached Little Otter Creek at about dawn.[92] They quickly covered the last two miles to Liberty and rejoined the Army of the Shenandoah to begin the long and dangerous journey to West Virginia. Lynchburg had survived.

The saddest part of Hunter's abortive attempt to take Lynchburg, and forgotten in that tale of desperation and deception, were the Union POWs who saw yet another hope of deliverance vanish. Their camp was within three miles of the Union headquarters, but there was never any hope of its inmates being liberated. Confederate soldiers from states other than Virginia were still stationed there, and by 1864, there was a large cavalry depot based at the Fair Ground.[93] There were Confederate troops massed on all sides of the site, so while the sounds of battle echoed all around the captives, no Union troops ever came close enough to penetrate the perimeter of the camp. The officers quartered

Chapter 5. The Lynchburg Campaign

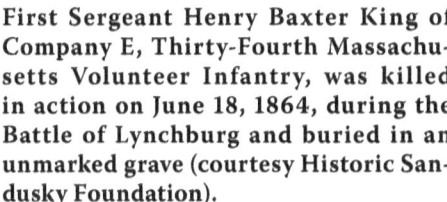

First Sergeant Henry Baxter King of Company E, Thirty-Fourth Massachusetts Volunteer Infantry, was killed in action on June 18, 1864, during the Battle of Lynchburg and buried in an unmarked grave (courtesy Historic Sandusky Foundation).

Private Melker Jeffreys of Company E, Fifteenth West Virginia Volunteer Infantry, was wounded during the Battle of Lynchburg on June 18, 1864, and had his right arm amputated below the elbow, but he survived (courtesy Historic Sandusky Foundation).

downtown had even less chance of liberation as they heard Early's soldiers falling into line, bound for the outer defenses.

As Early pursued Hunter, he sent more prisoners to Lynchburg, where they quickly taxed the facilities set aside for Union soldiers. It appears that prisoners taken during the Battle of Lynchburg and Hunter's retreat were housed in tobacco warehouses in the city. Private Frank Reader of the Fifth West Virginia Cavalry was captured on June 20, arrived in Lynchburg via the James River–Kanawha Canal on July 1, and was incarcerated in one of the warehouses. At no point in his memoir did he mention the POW camp at the Fair Ground. Answering the city's appeal, the Confederate government quickly ordered all Union prisoners in Lynchburg who were not being treated in a hospital to be shipped to Camp Sumter near Andersonville, Georgia, and all officers to Camp Oglethorpe in Macon, Georgia. Finally, after a month of waiting, uncertain of their fate, those inmates who were ambulatory boarded cattle cars, and the packed trains headed south on July 19, 1864.[94]

CHAPTER 6

The Convenience of Memory

On June 19, the day after the Battle of Lynchburg, Charles Button, editor of the *Lynchburg Daily Virginian*, was part of a group of men who rode out to the area that had been hotly contested 24 hours earlier. Much of the land was heavily wooded, but when they reached an open meadow that divided the property of Dr. William O. Owen from that of Mr. John B. Lee, they discovered, scattered about the field, the bodies of about 40 Union soldiers ranging in age from boys in their late teens to mature men with full beards.[1] In his *Lynchburg and Its People*, published in 1900, Aubrey Christian listed the number of dead at 100.[2] The Diuguid records listed 75 Union soldiers as "Unknown," obviously a cumulative number for 1862–1865. The Sanitary Commission in the autumn of 1866 exhumed 57 unknown Union soldiers and reburied them in the Poplar Grove Federal Cemetery in Petersburg, Virginia. Assuming that there were at least 20 bodies in the woods adjoining the abovementioned contested area as well as other Union dead along the line of battle, Christian's estimate appears to have been fairly accurate.[3]

The dead could not be identified because the scavengers who swarmed over the battlefield after the engagement had done their work with a thoroughness that shocked Button and his companions. Weapons, valuables, boots, and personal items were the most desirable, and once their clothes had been removed, it was impossible even to identify their regiments. Under the circumstances, a common grave was the only way to bury the bodies. So before the sun set and the full moon rose, they were interred by the same slaves who were pressed into service building makeshift fortifications two days earlier. In his editorial, Charles Button made a point of mentioning that three-quarters of them had died instantly with wounds to the head or heart, "thus showing the accuracy of that unerring aim which sent them to their last account."[4]

On February 17, 1864, the Confederate Congress passed a law

expanding the draft to all white males between the ages of 17 and 50.[5] Button closed this section of his editorial with the following passage for good reason: "We noticed one who seemed to be a stripling of scarce seventeen summers.... Alas! For the mother who will never learn the fate of the ... unhappy boy. Strange hands have now buried him out of sight, and his dust will mingle with mother earth in the land of those he came to despoil."[6] It was a reminder to his readers that their sons might soon be at risk of a similar fate. In the fall of 1864, Lynchburg boys of 17 were conscripted into the army along with every other white male in good health. Although not subject to the draft, male slaves were forced to work on fortifications and provide auxiliary services. Poor families were particularly hard hit when the breadwinner was drafted, and unfortunately, private charity was no longer able to supplement the needs of the less fortunate. Each day brought news of further casualties, and more slaves escaped to Union lines, leaving gaping holes in the workforce. Their future above the Mason-Dixon line might be uncertain, but at least they were free.

There remained the continuing challenge of more soldiers, both Union and Confederate, crowding into Lynchburg. Union dead were buried—either in the City Cemetery if they died in a hospital or in a hastily dug grave like the casualties of the recent battle. Those in the city hospitals were few compared to the Confederate sick and wounded, and those held at the Fair Ground or in tobacco factories were scheduled to be shipped to Georgia soon. The officers were bound for Camp Oglethorpe in Macon, while enlisted men and noncommissioned officers were sent to Camp Sumter near Andersonville.

Regular Confederate soldiers posed the most pressing problem, especially the Virginians stationed at Camp Davis, which was within easy walking distance of Buzzard's Roost, the cluster of brothels, dancehalls, and saloons that in three years had spread from the banks of the James River and Kanawha Canal to the lower end of Main Street. The outnumbered Lynchburg police force could not control them. The first provost marshal had enjoyed some success in containing the mayhem, but most of his successors had proven as ineffectual as the police. The authorities tried to limit the sale of alcohol, but that failed. Saloons might be closed, but some grocers kept their stores open by selling liquor from a jug hidden under the counter. Farmers in the Lynchburg area found shipping grain precarious at best, but once converted into moonshine, it could be concealed easily and delivered to customers within the city, with the authorities none the wiser. Not to be denied a

Chapter 6. The Convenience of Memory

bit of "rest and recuperation" whenever possible, Confederate soldiers stationed at the Fair Ground walked the extra miles to join the carousing that never seemed to end.

Many of the Lynchburg residents in 1861 had welcomed the thousands of soldiers who rendezvoused in their city; but by 1864, they wished the militiamen were elsewhere. It was no longer safe for respectable women to walk after dark in the heart of downtown even with a male escort because assaults and robberies were all too frequent. During the day, civilians were accosted by Confederate soldiers begging for money, food, or both. There were two serious unsolved fires in the fall of 1864 that destroyed stores and dwellings. Some believed these blazes were the work of a secret society of Union partisans called the Heroes of America. Confederate intelligence determined that some of their agents had connections in the city and the surrounding counties, but nothing was ever proved.[7] The rumors of a cell of Union saboteurs operating in the city that had circulated a year earlier reemerged, and the names of suspects were passed from one gossip to another. Officially, rowdy soldiers were to blame, but the arsonists were never discovered.

In the fall of 1862, Provost Marshal Thomas P. Turner had successfully dealt with the question of deserters taking refuge in the Lynchburg area. Two years later, the problem resurfaced but with a difference. The deserters of 1862 were from all over the Confederacy, but by the fall and winter of 1864, most of them were from the Lynchburg area. To all but the most sanguine supporters of the rebellion, it was apparent that the days of the Confederacy were numbered. The relentless campaign against the Army of Northern Virginia forced General Lee to assume a defensive position as General Grant slowly tightened the noose around Richmond, and General Sheridan's devastation of the Shenandoah Valley left the "breadbasket of the Confederacy" a smoldering ruin by the end of October. Two weeks later, General Sherman began his march to the sea, and five days before he reached his ultimate destination, General Thomas crushed the Army of Tennessee at the Battle of Nashville on December 15–16. Physically and emotionally exhausted, men left their units, often under cover of darkness, and headed home to families on the verge of starvation. While the number of those who deserted and returned to Lynchburg was small when compared to the rest of the Confederacy,[8] they were almost to a man poor, illiterate laborers who had been duped into fighting for a way of life that they had never shared. For them, it indeed had become a rich man's war and a poor man's fight.

From the late spring to the early fall, the food supply had been adequate for the needs of the population of Lynchburg, including the Confederate garrison and the Union prisoners; but with the arrival of colder weather, many went hungry. The holiday season of 1864 was particularly bleak, with acute shortages of fuel and food. Hoarding had been a problem since the war began, and even though it was condemned in the press and from the pulpit, it continued beyond the end of the war. Merchants were often the focus of public ire, being repeatedly reproached for raising prices for their own advantage, when actually the relentless inflationary spiral was to blame. Unfortunately, some merchants did lose their businesses trying to offer regular service to their customers during wartime. The extension of credit, even on a limited basis, to clients who were unable to pay because of the absence or death of the breadwinner ruined many a tradesman.

The situation improved slightly in January when the operation of the cartel was resumed with preference given to the exchange of ill or wounded prisoners. The damage done to the railroads during General Sherman's March to the Sea made shipping Union soldiers to Macon or Andersonville impossible, and due to the dilapidated status of the Southside Railroad, the journey to City Point from Lynchburg took longer than it did in 1862. Still, anything was preferable to being sent to Georgia. Union prisoners, whether in the camp or warehouse, spent only a few days at most in Lynchburg before they were on their way to City Point. The regular exchange had been resumed in part because it no longer gave the Confederacy an advantage. The drafting of 17-year-old boys and middle-aged men when the average lifespan of a white male in North America was 40 was a sign of desperation. Only a few die-hard secessionists refused to admit that the end of the war was near. With rampant inflation a reality and starvation a possibility for many poorer citizens, the city council bowed to public pressure and announced an open meeting to discuss the possibility of surrendering the city to the Union forces in the area.

The meeting was originally scheduled in Dudley Hall on February 28, 1865, but it was not held until March 3. John M. Speed, who had represented Lynchburg in Richmond during the secession crisis of 1861, presided, and a number of the city's prominent citizens spoke during the lengthy session.[9] The Lincoln administration, acting through its commanders in the field, offered generous terms to those communities willing to surrender. If the city voluntarily submitted to occupation by Federal troops after the evacuation of the Confederate wounded and the release of all Union POWs, there would be a subsequent easing

Chapter 6. The Convenience of Memory

of shortages of food and fuel. Confederate soldiers in Lynchburg and its environs were to be informed that they were subject to capture if they remained in place. Once a military government of occupation was established, the federal government promised to supply the citizens' basic needs until the end of hostilities. The debate lasted until after midnight, but it was finally resolved by voting to continue the struggle.[10] Within days of this decision, the rumor reached the city that General Sheridan was approaching Lynchburg. Stripped of most of their able-bodied males, their home guard units both depleted and poorly armed, and their crumbling defenses unmanned, Lynchburgers panicked. There was an attempt to raise a company of boys to resist the invasion, but only a few volunteered.[11] Luckily for Lynchburg, Sheridan headed toward Petersburg, unaware that he might have taken the city without a fight.[12]

On March 24, 1865, the *Lynchburg Daily Virginian* ceased publication; the *Lynchburg Republican* had already stopped its press for lack of supplies.[13] With the telegraph and refugees, both civil and military, as the only sources of information, apprehensive was the best word to describe Lynchburg in that fateful month of April 1865. Thanks to the efforts of General Early the previous June, the city had been spared the physical destruction that left Winchester in ruins, but in the spring of 1865, many in the Hill City anticipated a similar fate. On April 2, Lee abandoned Richmond while his retreating troops put parts of the Confederate capital to the torch. There were rumors that Lee was heading westward toward Lynchburg, which still held vital medical and food supplies for the Army of Northern Virginia as well as intact rail connections. On April 6, state officials confirmed those reports as they began arriving in Lynchburg by way of the canal. For barely 24 hours, Lynchburg was the unofficial capital of the Confederacy, and it was rumored that the next battle of the war might be fought on the hills above the James.

After the bureaucrats boarded the train to Danville on April 7, Confederate units immediately began to vacate the city.[14] By nightfall, only those servicemen who were too sick to move remained. With the evacuation of Camp Davis as well as the Confederate camp and horse depot at the Fair Ground, the population of the Hill City dropped by about 50 percent overnight, and the Lynchburg police force was able to keep the peace again unaided. Buzzard's Roost was empty except for local trade. The bewildered but hopeful Union prisoners, who were now few in number, waited to see what the next few days might bring. An uneasy quiet settled over the city. Although some assumed that the Union forces intended to destroy Lynchburg, in retrospect it was destined to remain the only major city in Virginia to be physically untouched by the war. The Union Army was more interested in the eight trains from Lynchburg filled with more medical and food supplies for the Army of Northern Virginia that were waiting at the Appomattox depot. Sheridan moved quickly from Farmville to Appomattox on April 8 and seized the supply trains.[15] As Lee advanced toward Lynchburg, he was trapped by Grant at Appomattox. On April 9, Palm Sunday, the end came quietly in the parlor of Wilbur McLean. When the news reached Lynchburg later that day, the foreboding became acute.

Early on the morning of April 11, Major General John Gibbon, who was in charge of the Appomattox headquarters of the Twenty-Fourth Army Corps, put Lieutenant Terrence Fitzpatrick, Company B, Fifth Pennsylvania Cavalry, in charge of a 14-man scouting party to reconnoiter Lynchburg.[16] When his troop prepared to enter the city, they were surprised to be met by Mayor William D. Branch and a small delegation of city leaders. Branch attempted to hand over control of the city to Fitzpatrick, who refused the offer because he was not authorized to accept it. To cover Branch's embarrassment due to his unfamiliarity with military protocol, Fitzpatrick carefully observed all the appropriate courtesies and promised that his commanding officer would respond to the mayor's request in proper form as soon as possible. The scouting party then hastily returned to Appomattox. Fitzpatrick reported to Gibbon, who immediately cut orders for Brigadier General Ranald S. Mackenzie to go to Lynchburg the next day and formally accept the surrender of the city.

Disconcerted by Branch's failure, and bowing to the inevitable, the city council met in a special session and voted that same afternoon, April 11, to surrender Lynchburg to General Grant or his designated representative as soon as possible. Then a delegation at once left for Appomattox. After a long day, Gibbon had gone to bed when he was informed at midnight of the deputation's arrival.[17] Quickly dressing in full uniform, he received the delegation, assuring them that Mackenzie was to travel to Lynchburg in the morning as the designated representative of General Grant. Having provided his unexpected guests with refreshments and a billet for the night, Gibbon returned to his quarters. Promptly after breakfast, Mackenzie and the Lynchburg delegation left Appomattox for Lynchburg. Arriving at half past one, he was met by the

Chapter 6. The Convenience of Memory

mayor and council on the bridge over the canal at Horseford Road and accepted the city's formal surrender.

Upon learning that Brigadier General James Dearing had been mortally wounded on April 6 during the Appomattox Campaign and was dying, Mackenzie immediately went to the Ladies Relief Hospital to see his West Point classmate. He ordered that Dearing neither be evacuated nor be required to take the oath of amnesty, thus granting him a pardon. The two men parted company after a brief visit. Mackenzie's concern for his friend earned him respect and compliments from the local elite whose support was essential for a peaceful restoration of federal authority.

Lynchburg's capitulation was front-page news in a number of Northern dailies, but the description in the April 13 edition of the *Chicago Tribune* was particularly sarcastic: "Lynchburg, long time Lee's kitchen garden, after defying for four years the threats of large and strong armies, has surrendered to a scouting party."[18] The demeaning term "kitchen garden" implied that Lynchburg's chief function was to keep the Army of Northern Virginia fed—quite a descent from its former status as the nation's second wealthiest city per capita.

One of the responsibilities of the commander of the Lynchburg district was the proper disposal of public property that belonged to the defunct Confederate government. Upon his entry into Lynchburg, Mackenzie notified Gibbon that there was "an immense quantity of public property there."[19] Also, Mackenzie immediately implemented General Orders No. 42, which directed that all Union POWs be transferred to Camp Parole at Annapolis, Maryland. Only those who were still hospitalized and not ambulatory remained. There were some concerns about the newly freed slaves, but the Federal soldiers and the leaders of the free Black community carefully monitored their jubilee at the Fair Ground. There was a certain irony that the former slaves chose to celebrate their newly granted freedom at the place where so recently Confederate soldiers had bivouacked and Union prisoners had endured captivity.[20] Late Good Friday night, April 14, the provost marshal received a telegraph message stating that President Lincoln had been shot, but it was not until the following day that another telegram confirmed the news of his death, an event greeted with disquiet and fear. The South had lost its best hope for a relatively nonpartisan reunion of the nation. Easter was a somber event as Northerners and Southerners filled the churches of Lynchburg to mark the end of the war and the beginning of the ecclesiastical year. The South's future was already

Some of the Union soldiers stationed in Lynchburg during Reconstruction (courtesy Lynchburg Museum System).

grim; now with the shock of Lincoln's violent assassination and the unexpected succession of Vice President Andrew Johnson, it was also uncertain.

After two years of lobbying and seemingly endless debate, President Lincoln finally signed the Freedmen's Bureau Act into law on March 3, 1865. Although it lasted until July 1872, the Freedmen's Bureau was supposed to expire at the end of a year because many members of Congress as well as some students of statutory law believed that the government was exceeding its powers as set forth in the Constitution. The Bureau of Refugees, Freedmen, and Abandoned Lands was actually the first welfare agency created by the federal government. Headed by Major General Oliver O. Howard, it dispensed food and medical aid and provided educational opportunities to all who were in need regardless of race. As soon as Lynchburg was occupied by federal troops, the Freedman's Bureau was opened in a building on Main Street with Captain Robert S. Lacey in charge.[21] The dispensing of medicine and food provoked complaints of too much traffic on Main Street, and for some whites, providing educational opportunities for former slaves of all ages was taking freedom too far. Creating and preserving a permanent underclass of illiterate whites had suited the agenda of the Richmond

Chapter 6. The Convenience of Memory

Junto and its allies, but they were no longer in control of the Commonwealth of Virginia. The classes offered by the Freedmen's Bureau were well attended despite both overt and covert intimidation; but in case of serious trouble, Lacey and his successors had the protection of the U.S. Army until early in 1870, when Reconstruction ended in Virginia.

When Mackenzie and the troops under his command left Lynchburg for Farmville, Virginia, on April 17, his place was taken by Brevet Brigadier General J. Irvin Gregg, assisted by Lieutenant Colonel Alender P. Duncan as provost marshal. As the newly appointed commander of the Lynchburg military district, Gregg supervised an area that included the counties of Amherst, Appomattox, Bedford, Campbell, Franklin, Henry, Nelson, Patrick, and Pittsylvania.[22] His staff was charged with administering the oath of allegiance to the United States to all adult males who had served the Confederate States in any capacity. Lynchburg's two newspapers resumed publication in May 1865, and their carefully censored editions were used to disseminate federal directives, particularly the necessity of taking the oath as soon as possible.

Initially, the public reception of Gregg and his staff was somewhat guarded, but by several actions, he quickly gained the support of community leaders. To keep the soldiers under his command under control and orderly during the early months of presidential reconstruction, Gregg ordered his provost marshal to confiscate the local supplies of liquor and close all the businesses in Buzzard's Roost. Next, the prostitutes were arrested and detained in a tobacco warehouse that was converted into a workhouse. However, these measures proved to be only temporary solutions to old problems. Whereas the general and his staff were accepted into Lynchburg polite society, average Lynchburgers generally did not fraternize with ordinary Union soldiers. Upon their arrival in the Hill City, the "Boys in Blue" were welcomed in Buzzard's Roost, but the orders that closed these establishments also stopped the flow of federal currency into the local economy. The prostitutes had made monetary contributions to the war effort, and with the coming of peace, some continued to help their poorer neighbors. During Reconstruction, they seldom failed to answer the need for charity, but they gave their money through third parties.[23] Yielding to public pressure, attempts to control morality ended; business returned to normal in Buzzard's Roost, but controlling the sordid side of life in Lynchburg remained a problem long after the end of Reconstruction in Virginia.

One reason that Lynchburg's economy was in shambles was due to the Confederate government repeatedly ordering all farmers to grow edible crops and not tobacco, and by the time of the surrender, the fields were already plowed and planted with foodstuffs. With the repeated prohibitions against growing *Nicotiana tabacum*, plugs of tobacco became more valuable than bullion; but by 1865, even this form of "money" was depleted. Since the tobacco that had formerly made Lynchburg rich was no longer available, the tobacco factories could not reach their normal production capacity for over a year. Warehouses were empty, save for scant evidence that they had recently been used to shelter the wounded and dying. After emancipation, many of the enslaved tobacco factory workers who had been assigned to war duties in 1863 merged into the general population. Many stores were vacant, their goods having disappeared months or years earlier. Veterans in patched or tattered uniforms mingled with freed slaves from the surrounding counties, wandering up and down the dusty streets looking for work or seeking a bit of early spring sunshine in the deserted doorway of a dilapidated building. For a time, it seemed that the only people in Lynchburg regularly earning a livelihood were the Union soldiers and the employees of Buzzard's Roost.

One component of a healthy economy was a workforce composed of loyal citizens committed to restoring national unity. Gregg was anxious that every male who was required to take the oath of allegiance to the United States do so quickly and then reenter the workforce; thus, his provost marshal, operating in the lobby of the Warwick Hotel on Main Street, was kept busy from morning until night.[24] Soldiers administering the oath in the counties that composed the Lynchburg district also reported very positive responses.[25] Gregg also sought to dispose of the public property that remained in Lynchburg, especially food supplies that had been allocated to the Confederate Army. Once the needs of the hospitals were satisfied, the remainder was distributed to the poor.[26] This expediency was temporary, as Gregg wanted to provide more opportunities for people to return to work as soon as possible. Tobacco had been the key to Lynchburg's wealth before the war, and it was potentially the solution to the city's postwar poverty. Although the Confederate government had routinely checked to make sure that farmers were growing produce, many had continued to cultivate small amounts of tobacco in out-of-the-way places. As the oath was being administered in surrounding counties, supplies of tobacco were discovered, which, when combined, amounted to a modest harvest. Now farmers could sell their tobacco for federal currency, creating the possibility that factories could reopen on a limited basis. By the end of May 1865,

Chapter 6. The Convenience of Memory

Gregg estimated that the value of the Lynchburg-area tobacco ready for processing was $15,000.[27] The problem was persuading factory owners to risk their carefully guarded assets in a venture that might fail or succeed beyond their expectations.

With the outbreak of war in 1861, specie suddenly vanished from circulation, and both belligerents resorted to issuing unpopular paper money. Rather than purchase Confederate bonds or exchange gold and silver coins for Confederate script, a number of astute Southerners hid their prewar gold and silver coins or deposited them in a Northern bank awaiting the end of the war. In his memoir, Captain Charles Minor Blackford relates arriving in Lynchburg around sundown on June 10, 1865, after a journey from Charlottesville that took over 12 hours, much of it on foot. Fortunately, shortly after he arrived, he met an old friend—William T. Booker, the tobacconist. Embarrassed but also desperate, Blackford asked if he might borrow five dollars whereupon Booker offered him five 20-dollar gold pieces. Blackford accepted one and immediately sent it to his wife in Charlottesville.[28] The wealth of men and women like Booker resulted in the founding of two new banks in August 1865—the First National on August 11 and the Lynchburg National on August 23.[29]

Toward the end of the summer, Gregg received orders for his next assignment, and Brigadier General N.M. Curtis moved into the commander of the Lynchburg district's office in the courthouse. As the commercial pulse of Lynchburg began to quicken, Curtis devoted his efforts to establishing a system of free public elementary education for all children in Lynchburg. Having faced decades of resistance by the Virginia General Assembly to public schools, Curtis assembled some members of the local clergy to assist in the formation of an educational system financed with fines levied for minor offenses. He proposed four public schools, two for white students and two for Black students, in both cases separated by gender. The ministers drew up a list of prominent laymen to comprise Lynchburg's first school board.[30] There were also separate private schools for white boys and girls whose parents could afford the tuition. Educating their children with Blacks and poorer whites was seen as a threat to the established social order, but with the Union Army in charge, there was little the elites could do but grumble. The first teachers were soldiers—enlisted men—who taught without pay because it was their assigned duty. Some who had been schoolmasters before they entered the service volunteered, and all of them had at least a grammar school education.[31] Perhaps the most positive accomplishment of Reconstruction in Lynchburg was the creation of a public education system, which in time became the city's pride.

John Richard Dennett, staff writer for the New York–based journal *The Nation*, which first appeared on newsstands in July 1865, arrived in Lynchburg on July 25 just as Curtis was preparing to replace Gregg as the commander of the Lynchburg district. The Hill City was Dennett's first stop after Richmond in a nine-month tour that took him through Virginia, the Carolinas, Georgia, Alabama, Louisiana, and Mississippi. His assignment in Lynchburg was to inform his readers of the present condition of what had been a formerly wealthy community, and his initial assessment was harsh: "The rough little city is built on several round-topped hills that descend abruptly to the banks of the James, which is here an insignificant stream at the bottom of a rocky valley hardly wider than the river's bed. The streets, which run towards the water, are almost precipitous, and all the streets, whether steep or not, are dirty and ill-paved."[32] Using Lynchburg as his base, Dennett explored central Virginia on horseback until August 29 when he left for North Carolina. He wanted to assess the effects of emancipation on race relations among members of the working class. Whereas he attended a lesson in the new school for Black children and was impressed by what he saw,[33] Dennett made no mention of the two new banks that were founded while he was still there. They were the stimulus that, within a year, began the transformation of Lynchburg from a run-down city into the metropolis of southwestern Virginia.

As the economic life of the community began to quicken, there was stiff competition for jobs. However, Black workers in Lynchburg usually did not have to vie with white workers to fill vacancies in the tobacco factories because these tasks had been performed by slaves before the war. The stiffest competition lay with Black migrants from the neighboring counties. By October 1865, the Freedmen's Bureau was feeding 1,000 refugees a week, many of them living at the Fair Ground in shelters fashioned from debris left by Confederate soldiers, horse trainers, and Union POWs.[34] With the approach of colder weather, there was one attempt to ease the overcrowding by reviving a program for resettling free Blacks in Africa, which had met with only limited success in the 1820s. Under the auspices of the newly formed Lynchburg Emigration Society (LES), on October 31, 1865, 150 former slaves left for an uncertain future in Liberia.[35] Because of the cost in time and money for such a small group as well as the lack of support in the Black community, the LES soon disbanded.

Chapter 6. The Convenience of Memory

Two months after Dennett headed south and a few days after the departure of the emigrants, another journalist, Whitelaw Reid, arrived in Lynchburg. He began his career as a war correspondent for the *Cincinnati Gazette*, but in 1868, two years after the publication of his book *After the War: A Southern Tour, May 1, 1865, to May 1, 1866*, Horace Greeley hired him as a reporter for the *New York Herald*. Reid covered the same territory as Dennett, but their views of the postwar South were often quite different. After a tedious journey from Richmond through land badly scarred by the war, he arrived at his destination. "Perched among its hills, and defended by nature's fortifications, Lynchburg had seen little of the immediate horrors of war.... Men had consequently escaped to some degree, the impoverishing effects of the rebellion. Business seemed brisk; the farmers of the surrounding country were prosperous, and lands were not largely offered for sale."[36]

On the way to Lynchburg, Reid was assured by one of his fellow passengers that half a million dollars in specie was in Lynchburg banks, that there was plenty of tobacco just waiting to be processed, and that former slaves who were willing to work were doing well. Reid quickly discovered that merchants and customers alike were just as suspicious of "greenbacks" as their Northern neighbors. Many a patriotic Virginian had suffered major losses converting gold and silver coins into Confederate currency, which eventually became worthless. They were reluctant to take that chance again. The Hill City was swarming with investors from the North, especially from Baltimore. Like Dennett before him, Reid learned that farmers in the Lynchburg district had been growing small crops of tobacco despite the Confederate government's prohibition, and he discovered that free Black men working in the city's refurbished hotels were making $20 a month plus tips for carrying luggage and polishing boots, which was at least $5 more than their Richmond counterparts.[37] Boarding the train for Bristol, Virginia, on a frosty morning in early November, Whitelaw Reid began the next segment of his long journey. Unlike Dennett, he was very impressed by what he had encountered during his brief stay in the Hill City.[38]

When Andrew Johnson became president after Lincoln's death on April 15, 1865, he made it clear that fundamentally he intended to follow the reconstruction policy devised by his predecessor. Initially, this was a wise move on Johnson's part because Lincoln already was considered a martyr by many, and opposing any policy conceived by the Great Emancipator was deemed disrespectful. All ordinary citizens who had served in the Confederate military and took the oath of allegiance to the United States had received a pardon and amnesty. Confederate civil and military officers as well as the very wealthy were to be considered on a case-by-case basis, but hoping to gain extra votes in the presidential election of 1868, Johnson granted thousands of pardons to ex–Confederates who should have been disenfranchised. It was an ill-conceived strategy that compromised Johnson's presidency and forced the former Confederate states to endure a far more severe form of Reconstruction once the Republicans were in complete control of the government. The oath takers were eligible to serve as delegates to state conventions charged with restoring a legitimate government. This process included repudiating secession, disavowing all state debts incurred between 1861 and 1865, and ratifying the 13th Amendment which abolished slavery. These newly constituted legislatures could not compensate slave owners for the loss of their labor force, so instead, they fashioned "Black codes" that restricted the rights of all African Americans, not only the freed slaves. When the 39th Congress met in December 1865, the more Radical Republicans in the House and Senate began the process of dismantling the Black codes while denying former Confederate males their civil rights. Johnson refused to make any concessions to Congress; in the end, his stubbornness and racism drove moderate Republicans into an alliance with the radicals.

Throughout the United States, there were many vacant chairs at dinner tables on December 25, 1865, but although the celebration was somewhat muted, the country was at peace. A number of shops along Lynchburg's Main Street boasted newly painted facades, windows decked with greenery, and consumer goods not seen in half a decade. The holiday fell on a Monday that year, so Saturday was devoted to visits to friends and family as well as modest parties. Sunday was a mixture of solemnity, rejoicing, and offering food, clothing, and money to those less fortunate. When toasts were raised to welcome the New Year, it was hoped that 1866 held the promise of better times to come. It proved to be a mixed blessing.

Jacob Eschbach Yoder arrived in Lynchburg in March 1866 as a new teacher at the Freedmen's Bureau. Born on February 22, 1838, in Gilbertsville, a few miles to the northwest of Philadelphia, Yoder was a Baptist of Mennonite descent.[39] Under the sponsorship of the Pennsylvania Freedmen's Relief Association, which was supported by the Society of Friends, Yoder accepted the challenge of reintroducing the residents of Lynchburg to the principles of their Quaker founder, especially equality.[40] However, the fate of the Freedmen's Bureau was already

Chapter 6. The Convenience of Memory

in question when Yoder became the principal of the Camp Davis school, located in one of the barracks that had been built to house Confederate officers from Virginia.

Lyman Trumbull of Illinois had introduced a bill in the U.S. Senate on January 5, 1866, which extended the operations of the Freedmen's Bureau but with no mention of an expiration date. It easily passed the Senate, and on February 13, the House of Representatives approved it. President Johnson vetoed it on February 19, outlining several reasons. He considered it to be a wartime measure that required a specific termination time, it infringed on states' rights as set forth in 10th Amendment of the U.S. Constitution,[41] and it used the power of the federal government to provide aid and services to a specific group of citizens.[42] The Radical Republicans did not challenge his veto because they were already working on a less controversial renewal bill. A packed public meeting held in Lynchburg on February 22, 1866, endorsed the policies of President Johnson, but it was only a symbolic display by white citizens. Although the future of the Freedmen's Bureau was uncertain, Yoder and his fellow teachers continued their work amid threats and harassment.

Congress passed a bill making African Americans full citizens in March 1866, and Johnson vetoed this civil rights bill. Congress then overrode his veto. In April, Congress passed the 14th Amendment, the first federal effort to restrict state control of civil and political rights. Among the Southern states, only Tennessee approved it and thereby avoided further reconstruction. The struggle between the president and Congress was approaching a climax. Although former Confederate states had been forced to ratify the 13th Amendment, which initially proved to be only an empty formality, real equality remained elusive. The Freedmen's Bureau and the U.S. Army sought to impede the enforcement of the Black codes but with limited success. A more moderate bill extending the life of the Freedmen's Bureau for two years was approved by Congress on July 3, but Johnson vetoed it. Congress once again overrode his veto on July 16, and the Supplementary Freedmen's Bureau Act became law. Protected by federal troops, Yoder and his colleagues at the Freedmen's Bureau were able to continue their own war against illiteracy.

There was also the issue of establishing national cemeteries for Union dead whose graves were scattered throughout the South. In July 1862, President Lincoln had signed a bill that authorized the purchase of land for military cemeteries, and at the end of the war, Brevet

Lieutenant Colonel James Miles Moore of the U.S. Quartermaster's Corps was tasked with securing a suitable site on which to establish a national military cemetery near Richmond. He chose a farm south of Petersburg that became Poplar Grove National Cemetery. Its name was taken from the rustic chapel built there by the men of the Fiftieth New York Volunteer Engineers who bivouacked on the farm during the Petersburg Campaign. It was here that the majority of the Union soldiers who died as POWs or were killed during the Battle of Lynchburg were reinterred. Early in 1866, the Burial Corps began to move remains to the new cemetery from nearly 100 separate burial sites in the Petersburg area. They then searched nine counties in the area for other hastily buried Union soldiers. Lynchburg was the westward limit of their territory. The Burial Corps consisted of 100 men, 40 mules, 10 horses, and 10 army wagons. They examined battle sites with much the same meticulous care later associated with modern archaeologists; they continued their work, weather permitting, through 1869. However, barely one-third of the remains recovered were positively identified.[43] Despite their efforts, there are still solitary Confederate and Union graves scattered throughout Virginia, including Lynchburg and its surrounding counties.

On October 1, 1866, the Burial Corps, accompanied by representatives of the U.S. Sanitary Commission, arrived at Lynchburg's City Cemetery to begin the work of disinterring the coffins of the Union soldiers who had died in Lynchburg as POWs.[44] The employees of George A. Diuguid who had carefully recorded all the available data on each man at the time of their original burial made this task much easier. Diuguid noted at the end of his record book the instructions he gave to those in charge of the operation: "The Federal Government in the removal of their dead from this place began at what I call No. 1 in 1st line 1st lot and numbered the coffin proceeding numerically in the row and going back to foot of No. 1 calling it II and so through the squares. Oct. 14th, 1866 G.A. Diuguid."[45]

Just outside the cemetery, at least half a dozen tents were erected to process the coffins recovered using Diuguid's guide, as well as the remains recovered from the areas contested in June 1864. Unfortunately, most of the casualties from the Battle of Lynchburg could not be identified. However, each soldier's remains were placed in a wooden coffin brought from Petersburg. Their headstones bore the designation "Unknown." Charles Button closed his remarks on the work of the Burial Corps of the United States with the following: "Those remains are

Chapter 6. The Convenience of Memory

to be taken with pious care to a national cemetery for sepulture, where monuments will be erected, flowers planted and every fitting demonstration of honor to the dead be paid. That is all right enough; a grateful country should honor those who died beneath its flag."[46] The empty Union graves were filled, in time grass covered the spot, and "Yankee Square" was forgotten. Poignantly, perhaps, among the men who helped open and later fill those empty graves were some who originally dug them. Then, they were slaves; but in the bright October weather of 1866, they were free and paid a fair wage for their labor. A few Union graves were not disturbed. They included soldiers from the U.S. Colored Troops who were not buried with the white soldiers but in "Negro Row," as well as Union dead who were mistaken for Confederates because they were from Union regiments raised in states that had seceded from the United States.

It was ironic that while the Burial Corps was uncovering the coffins of Union soldiers who died at the Fair Ground, a group of local, socially elite residents were planning to hold a fall festival in that same space. In 18 months, those 30 acres had been used as the site of celebration of freedom by former slaves, the location of temporary housing for the poor, and in November 1866 as the location of a medieval-style tournament. Because the novels of Sir Walter Scott were very popular in the United States, particularly in the South, it surprised no one that the young people of Lynchburg organized such an event. It was a not-so-subtle way of celebrating a way of life that was forever gone—if it had ever existed in the first place. There was a large crowd of all ages who enjoyed the festivities which ended with a grand ball held at the Cabell house, where a queen of love and beauty was crowned.[47]

The 14th Amendment had been the main issue in the bitterly contested congressional election of 1866. When the votes were counted, the Radical Republicans had won a solid majority. The continuing debate over the fate of the South, which began in December 1866, ended with the Reconstruction Act of 1867, which passed on February 20. The Confederate states, excluding Tennessee, which had already ratified the amendment, were divided into five military districts, each under the authority of a Union general. Once each of the former Confederate states approved the 14th Amendment and it became part of the Constitution,[48] the state would be readmitted to the Union and Reconstruction ended. President Johnson rejected the act on March 2, and predictably, that same day Congress overrode his veto. Congressional reconstruction began on March 5, and a week later Major General John M. Schofield assumed command of Military District One, which included Virginia and the District of Columbia. Schofield placed Brevet Major General Orlando B. Wilcox in charge of Lynchburg.

Wilcox, like Curtis, Gregg, and Mackenzie before him, quickly gained the acceptance of the local middle and upper classes. However, Union soldiers newly stationed in the city became a problem; like their predecessors, they soon found their way to the bawdy houses and bars along Jefferson Street. Although the money they spent on their leisurely pursuits was a welcome addition to the local economy, their brawls and drunkenness threatened military discipline and public order. In the summer of 1867, with his patience at an end, Wilcox ordered Provost Marshall Lieutenant Colonel George P. Buell to issue and enforce General Order No. 61, which closed the bordellos at "Buzzard's Roost," "Tin Shingles," and "Curl's Row."[49] Even pushing one of the shanties into the river with the residents still inside only briefly deterred the disreputable businesses now confined to the banks of the James River–Kanawha Canal.[50]

The Virginia General Assembly finally approved both the 14th and 15th Amendments to the Constitution on October 8, 1869, and on January 24, 1870, Virginia was readmitted to the Union. The 16 years between the end of Reconstruction in the Old Dominion and the centennial celebration of Lynchburg's incorporation as a town witnessed tremendous changes in the Hill City. Approved in July 1869, the new Virginia Constitution provided for a system of public education financed by both the state and local governments. Building on General Curtis' establishment of four public schools in 1865, the citizens of Lynchburg were ready to expand the system already in place, and on April 5, 1871, nine free public schools were opened. As was typical for the era, children were separated by sex, religion, and race.

That spring, with the departure of federal troops and their continuous protection, Jacob Yoder, the superintendent of the Freedmen's school, as well as the men, women, and children who were his students were subjected to seemingly constant intimidation, but they persevered. Although the work of the Freedmen's Bureau technically ended in December 1868, some of its programs continued to operate until 1872. Remedial education for adults became the concern of the Black churches, while the children were absorbed into the new Lynchburg schools. Jacob Yoder remained in charge of the education of Black children of the Hill City until his death in 1905.

Chapter 6. The Convenience of Memory

In the census of 1860, the proportion of free Blacks in the population of Lynchburg had been less than that in other Virginia cities, but under freedmen's leadership, an independent Black community began to grow and evolve after the war. They were particularly active in founding and leading the new churches and fraternal organizations which became the centers of Black community life. They actively supported the Freedmen's school and the public schools because they understood the value of education and the necessity of mastering a trade other than the menial tasks associated with the processing of tobacco. Slowly, under their tutelage, a generation of youngsters grew to maturity free of the stigma of slavery, ready to assume what they considered their rightful place in society despite the hostility of those who should have been their natural allies.

In February 1872, the first high school for white students opened. Under pressure from members of the privileged class who feared that poorer children might assume that an education entitled them to a position of equality with their betters, the city council closed the high school in 1877, using the excuse of rising costs. This attitude was not confined to Lynchburg, Virginia, or the South. At the end of the 19th century, free secondary education was considered by many as a potential threat to the established social order. Some even cited scripture to support their position: "Knowledge puffeth up," or to put it in layman's terms, "Education makes people biggity."[51] The first superintendent of the Lynchburg school system, Abram Biggers, who served from 1870 until 1878, fought for the reopening of the high school, and soon a majority of the electorate supported him. Those councilmen who opposed secondary education lost their seats in the next election, and the newly installed city council ratified the will of the people by reopening the high school in the fall of 1879.[52] Biggers did not live to savor this victory because his tireless efforts on behalf of secondary education hastened his death from tuberculosis on March 28, 1879. Three years later, Jackson Street High School for Black students was opened under the supervision of Jacob Yoder.[53]

Because of the damage done to the canal by the floods in 1870 and 1877, a new bridge from the city to Amherst County was a necessity. On August 14, 1878, the new toll-free iron bridge was opened.[54] These events reinforced the arguments of those who lobbied for the railroads. It took months at best to repair damage to the old canal whereas impaired stretches of railroad could be mended in days, if not hours. Railroad fever seized the nation, including Lynchburg, after the end of the war. In 1866, the city government pledged $60,000 toward the construction of the Lynchburg-Danville Railroad while the citizens raised another $200,000 for the new link to Southside and North Carolina.[55] Lynchburg had been one of the most important rail hubs in the Upper South before and during the war, and this latest enterprise was intended to be the first step in reestablishing Lynchburg's place in the nation's transit system.

In the immediate postwar period, the economy of the United States grew at an almost dizzying pace, especially in transportation. American railroads used coal and steel at an incredible rate, which stimulated further growth in both these industries. Since the future of transportation lay in an interconnected rail system that linked the East and West Coasts and points in between, investors and speculators were attracted to coal, steel, and railroad shares. In 1879, the Norfolk and Western Railway had absorbed the rail lines that had served central Virginia since 1852 and had become Virginia's link to the transcontinental system. The Norfolk and Western Railway purchased most of the property and completely dominated the future development of the small town of Big Lick near Salem, Virginia, transforming it into Roanoke, the new metropolis of southwest Virginia. The immense railroad systems seldom established their terminals and junction points in places they could not completely control.

Seven years before his death on March 27, 1869,[56] Samuel Miller, a recluse who was reported to be the wealthiest man in Lynchburg, announced his intention to build and endow an orphanage for girls just inside the city limits on a 46-acre tract of land that included a portion of the Fair Ground. At that same time, Miller transferred to the city a large tract of land adjacent to the Fair Ground, which over time was developed as a park and named in his memory.[57] In his will, Miller also bequeathed $20,000 to Lynchburg for the construction of a second reservoir in the College Hill section of the community.[58] The Lynchburg Female Orphan Asylum was completed in 1872 and opened in 1875. Three stories high with four-story towers flanking its entrance, externally it evoked the somber era in which it was constructed—an ever-deepening depression. Over time, landscaping and the laughter of children softened its grim facade. The old Fair Ground was slowly being repurposed piece by piece.

A Virginia inventor, James Albert Bonsack, received two patents for a cost-effective cigarette rolling machine in 1881, one on March 8 and the other on October 4, 1881.[59] After Bonsack and James Buchanan

Chapter 6. The Convenience of Memory

Duke formed their partnership,[60] Durham, North Carolina—Duke's hometown—became the new "Tobacco City." Ironically, Bonsack originally manufactured his revolutionary machines in the Hill City. Fortunately, a generation before the Civil War, the city's economy began to evolve from total dependence on tobacco to a more diverse base, which gave it the steadiness to weather the various economic storms of the late 19th century. Over time, milling, printing, steel, machine-made furniture, shoes, nails, pharmaceuticals, leather goods, retail establishments,[61] and colleges—both single-sex and coeducational—replaced tobacco as the foundations of the city's economy.[62] However, since the opportunities required by these new enterprises were skilled positions, this long-anticipated diversity did not immediately mean improved conditions for poor white laborers. These jobs not only entailed specialized training but also varying levels of education. Thus, immediately after the war, many illiterate white workers were finally forced by necessity to take jobs in the tobacco factories formerly reserved for slaves.

Out of desperation and necessity, there evolved a common cause that briefly transcended racial barriers, and for a while in the 1880s, the Lynchburg laboring class dominated the political life of the city—even electing two former slaves to the city council. Jefferson Anderson and Henry Edward were freely elected to the city council from a predominantly Black ward.[63] For the wealthy members of the post–Civil War generation, the Readjuster Party was the realization of their worst nightmare and required a political shift. Poor whites had been dismissed with contempt for years; now the power brokers began to court them seriously. As the literacy rate in this segment of the population began to slowly rise with the advent of free public schools, their threat to the status quo became even more dangerous. In the end, an appeal to an almost innate racism among nearly all poor whites restored the power base of the establishment. Some of those men involved in the tobacco industry in Lynchburg as well as old-school politicians regarded the southward migration of tobacco manufacturing as a positive development because many of the Black workers who had tried to organize unions in Lynchburg moved south to Danville and Durham looking for better-paying jobs. By 1886, the traditional conservatives were once again in control of the Hill City. The depression of the last decade was a fast-fading memory, and Lynchburgers were preparing for an anniversary that celebrated a romantic past, present economic successes, and a promising future.

The centennial of the granting of a town charter to Lynchburg by the General Assembly was celebrated on October 12–15, 1886. "It was also to be an agricultural and industrial exposition—a showcase of everything Central Virginia had to offer the Commonwealth and the Nation."[64] The weather was perfect—crisp evenings and warm days—Charles Button, editor of the *Lynchburg Daily Virginian*, heralded the opening day. "Everybody is coming. The old and the young, of all sizes, sexes, and conditions, and without regard to creed, color, clime.... We are ready to entertain every man, woman, and child with the first reds and golds of autumn under a cloudless sky of deep blue—except for clouds and light rain on the morning of October 14th."[65] It was ironic that the full moon on the night of October 13 was popularly known as the "hunter's moon."[66] The festivities were held at the Fair Ground and Miller Park, which already showed the results of careful landscaping, including the spot where the centennial oak was planted and dedicated at the end of November. The committee that planned and supervised the gala was composed of influential men from government and industry, but volunteers—both women and men—from all classes and races did the work that made it an event to remember.[67] The railroads that serviced Lynchburg offered special fares to people traveling to the Hill City, and it was estimated that between 50,000 and 75,000 took advantage of the offer. Every available room in the city was booked,[68] and local eateries were filled during the week of October 10–16.

The Fair Ground and Miller Park were not the only venues used for the centennial celebration. The city's elegant opera house, built at the corner of Main and 11th streets in 1878–1879, not only presented theater and musical performances but also hosted lectures and public meetings. The Music Committee also chose to treat everyone to a series of free outdoor band concerts. Louis Weber was the leader of a band that was very popular in Washington City, a number of Virginia resorts, and colleges, including the University of Virginia and Washington and Lee University.[69] From the opening day of the fair until its closing, the Louis Weber Band performed from nine to 11 every morning, four to six every afternoon, and eight to 10 every evening. A portion of Church and 9th streets in front of the Firemen's Memorial Fountain framed by Augustus Forsberg's ornamental steps at the base of Court House Hill was closed to wheeled traffic.[70] There were also several local and regional bands, including one from Salem, Virginia, that played during the Centennial Fair,[71] but it was the Louis Weber Band that drew massive crowds every time they took their places by the fountain.

On the first morning of the fair, the initial crowd—composed

Chapter 6. The Convenience of Memory

The 1886 centennial arch across Main Street proclaims, "Welcome Strangers to Our Gates" (courtesy Lynchburg Museum System).

primarily of locals—was smaller than anticipated because from nine o'clock when events began until noon, there were only speeches and prayers. By one o'clock, when the races—sack, foot, mule, and horses—began, throngs filled the Fair Ground and Miller Park. Meanwhile, Main Street was teeming with out-of-town visitors marveling at the numerous banners that adorned every available space not blocked by telephone and telegraph wires.[72] On October 13, more than 5,000 people packed the Fair Ground, and the headline in the *Lynchburg Daily Virginian* proclaimed, "THE FAIR GROUNDS, The Largest Crowd Ever Known at the Fair."[73] Charles Button obviously had no reason to recall

June 17, 1862, when he covered the arrival of the first Union POWs to join the thousands of Confederate soldiers already bivouacked there.

The following day, there were intermittent showers in the morning, which led to the cancellation of a speech by Charles M. Blackford, but by afternoon, the skies were clear, and the regularly scheduled activities resumed. Virginia governor Fitzhugh Lee was supposed to attend the centennial celebration on October 14, but he canceled at the last minute.[74] Governor Lee was a nephew of General Robert E. Lee, and on October 15, 1885, he had held a huge political rally at the Fair Ground seeking the support of the Lynchburg voters in his campaign for governor.[75] In place of one more political speech, the attendees at the Fair Ground were treated to fireworks, military precision completions by local militia units, and more horse races. The centennial celebration and fair ended on Friday, October 15, and by Saturday evening, most of the visitors were gone, the banners had been removed from Main Street, and the streets were quiet except for those in Buzzard's Roost.

* * *

The Fair Ground was deserted, and only the light from the waning moon cast shadows through the trees that once sheltered Union soldiers weary from marching to an uncertain future. The Fair Ground where they had waited for release had changed drastically in almost a quarter century, serving many purposes since the prisoners had departed, and it would perform many more in the future. As the sapling oaks of 1862 grew into massive trees, the land not only protected orphans, but it became a park, a residential neighborhood, a shopping precinct, and finally, the site of a public high school, which became one of the finest in the country, serving the children of Lynchburg regardless of gender, race, or creed. Most of the Union soldiers who braved the summer heat and winter cold were reared in communities where access to free education was their birthright, and this school, mellowed by time, resting where they slept and dreamed of home, is a fitting memorial to their sacrifice which must never be forgotten.

Appendix A:
Burial Records for POWs, 1862–1865

This appendix lists Union POWs who died in Lynchburg, Virginia, from 1862 to 1865, for whom burial records exist. They are listed by death date, then alphabetically.

Key

ANC: Alexandria National Cemetery
GNC: Gettysburg National Cemetery
PGNC: Poplar Grove National Cemetery
*** Denotes soldiers who did not die under normal circumstances, e.g., suicide.

In the 19th century, it was common practice to deny suicides burial in consecrated ground. In May 1864, Corporal John Robinson was shot by a guard. By the spring of 1864, most of the guards at the POW camp were civilians, and Robinson was buried quickly to avoid the implications of an unarmed POW being killed by a civilian.

Diuguid Soldiers Book (DSB) is the form used in this appendix to refer to "Soldier Book Record of Burials."

April 1862 (one death)

Smith, Private Wallace, 54th New York Volunteer Infantry, Company C
  Died: April 24, 1862, at Warwick House Hotel
  Buried: City Cemetery, no. 10, 2nd line of Lot 168, DSB, vol. I, 14
  Listed in the DSB as "Unknown Man"
  PGNC Number: 4787

June 1862 (seven deaths)

Bower, Private Joseph, 64th New York Volunteer Infantry, Company K
  Died: June 17, 1862, at John Brown's stable

Appendix A

 Buried: City Cemetery, no. 6, 1st line of Lot 169, DSB, vol. I, 30
 PGNC Number: 4582

Dowling, Private Patrick, 1st West Virginia Volunteer Light Artillery, Battery B
 Died: June 19, 1862, at the Fair Ground (POW camp)
 Buried: City Cemetery, no. 6, 5th line of Lot 172, DSB, vol. I, 17
 PGNC Number: 4726

Lambden, Private John, 1st Maryland Volunteer Infantry, Company B
 Died: June 19, 1862, at John Brown's stable
 Buried: City Cemetery, no. 5, 4th line of Lot 171, DSB, vol. I, 31
 PGNC Number: 4735

Rucker, Private John W., 25th Ohio Volunteer Infantry, Company I
 Died: June 24, 1862, at the Fair Ground (POW camp)
 Buried: City Cemetery, no. 4, 3rd line of Lot 172, DSB, vol. I, 32
 PGNC Number: 4733

Walton, Private John W., 27th Indiana Volunteer Infantry, Company H
 Died: June 25, 1862, at the Fair Ground (POW camp)
 Buried: City Cemetery, no. 10, 4th line of Lot 173, DSB, vol. I, 32
 PGNC Number: 4727

Barker, Private John H., 14th Indiana Volunteer Infantry, Company D
 Died: June 30, 1862, at the Fair Ground (POW camp)
 Buried: City Cemetery, no. 1, 2nd line of the Yankee Square, DSB, vol. I, 34
 PGNC Number: 4714

Strepler, Private Jacob, 27th Pennsylvania Volunteer Infantry, Company D
 Died: June 30, 1862, at the Fair Ground (POW camp)
 Buried: City Cemetery, no. 1, 1st line of the Yankee Square, DSB, vol. I, 34
 PGNC Number: 4596

July 1862 (57 deaths)

Peatt, Private Henry, 1st Michigan Volunteer Cavalry, Company B
 Died: July 1, 1862, at the Fair Ground (POW camp)
 Buried: City Cemetery, no. 2, 1st line of the Yankee Square, DSB, vol. I, 34
 PGNC Number: 4716

Taylor, Private Joseph, 1st Vermont Volunteer Cavalry, Company G
 Died: July 2, 1862, at the Fair Ground (POW camp) of typhoid fever
 Buried: City Cemetery, no. 2, 2nd line of the Yankee Square, DSB, vol. I, 34
 PGNC Number: 4609

Randles, Private Charles, 25th Pennsylvania Volunteer Infantry
 Died: July 3, 1862, at the Fair Ground (POW camp)
 Buried: City Cemetery, no. 3, 6th line of the Yankee Square, DSB, vol. I, 46
 PGNC Number: 4729

Burial Records for POWs, 1862–1865

Chorarty, Private Henry, 8th New York Volunteer Infantry, Company F
Died: July 5, 1862, at the Fair Ground (POW camp)
Buried: City Cemetery, no. 3, 1st line of Yankee Square, DSB, vol. I, 36
PGNC Number: 4586

Garfield, Private Henry Darius, 1st Michigan Volunteer Cavalry, Company B
Died: July 5, 1862, at the Fair Ground (POW camp)
Buried: City Cemetery, no. 1, 3rd line of the Yankee Square, DSB, vol. I, 36
PGNC Number: 4584

Weik, Private John, 54th New York Volunteer Infantry, Company C
Died: July 5, 1862, at the Fair Ground (POW camp)
Buried: City Cemetery, no. 3, 2nd line of the Yankee Square, DSB, vol. I, 36
PGNC Number: 4605

Sly, Private Hiram, 29th Ohio Volunteer Infantry, Company E
Died: July 6, 1862, at the Fair Ground (POW camp)
Buried: City Cemetery, no. 2, 3rd line of the Yankee Square, DSB, vol. I, 36
PGNC Number: 4731

King, Private William C., 46th Pennsylvania Volunteer Infantry, Company F
Died: July 7, 1862, at the Fair Ground (POW camp)
Buried: City Cemetery, no. 3, 3rd line of the Yankee Square, DSB, vol. I, 37
PGNC Number: 4602

Donahue, Private Peter F., Independent Pennsylvania Volunteer Light Artillery, Battery E
Died: July 8, 1862, at the Fair Ground (POW camp)
Buried: City Cemetery, no. 4, 3rd line of the Yankee Square, DSB, vol. I, 37
PGNC Number: 4578

Cocks, Private John H., 1st Maryland Volunteer Infantry, Company G
Died: July 10, 1862, at the Fair Ground (POW camp)
Buried: City Cemetery, no. 6, 1st line of the Yankee Square, DSB, vol. I, 40
PGNC Number: 4594

Kettle, Private John W., 66th Ohio Volunteer Infantry, Company G
Died: July 10, 1862, at the Fair Ground (POW camp)
Buried: City Cemetery, no. 4, 2nd line of the Yankee Square, DSB, vol. I, 38
PGNC Number: 4601

Gatton, Private George W., 1st West Virginia Volunteer Cavalry, Company D
Died: July 12, 1862, at the Fair Ground (POW camp)
Buried City Cemetery, no. 4, 1st line of the Yankee Square, DSB, vol. I, 39
PGNC Number: 4592

Harps, Private David S., 29th Pennsylvania Volunteer Infantry, Company B
Died: July 14, 1862, at the Fair Ground (POW camp)
Buried: City Cemetery, no. 2, 4th line of the Yankee Square, DSB, vol. 1, 39
PGNC Number: 4612

Appendix A

Lannen, Private Dennis, 29th Pennsylvania Volunteer Infantry, Company E
Died: July 14, 1862, at the Fair Ground (POW camp)
Buried: City Cemetery, no. 5, 4th line of the Yankee Square, DSB, vol. I, 39
PGNC Number: 4714

Robison, Private Charles, 27th Indiana Volunteer Infantry, Company G
Died: July 14, 1862, at the Fair Ground (POW camp)
Buried: City Cemetery, no. 1, 4th line of the Yankee Square, DSB, vol. I, 39
PGNC Number: 4577

O'Shaughnessy, Private Michael, 27th Indiana Volunteer Infantry, Company B
Died: July 15, 1862, at the Fair Ground (POW camp)
Buried: City Cemetery, no. 5, 1st line of the Yankee Square, DSB, vol. I, 40
PGNC Number: 4597

Stewart, Private John, 29th Pennsylvania Volunteer Infantry, Company I
Died: July 15, 1862, at the Fair Ground (POW camp)
Buried: City Cemetery, no. 5, 2nd line of the Yankee Square, DSB, vol. I, 40
PGNC Number: 4732

Delano, Private Levi G., 1st Maine Volunteer Cavalry, Company M
Died: July 17, 1862, at the Fair Ground (POW camp)
Buried: City Cemetery, no. 6, 2nd line of the Yankee Square, DSB, vol. I, 41
PGNC Number: 4580

Guldner, Private Nicholas, 4th New York Volunteer Cavalry, Company H
Died: July 17, 1862, at the Fair Ground (POW camp)
Buried: City Cemetery, no. 3, 4th line of the Yankee Square, DSB, vol. I, 40
PGNC Number: 4720

Gosley, Private Hugh S., 5th Connecticut Volunteer Infantry, Company E
Died: July 18, 1862, at the Fair Ground (POW camp)
Buried: City Cemetery, no. 6, 4th line of the Yankee Square, DSB, vol. I, 41
PGNC Number: 4611

Wilcox, Private William S., 67th Ohio Volunteer Infantry, Company A
Died: July 18, 1862, at the Fair Ground (POW camp)
Buried: City Cemetery, no. 5, 3rd line of the Yankee Square, DSB, vol. I, 41
PGNC Number: 4613

Frier, Private Joseph, 1st (West) Virginia Volunteer Infantry, Company ?
Died: July 19, 1862, at the Fair Ground (POW camp)
Buried: City Cemetery, no. 6, 3rd line of the Yankee Square, DSB, vol. I, 41
PGNC Number: 4604

Hall, Private Fleming, 66th Ohio Volunteer Infantry, Company C
Died: July 19, 1862, at the Fair Ground (POW camp)
Buried: City Cemetery, no. 7, 4th line of the Yankee Square, DSB, vol. I, 41
PGNC Number: 4718

Burial Records for POWs, 1862–1865

Leach, Sergeant William, 3rd Wisconsin Volunteer Infantry, Company B
Died: July 19, 1862, at the Fair Ground (POW camp)
Buried: City Cemetery, no. 7, 2nd line of the Yankee Square, DSB, vol. I, 41
PGNC Number: 4752

Schaum, Private Rudolph G., 8th New York Volunteer Infantry, Company G
Died: July 19, 1862, at the Fair Ground (POW camp)
Buried: City Cemetery, no. 4, 4th line of the Yankee Square, DSB, vol. I, 41
PGNC Number: 4724

Ellsworth, Private Isaac, 10th Maine Volunteer Infantry, Company F
Died: July 21, 1862, at the Fair Ground (POW camp)
Buried: City Cemetery, no. 8, 4th line of the Yankee Square, DSB, vol. I, 42
PGNC Number: 4749

Hartmann, Private August C., 8th New York Volunteer Infantry, Company C
Died: July 21, 1862, at the Fair Ground (POW camp)
Buried: City Cemetery, no. 7, 1st line of the Yankee Square, DSB, vol. I, 42
PGNC Number: 4754

Jones, Private William H., 29th Ohio Volunteer Infantry, Company D
Died: July 21, 1862, at the Fair Ground (POW camp)
Buried: City Cemetery, no. 7, 3rd line of the Yankee Square, DSB, vol. I, 42
PGNC Number: 4606

Ziegler, Private Franz, 45th New York Volunteer Infantry, Company D
Died: July 21, 1862, at the Fair Ground (POW camp)
Buried: City Cemetery, no. 9, 4th line of the Yankee Square, DSB, vol. I, 43
PGNC Number: 4747

Bower, Private Marquis, 66th Ohio Volunteer Infantry, Company E
Died: July 22, 1862, at the Fair Ground (POW camp), shot by a guard
Buried: City Cemetery, no. 9, 3rd line of the Yankee Square, DSB, vol. I, 43
PGNC Number: 4607

Monk, Private Henry, 1st Maryland Volunteer Infantry, Company I
Died: July 22, 1862, at the Fair Ground (POW camp)
Buried: City Cemetery, no. 8, 1st line of the Yankee Square, DSB, vol. I, 43
PGNC Number: 4595

Murphy, Private Patrick, 27th Indiana Volunteer Infantry, Company H
Died: July 22, 1862, at the Fair Ground (POW camp)
Buried: City Cemetery, no. 9, 2nd line of the Yankee Square, DSB, vol. I, 43
PGNC Number: 4598

Sprague, Private Thomas, 4th Ohio Volunteer Infantry, Company I
Died: July 22, 1862, at the Fair Ground (POW camp)
Buried: City Cemetery, no. 8, 3rd line of the Yankee Square, DSB, vol. I, 43
PGNC Number: 4722

Appendix A

Johnte, Corporal John George, 5th Ohio Volunteer Infantry, Company H
Died: July 23, 1862, at the Fair Ground (POW camp)
Buried: City Cemetery, no. 8, 2nd line of the Yankee Square, DSB, vol. I, 42
PGNC Number: 4750

Brommel, Private H. Fritz, 8th New York Volunteer Infantry, Company F
Died: July 24, 1862, at the Fair Ground (POW camp)
Buried: City Cemetery, no. 1, 6th line of the Yankee Square, DSB, vol. I, 43
PGNC Number: 4614

Freischmann, Private Charles, 1st Maryland Volunteer Infantry, Company E
Died: July 24, 1862, at the Fair Ground (POW camp)
Buried: City Cemetery, no. 10, 4th line of the Yankee Square, DSB, vol. I, 44
PGNC Number: 4663

Munson, Private Enos, 46th Pennsylvania Volunteer Infantry, Company G
Died: July 24, 1862, at the Fair Ground (POW camp)
Buried: City Cemetery, no. 1, 5th line of the Yankee Square, DSB, vol. I, 43
PGNC Number: 4725

Trieschman, Private Charles F., 1st Maryland Volunteer Infantry, Company C
Died: July 24, 1862, at the Fair Ground (POW camp) of starvation
Buried: City Cemetery, no. 10, 4th line of the Yankee Square, DSB, vol. I, 44
PGNC Number: 4663

Witham, Private Charles W., 10th Maine Volunteer Infantry, Company G
Died: July 24, 1862, at the Fair Ground (POW camp)
His burial is not listed in the Diuguid records.
He was buried near the POW camp.

McCort, Private James, 111th Pennsylvania Volunteer Infantry, Company F
Died: July 25, 1862, at the Fair Ground (POW camp)
Buried: City Cemetery, no. 9, 1st line of the Yankee Square, DSB, vol. I, 44
PGNC Number: 4666

Swisher, Private John H., 66th Ohio Volunteer Infantry, Company B
Died: July 25, 1862, at the Fair Ground (POW camp)
Buried: City Cemetery, no. 10, 2nd line of the Yankee Square, DSB, vol. I, 44
PGNC Number: 4740

Vinyard, Corporal Harvey, 66th Ohio Volunteer Infantry, Company B
Died: July 25, 1862, at the Fair Ground (POW camp)
Buried: City Cemetery, no. 10, 3rd line of the Yankee Square, DSB, vol. I, 44
PGNC Number: 4664

Bremer, Private Andrew, 1st Maryland Volunteer Infantry, Company K
Died: July 28, 1862, at the Fair Ground (POW camp)
Buried: City Cemetery, no. 10, 6th line of the Yankee Square, DSB, vol. I, 45
PGNC Number: 4581

Burial Records for POWs, 1862–1865

Calhoun, Private George S., 62nd Ohio Volunteer Infantry, Company K
Died: July 28, 1862, at the Fair Ground (POW camp)
Buried: City Cemetery, no. 1, 5th line of the Yankee Square, DSB, vol. I, 45
PGNC Number: Unknown

Emmert, Private Philip, 1st Maryland Volunteer Infantry, Company I
Died: July 28, 1862, at the Fair Ground (POW camp)
Buried: City Cemetery, no. 11, 3rd line of the Yankee Square, DSB, vol. I, 45
PGNC Number: 4738

Hueninston, Private Newton P., 29th Ohio Volunteer Infantry, Company G
Died: July 28, 1862, at the Fair Ground (POW camp)
Buried: City Cemetery, no. 1, 6th line of the Yankee Square, DSB, vol. I, 45
PGNC Number: Unknown

Isaac, Private Peter, 27th Indiana Volunteer Infantry, Company D
Died: July 28, 1862, at the Fair Ground (POW camp)
Buried: City Cemetery, no. 9, 5th line of the Yankee Square, DSB, vol. I, 45
PGNC Number: 4748

Nichols, Corporal Langdon H., 1st Vermont Volunteer Cavalry, Company C
Died: July 28, 1862, at the Fair Ground (POW camp)
Buried: City Cemetery, no. 9, 6th line of the Yankee Square, DSB, vol. I, 45
PGNC Number: 4734

Zimmerman, Private Charles, 1st New York Volunteer Light Artillery, Battery I
Died: July 28, 1862, at the Fair Ground (POW camp)
Buried: City Cemetery, no. 10, 5th line of the Yankee Square, DSB, vol. I, 45
PGNC Number: 4590

Hardison, Private Hiram P., 1st Maine Volunteer Cavalry, Company E
Died: July 29, 1862, at the Fair Ground (POW camp)
Buried: City Cemetery, no. 11, 5th line of the Yankee Square, DSB, vol. I, 45
PGNC Number: 4736

Herring, Private Daniel, 55th Ohio Volunteer Infantry, Company A (musician)
Died: July 29, 1862, at the Fair Ground (POW camp)
Buried: City Cemetery, no. 11, 4th line of the Yankee Square, DSB, vol. I, 44
PGNC Number: 4589

Hess, Private Henry, 55th Ohio Volunteer Infantry, Company C
Died: July 29, 1862, at the Fair Ground (POW camp)
Buried: City Cemetery, no. 11, 4th line of the Yankee Square, DSB, vol. I, 45
PGNC Number: 4744

Pike, Private William H., 10th Maine Volunteer Infantry, Company G
Died: July 29, 1862, at the Fair Ground (POW camp)
Buried: City Cemetery, no. 11, 2nd line of the Yankee Square, DSB, vol. I, 45
PGNC Number: 4746

Appendix A

Andrews, Private Charles E., 8th Vermont Volunteer Infantry, Company E
Died: July 30, 1862, at the Fair Ground (POW camp)
Buried: City Cemetery, no. 3, 5th line of the Yankee Square, DSB, vol. I, 46
PGNC Number: 4719

Bader, Private Henry, 1st Maryland Volunteer Infantry, Company K
Died: July 31, 1862, at the Fair Ground (POW camp)
Buried: City Cemetery, no. 7, 5th line of the Yankee Square, DSB, vol. I, 46
PGNC Number: 4610

Ferdun, Private George E., 28th New York Volunteer Infantry, Company G
Died: July 31, 1862, at the Fair Ground (POW camp)
Buried: City Cemetery, no. 12, 3rd line of the Yankee Square, DSB, vol. I, 46
PGNC Number: 4745

Moore, Private John T., 66th Ohio Volunteer Infantry, Company E
Died: July 31, 1862, at the Fair Ground (POW camp)
Buried: City Cemetery, no. 10, 6th line of the Yankee Square, DSB, vol. I, 46
PGNC Number: Unknown

August 1862 (11 deaths)

Dockham, Private George A., 1st Maine Volunteer Cavalry, Company M
Died: August 2, 1862, at the Fair Ground (POW camp)
Buried: City Cemetery, no. 4, 5th line of the Yankee Square, DSB, vol. I, 47
PGNC Number: 4587

Preacher, Private Bruno, 1st Maryland Volunteer Infantry, Company F
Died: August 2, 1862, at the Fair Ground (POW camp)
Buried: City Cemetery, no. 4, 6th line of the Yankee Square, DSB, vol. I, 47
PGNC Number: 4730

Weeks, Private Joseph, 10th Maine Volunteer Infantry, Company B
Died: August 2, 1862, at the Fair Ground (POW camp)
Buried: City Cemetery, no. 12, 6th line of the Yankee Square, DSB, vol. I, 47
PGNC Number: 4600

Kettering, Private Samuel, 3rd Maryland Volunteer Infantry, Company F
Died: August 4, 1862, at the Fair Ground (POW camp)
Buried: City Cemetery, no. 12, 5th line of the Yankee Square, DSB, vol. I, 48
PGNC Number: 4739

Roberts, Private Daniel S., 10th Maine Volunteer Infantry, Company B
Died: August 4, 1862, at the Fair Ground (POW camp)
Buried: City Cemetery, no. 12, 4th line of the Yankee Square, DSB, vol. I, 48
PGNC Number: 4741

Younger, Private John, 27th Indiana Volunteer Infantry, Company D
Died: August 4, 1862, at the Fair Ground (POW camp)

Buried: City Cemetery, no. 8, 6th line of the Yankee Square, DSB, vol. I, 48
PGNC Number: 4603

Barrett, Private Merritt C., 1st Vermont Volunteer Cavalry, Company H
Died: August 5, 1862, at the Fair Ground (POW camp) of scurvy
Buried: City Cemetery, no. 7, 5th line of the Yankee Square, DSB, vol. I, 49
Exhumed and returned to his parents in Vermont

Boyd, Private C. William, 27th Indiana Volunteer Infantry, Company E
Died: August 6, 1862, at the Fair Ground (POW camp) of typhoid
Buried: His burial is not listed in the Diuguid records.
He was buried near the POW camp.

Wheeler, Private George E., 1st Maryland Volunteer Infantry, Company A
Died: August 8, 1862, at the Fair Ground (POW camp)
Buried: City Cemetery, no. 11, 1st line of the Yankee Square, DSB, vol. I, 50
Exhumed and returned to his parents in Maryland

Reed, Private Charles E., 12th Massachusetts Volunteer Infantry, Company F
Died: August 9, 1862, at the Fair Ground (POW camp)
Buried: City Cemetery, no. 13, 5th line of the Yankee Square, DSB, vol. I, 50
PGNC Number: 4760

Kinerson, Private Albert, 1st Vermont Volunteer Cavalry, Company D
Died: August 15, 1862, somewhere between the Fair Ground and Annapolis, Maryland, of typhoid fever. His remains were shipped back to Vermont.
Buried: The Peacham Corner Cemetery in Peacham, Caledonia County, Vermont

November 1862 (one death)

Berry, Private James, 55th Ohio Volunteer Infantry, Company K
Died: November 15, 1862, at the Fair Ground
Buried: His burial is not listed in the Diuguid records.
He was buried near the POW camp.

January 1863 (one death)

Bronson, Private Lewis C., 34th Illinois Volunteer Infantry, Company F
Died: January 26, 1863, at Burton's tobacco factory
Buried: City Cemetery, no. 6, 4th line, Lot 187, DSB, vol. II, 97
PGNC Number: 4665

March 1863 (five deaths)

Pitcher, Private Horace M., 19th Michigan Volunteer Infantry, Company I
Died: March 20, 1863, at Crumpton's tobacco factory

Appendix A

Buried: City Cemetery, no. 2, 2nd line of Lot 187, DSB, vol. II, 108
PGNC Number: 4599

Beechner, Private John, 19th Michigan Volunteer Infantry, Company G
Died: March 21, 1863, at Knight's tobacco factory
Buried: City Cemetery, no. 9, 2nd line of Lot 199, DSB, vol. II, 108
PGNC Number: 4723

McGinnis, Private John C., 33rd Indiana Volunteer Infantry, Company A
Died: March 25, 1863, at Knight's tobacco factory
Buried: City Cemetery, no. 2, 2nd line of Lot 199, DSB, vol. II, 109
PGNC Number: 4593

Mason, Private Asa, 85th Indiana Volunteer Infantry, Company C
Died: March 27, 1863, at Knight's tobacco factory
Buried: City Cemetery, no. 7, 2nd line of Lot 199, DSB, vol. II, 109
PGNC Number: 4591

McBaird, Private James, 85th Indiana Volunteer Infantry, Company C
Died: March 27, 1863, at Christian's tobacco factory
Buried: City Cemetery, no. 8, 2nd line of Lot 199, DSB, vol. II, 109
PGNC Number: 4737

April 1863 (three deaths)

Jones, Private Owen R., 22nd Wisconsin Volunteer Infantry, Company F
Died: April 7, 1863, on an eastbound train of the Virginia and Tennessee Railroad
Buried: City Cemetery, no. 3, 5th line of Lot 199, DSB, vol. II, 110
PGNC Number: 4721

York, Sergeant Calvin B., 33rd Indiana Volunteer Infantry, Company A
Died: April 11, 1863, at Miller's tobacco factory
Buried: City Cemetery, no. 4, 4th line of Lot 199, DSB, vol. II, 111
PGNC Number: 4585

Robinson, Private Richard, 21st Michigan Volunteer Infantry, Company G
Died: April 27, 1863, at Burton's tobacco factory
Buried: City Cemetery, no. 2, 1st line of Lot 184, DSB, vol. II, 112
PGNC Number: 4742

May 1863 (two deaths)

Remington, Sergeant Francis A., 85th Indiana Volunteer Infantry, Company G
Died: May 1, 1863, at Miller's tobacco factory
Buried: City Cemetery, no. 3, 1st line of Lot 184, DSB, vol. II, 113
PGNC Number: 4761

Robinson, Captain Horace, 55th Ohio Volunteer Infantry, Company G
Died: May 10, 1863, location unknown
Buried: Farewell Retreat Cemetery, Republic, Seneca County, Ohio

December 1863 (one death)

Lapier, Private John B., 34th Massachusetts Volunteer Infantry, Company E
Died: December 3, 1863, at Massie's tobacco factory
Buried: City Cemetery, no. 1, 1st line of Lot 185, DBS, vol. II, 127
PGNC Number: 4935

February 1864 (one death)

Fergason, Private John L., 2nd North Carolina Mounted Volunteer Infantry, Company I
Died: February 25, 1864, at Ferguson's tobacco factory
Buried: City Cemetery, no. 1, 1st line of Lot 185, DSB, vol. II, 131
He is still buried in Lynchburg.

May 1864 (three deaths)

Carl, Private Frank W., 5th New York Volunteer Cavalry, Company F
Died: May 5, 1864, at Crumpton's tobacco factory
Buried: City Cemetery, no. 7, 4th line of Lot 2, DSB, vol. II, 135
PGNC Number: 4635

Glover, Private John F., 140th New York Volunteer Infantry, Company G
Died: May 7, 1864, at Crumpton's tobacco factory
Buried: City Cemetery, no. 4, 1st line of Lot 2, DSB, vol. II, 135
PGNC Number: 4765

Lennox, Private Samuel, 8th New York Volunteer Cavalry, Company C
Died: May 29, 1864, at Miller's tobacco factory
Buried: City Cemetery, no. 1, 1st line of Lot 1 in the far corner, DSB, vol. II, 140
PGNC Number: 4775

June 1864 (18 deaths)

Smith, Private William, 6th New Hampshire Volunteer Infantry, Company A
Died: June 2, 1864, at Camp Nicholls
Buried: City Cemetery, no. 2, 1st line of Lot 1 in the far corner, DSB, vol. II, 158
PGNC Number: 4786

Eustice, Private William, 7th Wisconsin Volunteer Infantry, Company C
Died: June 8, 1864, at Saunders' tobacco factory
Buried: City Cemetery, no. 3, 1st line of Lot 1, DSB, vol. II, 144
PGNC Number: 4646

Appendix A

Halsey, Private Joseph C., 5th Michigan Volunteer Infantry, Company B
Died: June 10, 1864, at Crumpton's tobacco factory
Buried: City Cemetery, no. 4, 1st line of Lot 1 in the far corner, DSB, vol. II, 144
PGNC Number: 4642

Boose, Sergeant Moses, 11th Pennsylvania Volunteer Infantry, Company A
Died: June 11, 1864, at Crumpton's tobacco factory
Buried: City Cemetery, no. 5, 1st line of Lot 1 in the far corner, DSB, vol. II, 145
PGNC Number: 4947

Condon, Private Elijah, 3rd Maine Volunteer Infantry, Company F
Died: June 12, 1864, at Camp Davis
Buried: City Cemetery, no. 6, 1st line of Lot 1 in the far corner, DSB, vol. II, 145
PGNC Number: 4789

Gibbs, Private Therone, New York Volunteer Heavy Artillery, Battery D
Died: June 14, 1864, at Crumpton's tobacco factory
Buried: City Cemetery, no. 8, 1st line of Lot 1 in the far corner, DSB, vol. II, 146
PGNC Number: 4789

Hernandez, Private Juan, 39th New York Volunteer Infantry, Company C
Died: June 14, 1864, at Crumpton's tobacco factory
Buried: City Cemetery, no. 7, 1st line of Lot 1 in the far corner, DSB, vol. II, 145
PGNC Number: 4784

Calas, Private Frederick, 61st New York Volunteer Infantry, Company B
Died: June 15, 1864, at Crumpton's tobacco factory
Buried: City Cemetery, no. 9, 1st line of Lot 1 in the far corner, DSB, vol. II, 146
PGNC Number: 4781

Davis, Private Charles C., 116th Ohio Volunteer Infantry
Died: June 20, 1864, at Pratt Hospital
Buried: City Cemetery, no. 10, 1st line of Lot 1 in the far corner, DSB, vol. II, 147
PGNC Number: 4956

Beckwith, Private George, 6th Michigan Volunteer Cavalry, Company C
Died: June 23, 1864, at Crumpton's tobacco factory
Buried: City Cemetery, no. 4, 2nd line of Lot 1 in the far corner, DSB, vol. II, 150
PGNC Number: 4791

Kelley, Quartermaster Sergeant John, 3rd West Virginia Volunteer Cavalry, Company I
Died: June 23, 1864, at the College Hospital
Buried: City Cemetery, no. 1, 3rd line of Lot 1 in the far corner, DSB, vol. II, 149
PGNC Number: 4794

McVey, Private James, 88th Pennsylvania Volunteer Infantry, Company D
Died: June 23, 1864, at Crumpton's tobacco factory
Buried: City Cemetery, no. 4, 2nd line of Lot 1 in the far corner, DSB, vol, II, 143
PGNC Number: 4792

VanOrder, Private Kimble, 15th New York Volunteer Cavalry, Company H
Died: June 24, 1864, at the College Hospital
Buried: City Cemetery, number and line of Lot 1 unknown, DSB, vol. II, 152
PGNC Number: Unknown

Green, Private William A., 7th West Virginia Volunteer Cavalry, Company I
Died: June 25, 1864, at the College Hospital
Buried: City Cemetery, no. 6, 2nd line of Lot 1 in the far corner, DSB, vol. II, 152
PGNC Number: 4774

Sears, Private William A., 34th Massachusetts Volunteer Infantry, Company H
Died: June 29, 1864, at the College Hospital
Buried: City Cemetery, no. 8, 2nd line of Lot 1 in the far corner, DSB, vol. II, 152
PGNC Number: 4783

Gatton, Private Jefferson, 116th Ohio Volunteer Infantry, Company A
Died: June 30, 1864, at the College Hospital
Buried: City Cemetery, no. 2, 3rd line of Lot 1 in the far corner, DSB, vol. II, 152
PGNC Number: 4776

Platenburgh, Private Peter, 111th New York Volunteer Infantry, Company D
Died: June 30, 1864, at Crumpton's tobacco factory
Buried: City Cemetery, no. 9, 2nd line of Lot 1 in the far corner, DSB, vol. II, 152
PGNC Number: 4770

Wood, Private Samuel D., 26th Michigan Volunteer Infantry, Company B
Died: Of starvation sometime after May 12, 1864, when he was taken prisoner at Spotsylvania Court House
Buried: His burial is not listed in the Diuguid records.
He was buried near the POW camp.

July 1864 (46 deaths)

Connelley, Private James, 7th Maine Volunteer Infantry, Company C
Died: July 1, 1864, at Saunders' tobacco factory
Buried: City Cemetery, no. 3, 3rd line of Lot 1 in the far corner, DSB, vol. II, 153
PGNC Number: 4630

Tripp, Private Ezra G., 37th Massachusetts Volunteer Infantry, Company A
Died: July 1, 1864, at Camp Davis
Buried: City Cemetery, no. 10, 2nd line of Lot 1 in the far corner, DSB, vol. II, 153
Reburied in the Silver Street Cemetery in Granville, Hampden County, Massachusetts

Fullmer, Private Isaiah, 148th Pennsylvania Volunteer Infantry, Company A
Died: July 2, 1864, at Crumpton's tobacco factory
Buried: City Cemetery, no. 4, 3rd line of Lot 1 in the far corner, DSB, vol. II, 153
PGNC Number: 4772

Appendix A

Sherman, Private Richard, 1st Michigan Volunteer Cavalry, Company C
Died: July 2, 1864, at Crumpton's tobacco factory
Buried: City Cemetery, no. 1, 1st line of Lot 2, DSB, vol. II, 153
PGNC Number: 4764

Fairbanks, Private Forrest G., 6th Michigan Volunteer Cavalry, Company D
Died: July 4, 1864, at Crumpton's tobacco factory
Buried: City Cemetery, no. 2, 1st line of Lot 2, DSB, vol. II, 154
PGNC Number: 4780

Schwartz, Private William, 48th Pennsylvania Volunteer Infantry, Company B
Died: July 5, 1864, at Massie's tobacco factory
Buried: City Cemetery, no. 6, 3rd line of Lot 1 in the far corner, DSB, vol. II, 154
ANC Number: 2256

Strikle, Corporal John M., 1st New York Volunteer Dragoons, Company F
Died: July 5, 1864, at Massie's tobacco factory
Buried: City Cemetery, no. 5, 3rd line of Lot 1 in the far corner, DSB, vol. II, 154
PGNC Number: 4961

Thornton, Private David M.C., 8th Michigan Infantry, Company C
Died: July 5, 1864, at Crumpton's tobacco factory
Buried: City Cemetery, no. 3, 1st line of Lot 2, DSB, vol. II, 154
PGNC Number: 4963

Fowler, Sergeant Thomas, 15th West Virginia Volunteer Infantry, Company A
Died: July 8, 1864, at the College Hospital
Buried: City Cemetery, no. 5, 1st line of Lot 2, DSB, vol. II, 155
PGNC Number: 4962

Burdett, Private Henderson F., 11th West Virginia Volunteer Infantry, Company G
Died: July 9, 1864, at Camp Davis
Buried: City Cemetery, no. 6, 1st line of Lot 2, DSB, vol. II, 155
PGNC Number: 4972

Jones, Private Jesse, 121st New York Volunteer Infantry, Company B
Died: July 9, 1864, at Crumpton's tobacco factory
Buried: City Cemetery, no. 8, 3rd line of Lot 1 in the far corner, DSB, vol. I, 155
PGNC Number: 4960

Boyce, Private John, 1st West Virginia Volunteer Light Artillery, Battery B
Died: July 10, 1864, at Crumpton's tobacco factory
Buried: City Cemetery, no. 8, 1st line of Lot 2, DSB, vol. II, 156
PGNC Number: 4785

Burial Records for POWs, 1862–1865

Bowen, Private Robert, 146th New York Volunteer Infantry, Company A (musician)
Died: July 11, 1864, at Crumpton's tobacco factory
Buried: Data not available
PGNC Number: Unknown

Coffren, Private Sebra F., 3rd Maine Volunteer Infantry, Company B
Died: July 11, 1864, at Crumpton's tobacco factory
Buried: City Cemetery, no. 9, 3rd line of Lot 1 in the far corner, DSB, vol. II, 156
PGNC Number: 4782

Pogan, Private Robert, 146th New York Volunteer Infantry, Company A
Died: July 11, 1864, at Crumpton's tobacco factory
Buried: Data not available
PGNC Number: Unknown

Dafoe, Private Edward, 1st Michigan Volunteer Cavalry, Company I
Died: July 12, 1864, at Crumpton's tobacco factory
Buried: City Cemetery, no. 7, 1st line of Lot 2, DSB, vol. II, 156
PGNC Number: 4640

Bardsley, Private John G., 1st West Virginia Volunteer Light Artillery, Battery B
Died: July 13, 1864, at the College Hospital
Buried: City Cemetery, no. 10, 3rd line of Lot 1 in the far corner, DSB, vol. II, 156
PGNC Number: 4632

Keller, Private Delevan, 111th New York Volunteer Infantry, Company K
Died: July 14, 1864, at Crumpton's tobacco factory
Buried: City Cemetery, no. 1, 2nd line of Lot 2, DSB, vol. II, 157
PGNC Number: 4766

Barnum, Private Isaac, 15th New York Volunteer Cavalry, Company E
Died: July 15, 1864, at Crumpton's tobacco factory
Buried: City Cemetery, no. 9, 1st line of Lot 2, DSB, vol. II, 157
PGNC Number: 4633

Hennessy, Private Michael, 15th New York Volunteer Cavalry, Company B
Died: July 15, 1864, at Crumpton's tobacco factory
Buried: City Cemetery, no. 10, 1st line of Lot 2, DSB, vol. II, 157
PGNC Number: 4763

Phillips, Private Theophilus C., 140th Pennsylvania Volunteer Infantry, Company I
Died: July 15, 1864, at Crumpton's tobacco factory
Buried: City Cemetery, no. 1, 3rd line of Lot 2, DSB, vol. II, 157
PGNC Number: 4768

Rice, Private Micah I., 29th Ohio Volunteer Infantry, Company D
Died: July 16, 1864, at Crumpton's tobacco factory

Appendix A

Buried: City Cemetery, no. 2, 3rd line of Lot 2, DSB, vol. II, 157
PGNC Number: 4954

Wickham, Quartermaster Sergeant John S., 135th Ohio Volunteer Infantry, Companies F and S
Died: July 16, 1864, at Crumpton's tobacco factory
Buried: City Cemetery, no. 2, 2nd line of Lot 2, DSB, vol. II, 157
Exhumed and reburied in Cedar Hill Cemetery, Newark, Licking County, Ohio

Bobson, Private Allen, 27th Ohio Volunteer Infantry, Company E, United States Colored Troops
Died: July 19, 1864, at Crumpton's tobacco factory
Buried: City Cemetery, Negro Row, DSB, vol. I, 158
He is still buried at the City Cemetery.

Rider, Sergeant John, 7th New York Volunteer High Artillery, Battery K
Died: July 19, 1864, at Crumpton's tobacco factory
Buried: City Cemetery, no. 3, 3rd line of Lot 2, DSB, vol. II, 158
PGNC Number: 4616

Rand, Private Jasper, 11th West Virginia Volunteer Infantry, Company B
Died: July 20, 1864, at Camp Davis
Buried: City Cemetery, no. 8, 3rd line of Lot 2, DSB, vol. II, 158
PGNC Number: 4617

Forbes, Corporal Daniel, 5th West Virginia Volunteer Infantry, Company B
Died: July 21, 1864, at Crumpton's tobacco factory
Buried: City Cemetery, no. 4, 3rd line of Lot 2, DSB, vol. II, 159
PGNC Number: 4618

Neal, Private James L., 11th New Hampshire Volunteer Infantry, Company A
Died: July 21, 1864, at Crumpton's tobacco factory
Buried: City Cemetery, no. 5, 3rd line of Lot 2, DSB, vol. II, 158
PGNC Number: 4615

Parker, Private John B., 3rd Maine Volunteer Infantry, Company I
Died: July 21, 1864, at Crumpton's tobacco factory
Buried: City Cemetery, no. 6, 2nd line of Lot 2, DSB, vol. II, 159
PGNC Number: 4762

State, Private William H., 6th New Hampshire Volunteer Infantry, Company K
Died: July 21, 1864, at Crumpton's tobacco factory
Buried: City Cemetery, no. 4, 2nd line of Lot 2, DSB, vol. II, 158
PGNC Number: 4965

Stout, Private George H., 6th Pennsylvania Volunteer Cavalry, Company G or M
Died: July 21, 1864, at Crumpton's tobacco factory

Buried: City Cemetery, no. 5, 2nd line of Lot 2, DSB, vol. II, 158
PGNC Number: 4945

Thompson, Private David, 110th Pennsylvania Volunteer Infantry, Company C
Died: July 23, 1864, at Camp Davis
Buried: City Cemetery, no. 7, 2nd line of Lot 2, DSB, vol. II, 159
PGNC Number: 4637

Hamilton, Private Evander B., 116th Ohio Volunteer Infantry, Company D
Died: July 24, 1864, at the College Hospital
Buried: City Cemetery, no. 6, 3rd line of Lot 2, DSB, vol. II, 159
PGNC Number: 4957

Love, Private Andrew, 183rd Pennsylvania Volunteer Infantry, Company C
Died: July 24, 1864, at Crumpton's tobacco factory
Buried: Data not available
PGNC Number: Unknown

McIntosh, Private Frank, 15th New York Volunteer Cavalry, Company G
Died: July 26, 1864, at Crumpton's tobacco factory
Buried: City Cemetery, no. 9, 2nd line of Lot 2, DSB, vol. II, 159
PGNC Number: 4631

Willard, Private James J., 57th Massachusetts Volunteer Infantry, Company G
Died: July 26, 1864, at Crumpton's tobacco factory
Buried: City Cemetery, no. 1, 4th line of Lot 2, DSB, vol. II, 159
PGNC Number: 4636

Wray, Corporal Thomas C., 72nd Pennsylvania Volunteer Infantry, Company E
Died: July 26, 1864, at Crumpton's tobacco factory
Buried: City Cemetery, no. 1, 5th line of Lot 2, DSB, vol. II, 159
PGNC Number: 4626

Morse, Private Jacob H., 5th New York Volunteer Cavalry, Company U
Died: July 27, 1864, at Crumpton's tobacco factory
Buried: City Cemetery, no. 3, 4th line of Lot 2, DSB, vol. II, 159
PGNC Number: Unknown

Farlow, Private Robert, 2nd Maryland Volunteer Infantry (Potomac Home Brigade), Company C
Died: July 28, 1864, at the College Hospital
Buried: City Cemetery, no. 2, 4th line of Lot 2, DSB, vol. II, 160
PGNC Number: 4638

McCluskey, Private John, 140th New York Volunteer Infantry, Company H
Died: July 28, 1864, at Crumpton's tobacco factory
Buried: City Cemetery, no. 7, 3rd line of Lot 2, DSB, vol. II, 160
PGNC Number: 4645

Appendix A

Clearnott, Private Joseph, 5th New Hampshire Volunteer Infantry, Company E
  Died: July 29, 1864, at the College Hospital
  Buried: City Cemetery, no. 2, 5th line of Lot 2, DSB, vol. II, 160
  PGNC Number: 4634

Redman, Private John, 5th New York Volunteer Cavalry, Company H
  Died: July 29, 1864, at Crumpton's tobacco factory
  Buried: City Cemetery, no. 8, 3rd line of Lot 2, DSB, vol. II, 160
  PGNC Number: 4647

Derr, Second Lieutenant Samuel A., 34th Ohio Volunteer Infantry, Company D
  Died: July 30, 1864, at the College Hospital
  Buried: City Cemetery, no. 4, 4th line of Lot 2, DSB, vol. II, 161
  PGNC Number: 4946

Stow, Sergeant Stephen L., 6th Michigan Volunteer Cavalry, Company B
  Died: July 30, 1864, at Crumpton's tobacco factory
  Buried: City Cemetery, no. 3, 5th line of Lot 2, DSB, vol. II, 161
  PGNC Number: 4966

Cooper, Private Eugene, 7th Michigan Volunteer Cavalry, Company F
  Died: July 31, 1864, at Crumpton's tobacco factory
  Buried: City Cemetery, no. 9, 3rd line of Lot 2, DSB, vol. II, 161
  PGNC Number: 4948

Robinson, Corporal John, 1st Maryland Volunteer Infantry, Company D
  Died: Sometime after May 8, 1864, shot by a Confederate guard
  Burial: He is not listed in the Diuguid records.
  He was buried near the POW camp at the Fair Ground.

August 1864 (16 deaths)

Olf, Private John, 126th New York Volunteer Infantry, Company E
  Died: August 1, 1864, at Crumpton's tobacco factory
  Buried: City Cemetery, no. 10, 3rd line of Lot 2, DSB, vol. II, 161
  PGNC Number: 4964

Dilcher, Private Henry, 122nd Ohio Volunteer Infantry, Company B
  Died: August 4, 1864, at Crumpton's tobacco factory
  Buried: City Cemetery, no. 4, 5th line of Lot 2, DSB, vol. II, 164
  PGNC Number: 4641

Gilson, Private Richard, 1st Potomac Home Brigade, Maryland Volunteer Cavalry, Company C
  Died: August 4, 1864, at Crumpton's tobacco factory
  Buried: City Cemetery, no. 5, 4th line of Lot 2, DSB, vol. II, 162
  He was reburied in the Maryland Plot of the GNC Section A, Number 7.

Burial Records for POWs, 1862–1865

Hammond, Private Leroy, 146th New York Volunteer Infantry, Company G
Died: August 4, 1864, location unknown
Buried: City Cemetery, no. 10, 2nd line of Lot 2, DSB, vol. II, 162
PGNC Number: Unknown

Lockwood, Private James E., 10th Vermont Volunteer Infantry, Company E
Died: August 8, 1864, at Crumpton's tobacco factory
Buried: City Cemetery, no. 6, 4th line of Lot 2, DSB, vol. II, 162
PGNC Number: 4951

Reed, Private Charles E., 12th Massachusetts Volunteer Infantry, Company F
Died: August 9, 1862, at the Fair Ground (POW camp)
Buried: City Cemetery, no. 13, 5th line of the Yankee Square, DSB, vol. II, 162
PGNC Number: 4760

Thorp, Corporal Nathan, 6th Pennsylvania Reserve Volunteer Infantry, Company C
Died: August 11, 1864, at Crumpton's tobacco factory
Buried: City Cemetery, no. 5, 5th line of Lot 2, DSB, vol. II, 163
PGNC Number: 4949

Barney, Private John P., 1st Delaware Volunteer Infantry, Company A
Died: August 12, 1864, at Crumpton's tobacco factory
Buried: City Cemetery, no. 6, 5th line of Lot 2, DSB, vol. II, 163
PGNC Number: 4790

Goggins, Private Andrew A., 31st Maine Volunteer Infantry, Company D
Died: August 12, 1864, at Crumpton's tobacco factory
Buried: City Cemetery, no. 8, 4th line of Lot 2, DSB, vol. II, 163
PGNC Number: 4771

Praynard, Private James P., 1st Delaware Infantry, Company A
Died: August 13, 1864, at Crumpton's tobacco factory
Buried: City Cemetery, no. 9, 3rd line of Lot 2, DSB, vol. II, 163
PGNC Number: 4622

Rapp, Private Levi, 149th Pennsylvania Volunteer Infantry, Company G
Died: August 13, 1864, at Crumpton's tobacco factory
Buried: City Cemetery, no. 9, 4th line of Lot 2, DSB, vol. II, 163
PGNC Number: 4955

Tourtellotte, Color Sergeant Chester A., 18th Connecticut Volunteer Infantry, Company H
Died: August 15, 1864, at the College Hospital
Buried: City Cemetery, no. 1, 1st line of Lot 3, DSB, vol. II, 163
PGNC Number: 4639

Rogers, Private Lawson H., 122nd Ohio Volunteer Infantry, Company H
Died: August 17, 1864, at Crumpton's tobacco factory
Buried: City Cemetery, no. 8, 5th line of Lot 2, DSB, vol. II, 164
PGNC Number: 4619

Appendix A

Ruck, Private Cyrus, 116th Pennsylvania Volunteer Infantry, Company G
Died: August 17, 1864, at the College Hospital
Buried: City Cemetery, no. 10, 4th line of Lot 2, DSB, vol. II, 164
PGNC Number: 4952

Stowell, Private Carlos A., 1st Vermont Volunteer Heavy Artillery, Company H
Died: August 22, 1864, at Crumpton's tobacco factory
Buried: City Cemetery, no. 9, 5th line of Lot 2, DSB, vol. II, 164
PGNC Number: 4986

Ballard, Private Joseph, 147th New York Volunteer Infantry, Company K
Died: August 26, 1864, at Crumpton's tobacco factory
Buried: City Cemetery, no. 10, 5th line of Lot 2, DSB, vol. II, 164
PGNC Number: 4959

September 1864 (10 deaths)

Leonard, Private Frank, 116th Pennsylvania Volunteer Infantry, Company H
Died: September 1, 1864, at Crumpton's tobacco factory
Buried: City Cemetery, no. 2, 1st line of Lot 3, DSB, vol. II, 165
PGNC Number: 4958

Stratton, Private Moses C., 6th Vermont Volunteer Infantry, Company B
Died: September 3, 1864, at Crumpton's tobacco factory
Buried: City Cemetery, no. 2, 2nd line of Lot 3, DSB, vol. II, 165
PGNC Number: 4969

Burr, Private Joel L., 4th United States Infantry, Company C
Died: September 6, 1864, at Crumpton's tobacco factory
Buried: City Cemetery, no. 3, 1st line of Lot 3, DSB, vol. II, 165
PGNC Number: 4643

Kenner, Captain Henry C., 4th United States Cavalry, Company A
Died: September 7, 1864, at Crumpton's tobacco factory
Buried: City Cemetery, no. 4, 1st line of Lot 3, DSB, vol. II, 165
Body exhumed in January 1866 and sent to Chattanooga, Tennessee

Sheehan, Private Michael, 150th Pennsylvania Volunteer Infantry, Company A
Died: September 7, 1864, at Crumpton's tobacco factory
Buried: City Cemetery, no. 3, 2nd line of Lot 3, DSB, vol. II, 165
PGNC Number: 4767

McGill, Private Samuel, 63rd New York Volunteer Infantry, Company C
Died: September 17, 1864, at Crumpton's tobacco factory
Buried: City Cemetery, no. 5, 1st line of Lot 3, DSB, vol. II, 165
PGNC Number: 4623

Donald, Private John, 1st Rhode Island Volunteer Light Artillery, Battery B
Died: September 20, 1864, at Crumpton's tobacco factory

Buried: City Cemetery, no.6, 1st line of Lot 3, DSB, vol. II, 165
PGNC Number: 4624

Monteith, Private William, 65th New York Volunteer Infantry, Company G
Died: September 20, 1864, at Crumpton's tobacco factory
Buried: City Cemetery, no. 4, 2nd line of Lot 3, DSB, vol. II, 165
PGNC Number: 4644

Arnold, Corporal William, 77th New York Infantry, Company B
Died: September 22, 1864, at Crumpton's tobacco factory
Buried: City Cemetery, no. 7, 1st line of Lot 3, DSB, vol. II, 166
PGNC Number: 4970

Kyle, Private Joseph F., 11th United States Infantry, Company D
Died: September 27, 1864, at Crumpton's tobacco factory
Buried: City Cemetery, no. 8, 1st line of Lot 3, DSB, vol. II, 167
PGNC Number: 4769

October 1864 (six deaths)

Coward, Private Charles A., 10th New Jersey Volunteer Infantry
Died: October 1, 1864, Massie's tobacco factory after being shot at the POW camp
Buried: City Cemetery, no. 10, 3rd line of Lot 3, DSB, vol. II, 167
Exhumed and reburied in Hightstown, New Jersey

Budd, Private Sebring, 1st Michigan Volunteer Cavalry, Company C
Died: October 16, 1864, at Crumpton's tobacco factory
Buried: City Cemetery, no. 3, 1st line of Lot 3, DSB, vol. II, 166
PGNC Number: 4935

Collins, Private James, 10th New Jersey Volunteer Infantry, Company G
Died: October 16, 1864, at Crumpton's tobacco factory
Buried: City Cemetery, no. 5, 2nd line of Lot 3, DSB, vol. II, 170
PGNC Number: 4973

Bowles, Private Almon E., 1st New Hampshire Volunteer Cavalry, Company L
Died: October 18, 1864, at Massie's tobacco factory
Buried: City Cemetery, no. 7, 2nd line of Lot 3, DSB, vol. II, 165
PGNC Number: Unknown

Sutton, Private Peter J., 15th New Jersey Volunteer Infantry, Company F
Died: October 18, 1864, at Massie's tobacco factory
Buried: City Cemetery, no. 2, 3rd line of Lot 3, DSB, vol. II, 168
PGNC Number: 4661

Cronshaw, Private John, 147th New York Volunteer Infantry, Company I
Died: October 26, 1864, at Crumpton's tobacco factory
Buried: City Cemetery, no. 6, 2nd line of Lot 3, DSB, vol. II, 168
PGNC Number: 4944

Appendix A

November 1864 (three deaths)

Moss, Private Jacob, 5th New York Volunteer Heavy Artillery, Company A
Died: November 2, 1864, at Crumpton's tobacco factory
Buried: City Cemetery, no. 3, 4th line of Lot 2, DSB, vol. II, 169
PGNC Number: 4627

Smith, Private Harrison H., 5th Vermont Volunteer Infantry, Company K
Died: November 4, 1864, at Crumpton's tobacco factory
Buried: City Cemetery, no. 8, 2nd line of Lot 3, DSB, vol. II, 169
PGNC Number: 4969

Welsh, Private John, 1st Maine Veteran Volunteer Infantry, Company K
Died: November 9, 1864, at Crumpton's tobacco factory
Buried: City Cemetery, no. 9, 2nd line of Lot 3, DSB, vol. II, 169
PGNC Number: 4971

December 1864 (five deaths)

Hartmann, Captain John B., 3rd New Jersey Volunteer Cavalry, Company C
Died: December 8, 1864, at Crumpton's tobacco factory
Buried: City Cemetery, no. 10, 2nd line of Lot 3, DSB, vol. II, 170
Exhumed and reburied in Philadelphia

Hunsaker, Private George, 1st United States Cavalry, Company A
Died: December 12, 1864, at Crumpton's tobacco factory
Buried: City Cemetery, no. 4, 3rd line of Lot 3, DSB, vol. II, 170
PGNC Number: 4936

Allen, Private Benjamin, 10th New Jersey Volunteer Infantry, Company G
Died: December 22, 1864, at Crumpton's tobacco factory
Buried: City Cemetery, no. 1, 4th line of Lot 3, DSB, vol. II, 170
PGNC Number: Unknown

Zulker, Private Benjamin C., 4th New Jersey Volunteer Infantry, Company D
Died: December 23, 1864, at Crumpton's tobacco factory
Buried: City Cemetery, no. 1, 5th line of Lot 3, DSB, vol. II, 170
PGNC Number: Unknown

Humphreys, Corporal Gabriel, 9th West Virginia Volunteer Infantry, Company D
Died: December 31, 1864, at Crumpton's tobacco factory
Buried: City Cemetery, no. 2, 4th line of Lot 3, DSB, vol. II, 170
PGNC Number: 4659

January 1865 (one death)

Warwick, Private Alfred, 3rd New Jersey Volunteer Cavalry
Died: January 22, 1865, at Crumpton's tobacco factory

Buried: City Cemetery, no. 2, 5th line of Lot 3, DSB, vol. II, 171
PGNC Number: Unknown

April 1865 (one death)

Almy, Corporal Frank M., 1st Massachusetts Volunteer Cavalry, Company D
 Died: April 30, 1865, shot during a fight on Bridge Street in Lynchburg
 Buried: City Cemetery, no. 3, 5th line of Lot 3, DSB, vol. II, 175
 Remains returned to his home in Newport, Rhode Island

June 1865 (one death)

Acker, Private Sidney E.A., 11th Michigan Volunteer Cavalry, Company M
 Died: June 3, 1865, at Pratt Hospital
 Buried: City Cemetery, no. 4, 5th line of Lot 3, DSB, vol. II, 175
 Remains returned to his parents in Rhode Island

Appendix B: Lynchburg Campaign Casualties, KIA/MIA

This appendix lists Union soldiers KIA/MIA during the Lynchburg Campaign, May 15–June 21, 1864, who are and are not buried in the City Cemetery. They are listed from highest rank to lowest, then alphabetically within rank.

2nd Easter Shore Maryland Volunteer Infantry

Chalron, Private Peter, Company I

2nd Maryland Volunteer Potomac Home Brigade

Crabtree, Private Martin, Company C
Gephart, Private Ernest, Company E

34th Massachusetts Volunteer Infantry

King, Sergeant Henry B., Company E
Breen, Corporal Dennis, Company H
Martin, Private Francis, Company K
Woodward, Private Seth A., Company D

5th New York Volunteer Heavy Artillery

Goswell, Private William, Company D
Jolly, Private James D., Company A

15th New York Volunteer Cavalry

Thompson, Corporal John, Company H
Carden, Private Patrick, Company A
Hawkins, Private William, Company B

Orton, Private Martin, Company B
Shum, Private Albert, Company L
Stanton, Private Silas, Company L

21st New York Volunteer Cavalry

Gage, Private Charles B., Company G[1]

8th Ohio Volunteer Cavalry[2]

Barber, Private William, Company K
Brant, Private Joseph, Company B
Dunlap, Private William H., Company A
Elson, Private Albert, Company G
Harrison, Private Battael V., Company K
Kenneke, Private Harman A., Company G
Martin, Private John R., Company G
Smith, Private John, Company C
Steen, Private John W., Company D

12th Ohio Volunteer Infantry

McCowen, First Sergeant Israel T., Company F
Shields, Corporal William C., Company A
Counsel, Private James D., Company D
Matson, Private James, Company C
Morse, Private William W., Company D
Townshend, Private Calvin W., Company B

23rd Ohio Volunteer Infantry

Decker, Private Alonzo, Company B
Steiber, Private Lewis, Company G

34th Ohio Volunteer Mounted Infantry

Conn, Corporal Daniel, Company B

36th Ohio Mounted Infantry

Thornburg, Corporal W.H., Company A
Thorn, Private Robert W., Company H[3]

91st Ohio Volunteer Infantry[4]

Stroup, First Lieutenant George B., Company D
Stiles, Sergeant Colvin, Company F

Bell, Corporal John, Company D
Dickey, Private William, Company I
Graham, Private Louis, Company C
McKee, Private Samuel L., Company I
Randall, Private William, Company F
Strausbaugh, Private Isaac, Company A
Swanger, Private James J., Company E

116th Ohio Volunteer Infantry

Blair, Private George, Company E
Boyd, Private James A., Company A
Coulter, Private George M., Company E
Fisher, Private William, Company F
VanHorn, Private Gilbert, Company I

123rd Ohio Volunteer Infantry

Dunn, Sergeant Samuel, Company F
Kiehl, Private Cyrus, Company F
McDonald, Private Savage, Company F

14th Pennsylvania Volunteer Cavalry

Sargent, Sergeant Cyrus B., Company F
Wolford, Sergeant Reyless, Company C
Curtis, Private Albert M., Company A
Hall, Private David L., Company F
Hedenthall, Private Joseph, Company A
Hudson, Private Alanson, Company F
Hull, Private Edmund J., Company A
McWilliams, Private James, Company C
Neifergold, Private Francis, Company A
Tingley, Private James, Company B

54th Pennsylvania Volunteer Infantry[5]

Marsh, Sergeant Simon, Company D
Levy, Corporal Joseph M., Company H
Schneider, Corporal Henry, Company B
Wendle, Corporal Jonathan L., Company C
Ellis, Private Nathan D., Company C
Firestone, Private Martin D., Company A
Groft, Private John, Company D
Hillegas, Private Nathaniel, Company K

Leadbeater, Private Leonard, Company E
Peck, Private Arthur, Company A
Pugh, Private John H., Company B
Reel, Private Hiram, Company C

1st West Virginia Volunteer Cavalry

Hoback, Corporal Alexander, Company D
Carter, Private James, Company H

1st West Virginia Volunteer Infantry

Simpson, Private Roberts J., Company I[6]

1st West Virginia Volunteer Light Artillery

Beardsley, Private John G., Battery D
Durbin, Private John W., Battery D
Gefner, Private Joseph, Battery A
Rust, Private William, Battery B

2nd West Virginia Volunteer Cavalry

Woodrum, Private James, Company H

3rd West Virginia Volunteer Cavalry

Wentz, Corporal William, Company M

5th West Virginia Volunteer Infantry

Thomas, Second Lieutenant David J., Company A
Waller, Sergeant Coleman B., Company K
Harrison, Private Solomon, Company D

7th West Virginia Volunteer Cavalry

Ballard, Sergeant Patterson, Company B
Green, Private William A. Company I

9th West Virginia Volunteer Infantry

Smith, Private Henry S., Company D

11th West Virginia Volunteer Infantry

Barr, First Lieutenant James, Company D

Appendix B

Mathews, Private James L., Company I
McPherson, Private Thomas, Company K
Proudfoot, Private Francis, Company C
Rexroad, Private Morgan, Company C
Sigler, Private John W., Company C
Smith, Private Francis M., Company C

12th West Virginia Volunteer Infantry

Steward, Private James M., Company F
White, Private James, Company K

14th West Virginia Volunteer Infantry

Prince, Private John E., Company D

15th West Virginia Volunteer Infantry

Hitt, Corporal Joseph W., Company B
Coonts, Private Philip, Company F
Daugherty, Private Daniel, Company K
Dulaney, Private Daniel, Company C
Kayser, Private John S., Company D
King, Private William, Company K
Lemon, Private Robert, Company C
Runner, Private George, Company E
Watkins, Private John, Company C

Chapter Notes

Introduction

1. *The War of the Rebellion: A Compilation of the Official Records of the Union and Confederate Armies*, series 2, vol. 4 (Washington, D.C.: Government Printing Office, 1899), 777.
2. William Best Hesseltine, *Civil War Prisons: A Study in War Psychology* (Columbus: Ohio State University Press, 1930), 68.
3. William Best Hesseltine, "Andersonville Revisited," *Georgia Review* 10, no. 1 (1956): 94.
4. Lonnie R. Speer, *Portals to Hell: Military Prisons of the Civil War* (Mechanicsburg, PA: Stackpole Books, 1997), 96.
5. Ibid., 159.
6. Ibid., 336.
7. Charles W. Sanders, Jr., *While in the Hands of the Enemy: Military Prisons of the Civil War* (Baton Rouge: Louisiana State University Press, 2005), 9.
8. Roger Pickenpaugh, *Captives in Blue: The Civil War Prisons of the Confederacy* (Tuscaloosa: University of Alabama Press, 2013), 40–41, 75, 109–111.
9. Paul J. Springer and Glenn Robins, *Transforming Civil War Prisons: Lincoln, Lieber, and the Politics of Captivity* (New York: Routledge, 2015).
10. Official Records, series I, vol. 37, pt. 1 (1891), 598.

Chapter 1

1. James Pinkney Bell, *Our Quaker Friends of Ye Olden Times* (Lynchburg: J.P. Bell, 1905), 145–147.
2. T. Gibson Hobbs, Jr., *The Canal on the James* (Lynchburg: Blackwell, 2009), 3.
3. Ibid., 110–111.
4. Ibid., 143–144.
5. Edward Hunt, ed., *Hunt's Merchant's Magazine and Commercial Review* 32, June 1855, 743; David R. Goldfield, *Urban Growth in the Age of Sectionalism: Virginia, 1847–1861* (Baton Rouge: Louisiana State University Press, 1977), 249. Three million dollars in 1855 had the purchasing power of $9,936,000 in 2022 dollars. Likewise, $1,623 had the purchasing power of $53,765. The whaling industry made New Bedford, Massachusetts, the wealthiest community per capita in the United States in 1855.
6. S. Allen Chambers, Jr., *Lynchburg: An Architectural History* (Charlottesville: University of Virginia Press, 1981), 88, 164–165.
7. W. Aubrey Christian, *Lynchburg and Its People* (Lynchburg: J.P. Bell, 1900), 50.
8. *Lynchburg Daily Virginian*, March 19, 1853, 2.
9. Chambers, 88, 164–165.
10. Christian, 162. Christian's statement that the clock had lain on a hillside rusting since 1850 seems to be hyperbole. It is highly unlikely that the vestry of Saint Paul's Episcopal Church would allow a valuable clock simply to rust.
11. Lib Wiley, *Alongside the River: A History of Lynchburg's Congregations* (Lynchburg: Lynchburg Bicentennial Commission, 1986), 42.
12. Charles H. Haskins and William I. Hull, *A History of Higher Education in Pennsylvania* (Washington, D.C.: Government Printing Office, 1902), 155–156.

Notes—Chapter 2

13. The Cumberland Presbyterian Church was founded in 1810 in Dickson County, Tennessee, during the Second Great Awakening (1790–1840). Its name is derived from the Cumberland River, which flows through Dickson County; Haskins and Hull, 157.
14. *Ibid.*
15. *Ibid.*
16. W. Harrison Daniel, "Old Lynchburg College," *Virginia Magazine of History and Biography* 88 (October 1980): 450.
17. Christian, 167–168.
18. Haskins and Hull, 57.
19. Christian, 157, 318.
20. Christian, 168.
21. Daniel, 463.
22. *Ibid.*, 453–454. Twenty thousand dollars had the purchasing power of $662,400, while $10,000 equals $331,200.
23. John Theodore Oakey, comp., "The Story of Old Lynchburg College," typed manuscript dated 1936 in the Jones Memorial Library Collection, 1.
24. Christian, 161, 169.
25. Chambers, 143.
26. *Ibid.*
27. Sarah LaRue Hopwood was the author of the college motto, "Christian Education, the Hope of the World."
28. Christian, 171.
29. Anne Royall, *Mrs. Royall's Southern Tour, or Second Series of the Black Book* (Washington, D.C.: Publisher unknown, 1830), 1:100–101.
30. Joseph Clarke Robert, *The Tobacco Kingdom: Plantation, Market, and Factory in Virginia and North Carolina, 1800–1860* (Gloucester, MA: Peter Smith, 1965), 182–183.
31. These statistics are based on the 1860 U.S. federal census and the 1860 U.S. federal census—slave schedules. David E. Booker and his son, James M. Booker, owned 13 slaves who worked in Booker's tobacco factory. David W. Burton, the owner of Burton's tobacco factory, had 11 slaves working for him. Christian's tobacco factory owned by Camillius Christian employed 22 slaves. Ten slaves worked in Crumpton's tobacco factory owned by William Crumpton. Thomas Ferguson and his male relatives operated Ferguson's tobacco factory with the labor of 15 slaves. John A. Read operated Read's tobacco factory with a labor force of 19 slaves. James Saunders and his brother, William Saunders, owned and operated Saunders' tobacco factory, which was the largest enterprise of its kind in the city with a labor force of 85 slaves. Benjamin B. Taliaferro operated Taliaferro's tobacco factory with a workforce of a dozen slaves.
32. Robert, *Tobacco Kingdom*, 203.
33. *Ibid.*, 181.
34. William Cullen Bryant, "Travels, Addresses and Comments," *Prose Writings of William Cullen Bryant*, ed. Parke Godwin (New York: D. Appleton, 1889), 2:24–26.
35. Susan L. Blackford, comp., and Charles M. Blackford, ed., *Memoirs of Life In and Out of the Army in Virginia During the War Between the States* (Lynchburg: Warwick House Publishing, 1996), 1:8.
36. Christian, 191.
37. *Ibid.*, 193.
38. *Ibid.*, xvi.
39. Blackford and Blackford, 1:14.
40. Christian, 195.
41. *Ibid.*, 195–196.
42. Blackford and Blackford, 1:17.
43. William M. Brown, *Marshall Lodge #39* (Staunton, VA: McClure, 1953), 203; Chambers, 115–118.
44. Christian, 201.
45. Richard Snow, *A Guide Book of Flying Eagle and Indian Head Cents* (Atlanta: Whitman Publishing, 2007), 21–22; Don Taxey, *The U.S. Mint and Coinage* (New York: Arco Publishing, 1966), 235–239.
46. Raymond Williamson, "Lynchburg Paper Money of 1862," *Lynch's Ferry* 8, no. 1 (Lynchburg: Lynchburg Historical Foundation, 1995): 16–19.

Chapter 2

1. "The Concert To-Night," *Richmond Enquirer*, December 20, 1850, 2.
2. There were few institutions of higher education for women in the United States before the Civil War, but

Notes—Chapter 2

there were two in Virginia, both founded in 1842: Augusta Female Seminary (now Baldwin University) and Valley Union Seminary (now Hollins University).

3. On May 24, 1856, John Brown led a raid on the small pro-slavery settlement at Pottawatomie Creek, Kansas. Attempts to find the murderers failed, but details of the "Pottawatomie massacre" filled newspapers countrywide. John Brown became a figure to be feared or cheered.

4. "Cardinal Democratic Principles on the Slavery Issue," *Richmond Enquirer*, October 25, 1859, 2.

5. William W. Freehling and Craig M. Simpson, *Showdown in Virginia: The 1861 Convention and the Fate of the Union* (Charlottesville: University of Virginia Press, 2010), xvi.

6. "Treatment of Prisoners of War—Yankee Justice and Magnanimity," *Richmond Enquirer*, July 9, 1861, 4.

7. "Resignations," *Richmond Daily Dispatch*, April 26, 1861, 1.

8. *Original Records*, pt. 2, 146; Series II, vol. 3, 683.

9. "The Great Battle," *Richmond Daily Dispatch*, July 16, 1861, 2; July 31, 1861, 2; August 2, 1861, 2.

10. Theodore Cazeau, *A Brief Account of the Thirteenth New York State Volunteer Regiment, 1861–1863* (Rochester: Historic Monograph Collection, Central Library of Rochester and Monroe County, 1925), 2.

11. Alfred Ely, *Journal of Alfred Ely: A Prisoner of War in Richmond* (New York: Appleton, 1862), 3.

12. Noted for his quick temper and sadistic treatment of POWs, Lieutenant David H. Todd was the half brother of Mary Todd Lincoln.

13. William H. Jeffrey, *Richmond Prisons, 1861–1862* (St. Johnsburg, VT: Republican Press, 1893), 10. Jeffrey assumed that Ely and his fellow prisoners were moved to Atkinson's warehouse, which was directly across Main Street. Sandra V. Parker, *Richmond's Civil War Prisons* (Lynchburg: H.E. Howard, 1990), 4, made a stronger case for them being moved next door to Howard's warehouse. Crossing Main Street with a large body of Union officers under guard would have been logistically difficult regardless of the time of day.

14. Ely, 98. In his narrative, Ely records that his cot cost 20 shillings—a common term for a quarter. In short, he paid $5.

15. Among the newspapers available for purchase by the prisoners were the *Richmond Enquirer*, *Daily Richmond Whig*, *Daily Richmond Dispatch*, *Richmond Weekly Enquirer*, *Weekly Dispatch*, *Semi-weekly Dispatch*, *Richmond Whig and Public Advertiser*, *Daily Richmond Enquirer*, and *Daily Richmond Examiner*. One copy of each available paper would be bought to be read aloud and then passed around the group.

16. Jeffrey, 10.

17. Ely, 100.

18. Jeffrey, 47; John S.C. Abbott, "Heroic Deeds of Heroic Men, XVI. The Capture, Imprisonment, and Escape," *Harper's New Monthly Magazine*, January 1867, 159.

19. Ely, 93.

20. *Ibid.*, 96, 103.

21. Colonel George Couper Gibbs (1822–1873) was a member of the Forty-Second North Carolina Infantry, although a native of Florida. He supervised the creation of the auxiliary POW camp in Salisbury, North Carolina, in December 1861 and the camp in Lynchburg, Virginia, in April 1862.

22. Ely, 106.

23. Colonel Gibbs accompanied the POWs to Charleston. Roger Pickenpaugh, *Captives in Blue: The Civil War Prisons of the Confederacy* (Tuscaloosa: University of Alabama Press, 2013), 13; Ely, 108.

24. In addition to being the librarian of the U.S. House of Representatives, Charles Lanman (1819–1895) was a noted author and artist, having studied with the leading painters of the Hudson River school.

25. Frederick F. Cavada, *Libby Life: Experiences of a Prisoner in Richmond, Virginia, 1863–64* (Philadelphia: J.B. Lippincott, 1865), 26.

26. Justin Glenn, *The Washingtons: A Family History*, vol. 1, *Seven Genera-*

tions of the Presidential Branch (El Dorado, CA: Savas Beatie, 2014–2015), 131; Robert J. Driver and Kevin C. Ruffner, *1st Battalion Virginia Infantry, 39th Battalion Virginia Infantry, 24th Battalion Virginia Partisan Rangers* (Lynchburg: H.E. Howard, 1996), 126.

27. Parker, 11; United States Sanitary Commission, *Narrative of Privations and Sufferings of United States Officers and Soldiers While Prisoners of War in the Hands of Rebel Authorities. Being the Report of a Commission of Inquiry, Appointed by the United States Sanitary Commission with an Appendix, Containing the Testimony* (Philadelphia: King and Baird, Printers, 1864), 44.

28. Robert Knox Sneden, *Eye of the Storm*, ed. Charles E. Bryan, Jr., and Nelson D. Langford (New York: Free Press, 2000), 4.

29. Frances H. Casstevens, *"Out of the Mouth of Hell": Civil War Prisons and Escapes* (Jefferson, NC: McFarland, 2011), 266; Lonnie R. Speer, *Portals to Hell: Military Prisons of the Civil War* (Mechanicsburg, PA: Stackpole Books, 1997), 91.

30. Frank L. Byrne, "Libby: A Study in Emotions," *Journal of Southern History* 24 (1958): 431.

31. Parker, 12.

32. Cavada, 141.

33. A corporal or sergeant equals two privates; a lieutenant equals four privates; a captain equals six privates; a major equals eight privates; 10 privates equal a lieutenant colonel; 15 privates equal a colonel; 20 privates equal a brigadier general; 40 privates equal a major general; and 60 privates equal a commanding general.

34. President Davis deplored everything Union general Benjamin F. Butler had done during his tenure as military governor of New Orleans (June–December 1862), but he was incensed by Butler ordering William B. Mumford's execution for tearing down the flag of the United States from the U.S. Mint and for issuing General Order 28, which declared that any woman who insulted or showed disrespect to a Union soldier was liable to arrest as a prostitute. Davis' repeated protests were ignored, so he retaliated by canceling the exchange program for 16 days, from December 22 to January 7, thus the Union POWs spent the entire Christmas season separated from their families.

35. This number included prisoners who were to be exchanged from other POW camps containing many from Salisbury. The officers among them were taken to Libby. "Exchange of Prisoners," *Richmond Daily Dispatch*, August 15, 1862, 1.

36. On September 8, 400 POWs from Belle Isle joined 100 from Libby and, under the command of Captain Montgomery, began the journey to the point of exchange. *Richmond Daily Dispatch*, September 8, 1862, 2.

37. Parker, 26.

38. "Belle Isle," *Richmond Dispatch*, January 17, 1863, 2.

39. *Richmond Dispatch*, May 13, 1863, 2.

40. George Haven Putnam, *A Prisoner of War in Virginia, 1864–5* (New York: G.P. Putnam's Sons, 1914), 19.

41. Asa B. Isham, Henry M. Davidson, and Henry B. Furness, *Prisoners of War and Military Prisons* (Cincinnati: Lyman and Cushing, 1890), 29.

42. Cavada, 23.

43. Joseph Janvier Woodward, *Outlines of the Chief Camp Diseases of the United States Armies as Observed During the Present War: A Practical Contribution* (Philadelphia: Lippincott, 1863), 116.

44. *Ibid.*, 47.

45. Putnam, 27.

46. Cavada, 47.

47. Joseph Ferguson, *Life-Struggles in Rebel Prisons: A Record of Suffering, Escapes, Adventures, and Starvation of the Union Prisoners* (Philadelphia: James A. Ferguson, Publisher, 1865), 34.

48. Cavada, 51, 55.

49. Parker, 49; Alva C. Roach, *The Prisoner of War and How Treated* (Indianapolis: Railroad City Publishing House, 1865), 60.

50. Parker, 89, 133.

51. U.S. Sanitary Commission, 39.

52. Cavada, 166.

53. "Yankee Prisoners Escape," *Richmond Examiner*, February 11, 1864, 1;

Notes—Chapter 3

"Important Escape of Yankee Prisoners—Over Fifty Feet of Ground Tunneled," *Richmond Dispatch*, February 11, 1864, 1.

54. Casstevens, 276.

55. Harrison C. Hobart, "Libby Prison—The Escape," *War Papers, Wisconsin Commandery, Military Order of the Loyal Legion of the United States* (Milwaukee: Burdick, Armitage and Allen, 1891), 1:394–409.

56. A week after the escape, February 15, Private Sneden was shipped to Andersonville. Angela Zombec, "Libby Prison," *Encyclopedia Virginia*, http://encyclopediavirginia.org/entries/libby-prison.

57. "Yankee Prisoners Escape," *Richmond Examiner*, February 11, 1864, 1; "Important Escape of Yankee Prisoners," *Richmond Dispatch*, February 11, 1864, 1; "Yankee Prisoners Escape," *Richmond Whig*, February 11, 1864, 1.

58. Cavada, 174, 176.

59. U.S. Sanitary Commission, 42.

60. Parker, 33.

61. Ibid., 34.

62. U.S. Sanitary Commission, 51.

63. Ibid., 106.

64. Casstevens, 196.

65. John W. Manning, "Brutal Murders at Belle Isle," *National Tribune*, September 2, 1882; Casstevens, 197–198.

66. Josephus Hopwood, *A Journey through the Years* (St. Louis: Bethany Press, 1932), 32. In 1903, Dr. Hopwood and his wife, Sarah LaRue Hopwood, founded Virginia Christian College, now the University of Lynchburg, on land contested during the Battle of Lynchburg, June 17–18, 1864. The campus is less than two miles from the location of the Union POW camp. Dr. Hopwood was a private in Company L, 7th Illinois Volunteer Cavalry.

67. "Belle Isle," *Richmond Daily Dispatch*, July 9, 1862, 1.

68. *Official Records*, Series II, vol. 4, 475.

69. Parker, 57.

70. Hopwood, 31.

71. Ibid., 32.

72. J. Osborn Coburn, *Hell on Belle Isle: Diary of a Civil War POW* (Bryan, OH: Faded Banner Publications, 1997), 64.

73. Parker, 62.

Chapter 3

1. John B. Floyd was governor of Virginia from 1849 to 1852 and secretary of war from 1857 to 1860, but his military career was both short and lackluster. Floyd took command of Fort Donelson on February 13, 1862, exactly a week after Brigadier General Ulysses S. Grant had taken Fort Henry. By February 15, it was obvious that Grant also intended to take Fort Donelson. The following day, Floyd turned his command of the fort over to Brigadier General Gideon Johnson Pillow, who then relinquished to Brigadier General Simon Bolivar Buckner. Floyd and Pillow escaped while Buckner surrendered to Grant. President Davis relieved Floyd of his command on March 11, 1862.

2. *Lynchburg Daily Virginian*, November 15, 1861, 3.

3. *Lynchburg Daily Virginian*, November 23, 1861, 2.

4. "The Reported Burning of Guyandotte Contradicted," *Lynchburg Daily Virginian*, November 23, 1861, 2.

5. "The Guyandotte Raid," *Daily Intelligencer*, November 13, 1861, 3.

6. This was not the current Forest Road.

7. Jeremy Francis Gilmer, *Lynchburg and Vicinity* (Richmond: Confederate Engineer Bureau, 1864), 2 maps.

8. W. Aubrey Christian, *Lynchburg and Its People* (Lynchburg: J.P. Bell, 1900), 198.

9. Charles E. Driscoll, *John J. Terrell, MD, Civil War Doctor to Man and Horse* (Lynchburg: Warwick House Publishers, 2020), 95.

10. Alice DuPuy Spencer, *"I Even Remember Where the Mud Puddles Were,"* ed. Joe Spencer (Lynchburg: Privately printed, 1997). This endnote refers to Mrs. Spencer's hand-drawn map of the location of the POW camp.

11. Charles H. Blinn, "Journal of C.H. Blinn, Private, Co. A 1st Vermont

Notes—Chapter 3

Cavalry," 2 vols. (Burlington, VT: Silver Special Collections, University of Vermont Libraries, 1862), 1:59.

12. City of Lynchburg, "Minute Book of City Council," March 8, 1862, vol. 3, 1851–1864 (Lynchburg: Jones Memorial Library).

13. *Official Records*, Series II, vol. 4, 779.

14. Charles Button, "Latest from the Army in the Valley," *Lynchburg Daily Virginian*, June 6, 1862, 3.

15. Charles Button, "Arrival of Yankee Prisoners," *Lynchburg Daily Virginian*, June 11, 1862, 3.

16. Michael Henry VanBuskirk, "Diary, 1862–1864," June 11, 1862, SC 1383, Special Collections Library, Western Kentucky University, Bowling Green.

17. *Ibid.*, June 12, 1862; Charles Button, "Yankee Prisoners," *Lynchburg Daily Virginian*, June 12, 1862, 3.

18. *Ibid.*

19. Charles Button, "A Caution," *Lynchburg Daily Virginian*, June 13, 1862, 3.

20. *Original Records*, Series II, vol. 7, 373.

21. Blinn, 43–46.

22. *New York, U.S., Federal Census, 1855*, 7.

23. Blinn, 46–48.

24. Ziba Roberts, "Diary," James S. Schoff Collection, William L. Clements Library, University of Michigan, Ann Arbor, May 26, 1862.

25. VanBuskirk, May 27 and 28, 1862.

26. Blinn, 47; VanBuskirk, May 28, 1862.

27. Blinn, 48.

28. *Ibid.*, 49–50, 56–57.

29. VanBuskirk, May 31, 1862.

30. Roberts, June 1, 1862.

31. Blinn, 52; VanBuskirk, June 3, 1862; Roberts, June 3, 1862.

32. Blinn, 51; VanBuskirk, June 3, 1862; Roberts, June 3, 1862.

33. VanBuskirk, May 31, 1862.

34. Roberts, June 3, 1862.

35. VanBuskirk, June 4, 1862.

36. Roberts, June 5, 1862.

37. Richard G. Williams, Jr., *The Battle of Waynesboro* (Charleston, SC: History Press, 2014), 17–18.

38. VanBuskirk, June 5, 1862.

39. Blinn, 52–55.

40. VanBuskirk, June 7, 1862.

41. Roberts, June 8, 1862.

42. Blinn, 54. Engineered by Claudius Crozet, the tunnel was begun in 1850 and opened to railroad traffic in 1858.

43. Roberts, June 9, 1862; VanBuskirk, June 10, 1862; Blinn, 53, 56.

44. VanBuskirk, June 10, 1862; Roberts, June 10, 1862; Blinn, 56.

45. Roberts, June 11, 1862; Blinn, 57.

46. Roberts, June 11, 1862; Blinn, 57.

47. *Official Records*, Series II, vol. 4, 777.

48. *Ibid.*

49. Blinn, 61, 66.

50. Charles Button, "Our Yankee Guests," *Lynchburg Daily Virginian*, June 13, 1862, 3.

51. Roberts, June 12, 1862.

52. VanBuskirk, June 12, 1862.

53. Blinn, 57.

54. Charles Button, "A Caution," *Lynchburg Daily Virginian*, June 13, 1862, 2.

55. Blinn, 58.

56. *Ibid.*

57. *Ibid.*, 59.

58. VanBuskirk, June 15, 1862.

59. Roberts, June 15, 1862.

60. *Official Records*, Series II, vol. 4, 779.

61. Blinn, 59.

62. Roberts, June 16, 1862.

63. *Ibid.*, June 17, 1862.

64. Blinn, 59; Edward P. Tobie, *History of the First Maine Cavalry, 1861–1865* (Boston: Press of Emery & Hughes, 1887), 43.

65. VanBuskirk, June 17, 1862.

66. Roberts, June 18, 1862.

67. *Official Records*, Series II, vol. 4, 779.

68. *Ibid.*, 779.

69. *Ibid.*, 788.

70. Blinn, 60.

71. Roberts, June 18, 1862.

72. Francis P. Pierpont, *Annual Report of the Adjutant General of West Virginia for the Year Ending December 31, 1864* (Wheeling, WV: John F.M. Dermot, Public Printer, 1865), 703.

73. "Diuguid Soldiers Book," manuscript in possession of the Old City Cemetery, Lynchburg, vol. I, 31.

Notes—Chapter 3

74. *West Virginia Soldiers Service Records: Private Patrick Dowling*, www.fold3.com/image#265743524.
75. Pierpont, 703.
76. Lucy Harrison Baber and Evelyn Lee Moore, *Behind the Old Brick Wall: A Cemetery Story* (Lynchburg: Lynchburg Committee of the National Society of the Colonial Dames of America in the Commonwealth of Virginia, 1968), 245; "Diuguid Soldiers Book," vol. I, 31.
77. Blinn, 60.
78. Private John W. Rucker, Company I of the Twenty-Fifth Ohio Volunteer Infantry, died at the Fair Ground on June 24, 1862, and was buried in the City Cemetery the same day. "Diuguid Soldiers Book," vol. I, 32; Baber and Moore, 245.
79. Blinn, 60.
80. "Diuguid Soldiers Book." The cost paid by the Confederate government for each burial is recorded as part of each entry, and it is the same for the men of both armies.
81. Gerald P. Fogarty, *Commonwealth Catholicism: A History of the Catholic Church in Virginia* (Notre Dame: University of Notre Dame Press, 2001), 169.
82. Blinn, 61.
83. "Diuguid Soldiers Book," vol. I, 30–51.
84. Blinn, 65; Roberts, June 27, 1862; VanBuskirk, July 2 and 19, 1862.
85. Blinn, 61.
86. Joseph Janvier Woodward, *Outlines of the Chief Camp Diseases of the United States Armies as Observed During the Present War* (Philadelphia: J.B. Lippincott, 1863), 23, 62, 69, 73.
87. Roberts, June 21, 1862.
88. VanBuskirk, June 21, 1862.
89. Blinn, 62, 63.
90. VanBuskirk, June 23, 1862.
91. Blinn, 61.
92. Roberts, June 24 and 26, 1862.
93. VanBuskirk, July 5, 1862.
94. Blinn, 65.
95. *Ibid.*, 64.
96. Roberts, July 7 and 8, 1862.
97. Blinn, 62.
98. Roberts, June 26–July 5, 1862.
99. Woodward, 253.
100. VanBuskirk, July 2, 4, and 12, 1862.
101. Blinn, 67–68. The first entry in his second volume was dated November 19, 1862, when he was a free man once again. Like so many other POWs who survived, he mustered out of service when his three-year term was completed, but he waited until November 18, 1864, to leave the service.
102. *Official Records*, Series II, vol. 4, 801, 822, 832, 833, 837, 838, 868. The tents, which were no longer needed, were shipped back to Richmond for use on Belle Isle.
103. VanBuskirk, July 19, 1862.
104. *Ibid.*, July 21 and 22, 1862.
105. "Diuguid Soldiers Book," vol. I, Private Marquis Bower, 43; Corporal Harry Vinyard, July 25, 44; Private John Swisher, July 2, 44; and Private John Moore, July 31, 46.
106. VanBuskirk, July 28, 1862.
107. *Ibid.*, August 8 and 9, 1862.
108. Roberts, August 9, 1862; VanBuskirk, August 10, 1862.
109. Walter Clark, ed., *Histories of the Several Regiments and Battalions from North Carolina in the Great War, 1861–65* (Goldsboro, NC: Nash Brothers, 1901), 2:792.
110. "Libby Prison," *Richmond Dispatch*, August 20 and 21, 1862.
111. Thomas P. Turner Compiled Service Record, M331, National Archives, Washington, D.C.
112. Arch Frederic Blakey, *General John H. Winder, C.S.A.* (Gainesville: University Press of Florida, 1990), 157–158.
113. *Official Record*, Series II, vol. 5, 795–797.
114. Charles Blinn, Ziba Roberts, and Michael VanBuskirk chose to not reenlist at the end of their three-year commitment. *1890 Veterans Schedules of the U.S. Federal Census*.
115. *Ibid.*, 127, 128, 130.
116. John R. McBride, *History of the Thirty-Third Indiana Veteran Volunteer Infantry During the Four Years of Civil War from Sept. 16, 1861, to July 21, 1865, and Incidentally of Col. Coburn's Second Brigade, Third Division, Twentieth Army Corps Including Incidents of the Great*

Rebellion (Indianapolis: William B. Burford, Printer and Binder, 1900), 74.
117. *Official Records*, Series I, vol. 23, pt. 1, 73.
118. Cecil K. Byrd, ed., "Journal of Israel Cogshall, 1862–1863," *Indiana Magazine of History* 42, no. 1 (March 1946): 77.
119. McBride, 78–79.
120. "Diuguid Soldiers Book," vol. I, 108–111, 113.
121. McBride, 84.
122. J.E. Brant, *History of the Eighty-Fifth Indiana Volunteer Infantry, Its Organization, Campaigns, and Battles* (Bloomington, IN: Cravens Bros., Printers and Binders, 1902), 24.
123. *Official Records*, Series II, vol. 7, 916–919.
124. Corporal Charles Smedley was a member of G Company, Ninetieth Pennsylvania Volunteer Infantry, and Private John W. Northrop was a member of F Company, Seventy-Sixth New York Volunteer Infantry.
125. Charles Mattocks, *"Unspoiled Heart": The Journal of Charles Mattocks of the 17th Maine*, ed. Philip N. Racine (Knoxville: University of Tennessee Press, 1994), 141.
126. John Worrell Northrop, *Chronicles from the Diary of a War Prisoner in Andersonville and Other Military Prisons of the South in 1864* (Wichita: Published by the author, 1904), 43.
127. *Ibid.*, 45.
128. Charles Smedly, *Life in Southern Prisons: From the Diary of Corporal Charles Smedley, of Company G, 90th Regiment Penn'a Volunteers, Commencing a Few Days Before the Battle of the Wilderness, in Which He Was Taken Prisoner, in the Evening of the Fifth Month Fifth Day, 1864* (Lancaster, PA: Published by the Ladies' and Gentlemen's Fulton Aid Society, 1865), 17.
129. Northrop, 43; Smedley, 17.
130. Northrop, 45.
131. "Diuguid Soldiers Book," vol. II, 170.
132. "Diuguid Soldiers Book," vol. II, 167.
133. *Official Records*, Series II, vol. 7, 98.
134. "Diuguid Soldiers Book," vol. II, 170.

Chapter 4

1. *Official Records*, Series II, vol. 4, 779.
2. Frank Wilkeson, *Turned Inside Out: Recollections of a Private Soldier in the Army of the Potomac* (Lincoln: University of Nebraska Press, 1997), xiii–xiv, 80, xvii.
3. *Ibid.*, 59.
4. *Ibid.*, 63.
5. Unscrupulous men joined a regiment, collected the bounty, and then disappeared. Under an assumed name, they repeated the process again and again. If they were caught and convicted, they were sent to prison. The term of incarceration depended on the state where the fraud was committed and where they were apprehended.
6. Wilkeson, 198.
7. *Ibid.*, 67.
8. *Ibid.*, 205.
9. *Ibid.*
10. Lynch Street, which was one block below Main Street, was renamed Commerce Street in the late 19th century. Wade's tobacco factory was used only briefly as a hospital and then probably only the first floor. Union officers were detained on the second and third floors. Peter W. Houck, *A Prototype of a Confederate Hospital Center in Lynchburg, Virginia* (Lynchburg: Warwick House Publishing, 1986), 144.
11. Charles Mattocks, *"Unspoiled Heart": The Journal of Charles Mattocks of the 17th Maine*, ed. Philip N. Racine (Knoxville: University of Tennessee Press, 1994), 136.
12. *Ibid.*, 138–140.
13. The Albemarle Female Institute was located at Jefferson and 10th streets; today, it is part of St. Anne's–Belfield School.
14. Mattocks, 140–141.
15. *Ibid.*, 141–142.
16. *Ibid.*, 142–143.
17. *Ibid.*, 143–144.
18. *Ibid.*, 145.
19. *Ibid.*, 146.
20. *Ibid.*, 147. Charles Mattocks survived the war, graduated from Harvard Law School, and had a distinguished career.

Notes—Chapter 4

21. John V. Hadley, *Seven Months a Prisoner* (Bellevue, WA: Big Byte Books, 2014 [1898]), 30.
22. *Ibid.*, 31.
23. *Ibid.*
24. *Ibid.*, 32.
25. Joseph Ferguson, *Life-Struggles in Rebel Prisons: A Record of Sufferings, Escapes, Adventures and Starvation of the Union Prisoners* (Philadelphia: James M. Ferguson, Publisher, 1865), 22–30.
26. *Ibid.*, 45.
27. *Ibid.*, 47–48.
28. *Ibid.*
29. *Ibid.*, 49.
30. *Ibid.*, 50.
31. *Ibid.*, 51.
32. Operating in the lower Shenandoah Valley, the Forty-Third Virginia Cavalry Battalion harassed Union units from 1862 until the end of the war. Led by Colonel John Singleton Mosby, the "Gray Ghost," they were authorized by the Partisan Ranger Act of 1862.
33. Charles A Humphreys, *Field, Camp, Hospital and Prison in the Civil War, 1863–1865* (Boston: Press of George H. Ellis, 1915), 115–116.
34. The designation of "factory" was applied to a structure where tobacco was processed or stored.
35. Humphreys, 117.
36. *Ibid.*
37. Houck, 21.
38. "Diuguid Soldiers Book," vol. II, 156–158; Lucy Harrison Baber, Lucy Harrison, and Evelyn Lee Moore, *Behind the Old Brick Wall: A Cemetery Story* (Lynchburg: Lynchburg Committee of the National Society of the Colonial Dames of America in the Commonwealth of Virginia, 1968), 248.
39. Charles Walter Amory was exchanged in September 1864, survived the war, and mustered out of service as a captain. A resident of Boston, he died on November 5, 1913 (*Boston Evening Transcript*, November 8, 1913, 30).
40. Humphreys, 118–119.
41. Captain Otey was the son of Mrs. Lucy Mina Otey who was in charge of the Ladies Relief Hospital at the corner of 6th and Main streets. He died of disease on September 15, 1864. W. Aubrey Christian, *Lynchburg and Its People* (Lynchburg: J.P. Bell, 1900), 232.
42. Psalm 137:1–9, KJV.
43. Humphreys, 146–148.
44. Thomas F. Wildes, *Record of the One Hundred and Sixteenth Regiment, Ohio Infantry Volunteers in the War of the Rebellion* (Sandusky, OH: I.F. Mack and Brother, Printers, 1884), 283.
45. *Ibid.*, 284.
46. *Ibid.*
47. *Ibid.*
48. The first Lynchburg College was founded in 1855, and its last session was 1860–1861. In 1919, the name of Virginia Christian College was changed to Lynchburg College. These two colleges were unrelated to each other. The first was an all-male military school; the second was from its beginning in 1903 coeducational. In 2018, the name of Lynchburg College was changed to the University of Lynchburg.
49. Houck, 26; Horace Herndon Cunningham, *Doctors in Gray: The Confederate Medical Service* (Baton Rouge; Louisiana State University Press, 1986), 50.
50. "Diuguid Soldiers Book," vol. I, 14.
51. Houck, 78. The original quote is cited in "Lynchburg Hospitals of the Past," *Lynchburg News*, February 1920, in the manuscript "Norvell Family Notebook" in Jones Memorial Library, 51–56.
52. "William Walker Hurt to Anne Norvell Otey Scott, August 30, 1936," manuscript letter from the Historic Sandusky collection at the University of Lynchburg.
53. Houck, 26–29.
54. Cunningham, 50; Houck, 30.
55. Houck, 24.
56. *Ibid.*
57. Jerald H. Markham, comp., *The Diuguid Records, 1861–1865, and Biographical Sketches* (Westminster, MD: Heritage Books, 2007), 17.
58. *Lynchburg Daily Virginian*, August 6, 1863, 2.
59. *Lynchburg Daily Republican*, September 15, 1863, 2.
60. Christian, 131.
61. *City of Lynchburg Deed Book*, 118, 165.
62. Houck, 18, 145.

63. Alva C. Roach, *The Prisoner of War and How Treated* (Indianapolis: Railroad City Publishing House, 1865), 64–66.

64. In the 19th century, slaked lime was in regular use in spaces where unpleasant odors might accumulate because it stopped decomposition and absorbed unpleasant smells. Once the lime had reduced the stench in the barn and pest house, it was replaced by white sand, which also absorbed odors but was not caustic like slaked lime.

65. Charles E. Driscoll, *John Jay Terrell, MD, Civil War Doctor to Man and Horse* (Lynchburg: Warwick House Publishers, 2020), 71–72.

66. George W. Watson, "The Slowest Mail of All," in *"This War Is an Awful Thing": Civil War Letters of the National Guards, the 19th and 90th Pennsylvania Volunteers*, ed. James Durkin and Jennifer M. Whitcome (Glenside, PA: J. Michael Santarelli Publishing, 1994), 256–262.

67. On page 262, Watson mentions that the hospital where he was taken was "surrounded by a cordon of sentinels." Frank S. Reader, *History of the Fifth West Virginia Cavalry, Formerly the Second Virginia Infantry, and of Battery G, First West Virginia Light Artillery* (New Brighton, PA: Daily News, 1890), 285, makes a similar reference to Crumpton's.

68. Watson, 263. After the war, Gamble was repaid every dollar he had loaned his old friend—in U.S. currency, not Confederate bills.

69. *Ibid.*, 264.

70. *Ibid.*, 267–268.

71. Edward Addison Craighill, *Confederate Surgeon: The Personal Recollections of E.A. Craighill*, ed. Peter W. Houck (Lynchburg: H.E. Howard, 1989), 71.

72. *Ibid.*, 78–79

73. *Ibid.*, 79.

74. S. Allen Chambers, *Lynchburg: An Architectural History* (Charlottesville: University of Virginia Press, 1981), 145.

Chapter 5

1. Ulysses S. Grant, *Personal Memoirs of U.S. Grant* (New York: Charles L. Webster, 1882), 2:121–123.

2. L. van Loan Naisawald, *The Battle of Lynchburg: Seize Lynchburg—If Only for a Single Day!* (Lynchburg: Warwick House Publishing, 2004), 9.

3. David Hunter Strother, *A Virginia Yankee in the Civil War: The Diaries of David Hunter Strother*, ed. Cecil D. Eby, Jr. (Chapel Hill: University of North Carolina Press, 1961), 231.

4. Weapons, uniforms, and boots supplied to the government were not always of acceptable quality—guns jammed or malfunctioned, and boots often did not survive the long, rough marches. Boots were also lost by soldiers who preferred to march barefooted. Leander Stillwell, who was raised on a farm in Illinois, mentioned in his memoir that many men preferred to march without boots or socks because it was more comfortable. With socks stuffed into each boot and the laces tied together, the boots were hung over the end of the rifle. Stillwell entered the Sixty-First Illinois Volunteer Infantry as a private and mustered out of the regiment as a first lieutenant. Leander Stillwell, *The Story of a Common Soldier in the Civil War, 1861-1865* (Erin, KS: Franklin Hudson Publishing, 1920), 107.

5. Wildes, 40.

6. Strother, 238–239.

7. *Ibid.*, 239. Tanned horsehide was used primarily to make shoes.

8. William Hanchett, *Irish: Charles G. Halpine in the Civil War* (Syracuse: Syracuse University Press, 1970), 111–112.

9. Strother, 239.

10. Edward A. Miller, Jr., *Lincoln's Abolitionist General: The Biography of David Hunter.* (Columbia: University of South Carolina Press, 1997), 175.

11. Strother, 246.

12. Hanchett, 117; Miller, 189.

13. *Official Records*, Series I, 598.

14. Strother, 248–250.

15. Edward S. Wilson, "The Lynchburg Campaign," in *Sketches of War History, 1861-1865: Papers Prepared for the Ohio Commandery of the Military Order of the Loyal Legion of the United States, 1890-1896*, ed. W.H. Chamberlain (Cincinnati: Robert Clarke, 1896), 138–139.

16. Charles J. Rawling, *History of the*

Notes—Chapter 5

First Regiment Virginia Infantry, Being the Narrative of the Military Movements in the Mountains of Virginia, in the Shenandoah Valley and East of the Blue Ridge During the War of the Rebellion, of the First Regiment Virginia Infantry Volunteers—Three Months' and Three Years' Service (Philadelphia: J.B. Lippincott, 1887), 177.

17. Strother, 252.
18. Rawling, 177.
19. J.J. Sutton, *History of the Second Regiment West Virginia Cavalry Volunteers during the War of the Rebellion* (Portsmouth, OH: Privately printed, 1892), 126.
20. *Richmond Dispatch*, October 6, 1864, 2.
21. William S. Lincoln, *Life with the Thirty-Fourth Mass. Infantry in the War of the Rebellion* (Worcester, MA: Press of Noyes, Snow, and Company, 1879), 306.
22. The official name of the campus of VMI is The Post.
23. George E. Pond, *Campaigns of the Civil War*, vol. 11, *The Shenandoah Valley in 1864* (New York: Charles Scribner's Sons, 1883), 30.
24. Strother, 253.
25. Pond, 30.
26. Strother, 252–253.
27. *Ibid.*, 253.
28. Henry A. Du Pont, *The Campaign of 1864 in the Valley of Virginia and the Expedition to Lynchburg* (New York: National American Society, 1925), 68.
29. Strother, 258.
30. Humphreys, 55.
31. Milton W. Humphreys, *A History of the Lynchburg Campaign* (Charlottesville: Michie Company, Printers, 1924), 54–55.
32. Strother, 255.
33. Charles G. Halpine, *Baked Meats of the Funeral: A Collection of Essays, Poems, Speeches, Histories, and Banquets* (New York: Carleton, Publisher, 1866), 312–313.
34. Du Pont, 68; Strother, 257; Miller, 194.
35. Miller, 196.
36. Lincoln, 306.
37. Charles H. Lynch, *The Civil War Diary, 1862–1865, of Charles H. Lynch, 18th Connecticut Volunteers* (Hartford, CT: Case, Lockwood and Bramard, 1915), 75.
38. Hanchett, 118.
39. Du Pont, 69; Miller, 118.
40. Strother, 256.
41. Rawling, 178.
42. Jeannie Cummings Harding, "Retaliation with Restraint: Destruction of Private Property in the 1864 Shenandoah Valley Campaign" (MA thesis, James Madison University, 2013), 24.
43. William C. Walker, *History of the Eighteenth Regiment Conn. Volunteers in the War for the Union* (Norwich, CT: Published by the committee, 1885), 249.
44. Strother, 256.
45. "Board of Trustees Meeting Minutes, August 4, 1864," *Board of Trustees Meeting Minutes Book, February 21, 1845–September 1873* (Lexington, VA: Washington and Lee University), 141.
46. Wildes, 104.
47. Rawling, 178–179.
48. Miller, 196.
49. Strother, 257.
50. Sutton, 127. Writing in 1892, Sutton was obviously recalling "Tiger John" McCausland burning Chambersburg, Pennsylvania, which occurred on July 16, 1864.
51. Walker, 250.
52. Lynch, 75.
53. Rawling, 178.
54. Strother, 257.
55. Lincoln, 307; Strother, 257–258.
56. Milton W. Humphreys, 57.
57. Strother, 258.
58. Milton W. Humphreys, 54–55.
59. Strother, 257; Milton W. Humphreys, 55.
60. Strother, 258.
61. Lincoln, 307.
62. Strother, 254.
63. Rawling, 179.
64. Walker, 250.
65. *Ibid.*, 251.
66. Lynch, 77.
67. Rawling, 181.
68. Strother, 262.
69. *Official Records*, Series I, pt. 1, 760.
70. Pond, 33.
71. Strother, 263.
72. Lincoln, 310.

Notes—Chapter 6

73. *Official Records*, Series I, pt. 1, 760.
74. Lincoln, 310.
75. William Hewitt, *History of the Twelfth West Virginia Volunteer Infantry, the Part It Took in the War of the Rebellion, 1861–1865* (Charleston, WV: Twelfth West Virginia Infantry Association, 1892), 146.
76. William C. Walker, *History of the Eighteen Regiment, Conn. Volunteers in the War for the Union* (Norwich, CT: Published by the Committee, 1885), 254; Stan Cohen, *Historic Springs of the Virginias* (Charleston, WV: Quarrier Press, 1981), 12.
77. Charles W. Bennett, Jr., ed., *"Four Years with the Fifty-Fourth": The Military History of Franklin Bennett, 54th Pennsylvania Volunteer Regiment, 1861–1865* (Richmond, VA: Privately printed, 1985), 45.
78. Wilson, 142.
79. Strother, 264.
80. Jubal A. Early, *A Memoir of the Last Year of the War for Independence in the Confederate States of America, Containing an Account of the Operations of His Command in the Years 1864 and 1865*, 2nd ed. (Lynchburg: Charles Button, 1867), 42.
81. *Official Records*, Series I, vol. 37, pt. 1, 99.
82. Lincoln, 310.
83. Pond, 86–87.
84. Wildes, 107.
85. Rawling, 183.
86. MOLLUS, the Military Order of the Loyal Legion of the United States, is a hereditary organization founded by Union officers shortly after the assassination of Lincoln to provide military leadership on a national level and prevent a possible coup. Membership is opened to male descendants of Union officers.
87. Wilson, 143.
88. William C. Walker, 255.
89. Charles M. Blackford, *Campaign and Battle of Lynchburg, Va., Delivered by Request of the Garland-Rodes Camp of Confederate Veterans of Lynchburg, Virginia, June 18, 1901* (Lynchburg: J.P. Bell, 1901), 22.
90. George S. Morris and Susan L. Foutz, *Lynchburg in the Civil War: The City, the People, the Battle* (Lynchburg: H.E. Howard, 1984), 46; Clifton Potter and Dorothy Potter, *Lynchburg: "The Most Interesting Spot"* (Lynchburg: Beric Press, 1985), 74–75.
91. Strother, 264.
92. William C. Walker, 258.
93. Charles E. Driscoll, *John Jay Terrell, MD, Civil War Doctor to Man and Horse* (Lynchburg: Warrick House Publishing, 2020), 95–96.
94. Frank S. Reader, *History of the Fifth West Virginia Cavalry, Formerly the Second Virginia Infantry, and of Battery G, First West Va., Light Artillery* (New Brighton, PA: Daily News, 1890), 283–286.

Chapter 6

1. Charles Button, "The Battle of Lynchburg," *Lynchburg Daily Virginian*, June 21, 1864, 1.
2. W. Aubrey Christian, *Lynchburg and Its People* (Lynchburg: J.P. Bell, 1900), 221.
3. Using data gleaned from the American Civil War Research Database, it appears that during the Battle of Lynchburg, 21 Union soldiers died on June 17th and 81 on June 18th, making a total of 102.
4. Button, *Lynchburg Daily Virginian*, June 21, 1864, 1.
5. James M. Matthews, *The Statues at Large of the Confederate States of America, Passed at the Fourth Session of the First Congress: 1863-4. Carefully Collated with the Originals at Richmond* (Richmond, VA: R.M. Smith, Printer to Congress, 1864), 211.
6. Button, *Lynchburg Daily Virginian*, June 21, 1864, 1.
7. Steven Elliott Tripp, *Yankee Town, Southern City: Race Relations in Civil War Lynchburg* (New York: New York University Press, 1997), 107.
8. *Lynchburg Daily Virginian*, January 21, 1865; Tripp, 109.
9. Christian, 233.
10. *Lynchburg Daily Virginian*, March 2, 1865.
11. Tripp, 159.

Notes—Chapter 6

12. Christian, 234.
13. *Ibid.*
14. *Official Records*, Series I, vol. 46, pt. 3, sec. 1, 633.
15. *Ibid.*, 635.
16. *Official Records*, Series I, vol. 46, pt. 1, sec. 2, 1246; Report of Brigadier General Ranald S. Mackensie, "The War News," *Daily Advertiser*, April 13, 1865.
17. *Official Records*, Series I, vol. 46, pt. I, sec. 2, 711.
18. *Chicago Tribune*, April 1, 1865, 1.
19. *Official Records*, Series I, 734. Major General Gibbon to Lieutenant General Grant, April 13, 1865.
20. Tripp, 161.
21. Tripp, 167.
22. *Official Records*, Series I, 1213. Special orders from Major General Ord, Army of the James.
23. Nancy J. Weiland, "The Bawdy Ladies of the Buzzard," *Lynch's Ferry* (Fall/Winter, 2001–2002): 39.
24. Christian, 239.
25. *Ibid.*, 240.
26. *Ibid.*
27. *Ibid.*
28. Susan L. Blackford, comp., and Charles M. Blackford, ed., *Life In and Out of the Army in Virginia During the War Between the States* (Lynchburg: J.P. Bell, 1894), 2:237.
29. Christian, 241.
30. *Ibid.*, 242–243.
31. John Richard Dennett, *The South as It Is, 1865–1866* (New York: Viking, 1967), 56.
32. *Ibid.*, 47.
33. *Ibid.*, 56–57.
34. Tripp, 166.
35. Christian, 246.
36. Whitelaw Reid, *After the War: A Southern Tour. May 1, 1865 to May 1, 1866* (New York: Moore, Wilstach, & Baldwin, 1866), 331.
37. *Ibid.*, 331, 332, 334.
38. *Ibid.*, 339.
39. Jacob E. Yoder, *The Fire of Liberty in Their Hearts: The Diary of Jacob Yoder of the Freedmen's School, Lynchburg, Virginia, 1866–1870*, ed. Samuel L Horst (Richmond: The Library of Virginia, 1996), xii.
40. *Ibid.*, xiv.
41. 10th Amendment of the U.S. Constitution: "The powers not delegated to the United States by the Constitution, nor prohibited by it to the States, are reserved to the States respectively, or to the people."
42. In 70 years, similar measures were a regular part of President Franklin Roosevelt's New Deal.
43. https://www.nps.gov/pete/learn/historyculture/poplar-grove-national-cemetery.htm.
44. *Lynchburg Daily Virginian*, October 13, 1866, 3; the City Cemetery was sometimes called the Methodist Cemetery although the land on which it was located was a gift from John Lynch who was a Quaker. Several Union soldiers are buried in other cemeteries in the city and in surrounding counties, but they were veterans who had become permanent residents after the war.
45. Notation by George A. Diuguid in the "Soldier Book Record of Burials, Confederate Section, Old City Cemetery, May 19, 1861–September 19, 1869."
46. *Lynchburg Daily Virginian*, October 17, 1866, 3.
47. Christian, 252.
48. South Carolina and Louisiana ratified the 14th Amendment on July 9, 1868, thus providing the necessary three-fourths majority to ensure its inclusion in the Constitution.
49. Weiland, 37.
50. *Lynchburg News*, August 23, 1867, 2.
51. Corinthians 8:1, AV.
52. Yoder, xxxi.
53. *Ibid.*
54. Christian, 317–318.
55. Phillip Lightfoot Scruggs, *The History of Lynchburg, Virginia, 1786–1946* (Lynchburg: J.B. Bell, 1971), 121.
56. Christian, 267.
57. S. Allen Chambers, *Lynchburg: An Architectural History* (Charlottesville: University of Virginia Press, 1981), 226.
58. Rosa Faulkner Yancey, *Lynchburg and Its Neighbors* (Richmond, VA: J.W. Ferguson and Sons, 1935), 189.
59. United States Patent Office, James A. Bonsack of Bonsack, Virginia,

Cigarette Machine Specifications Forming of Letters Patent No. 238,640, dated March 8, 1881. Application filed September 4, 1880 (Model). 10 pages. United States Patent Office, James A. Bonsack of Bonsack, Virginia, Cigarette Machine Specifications Forming of Letters Patent No. 247,795 dated October 4, 1881. Application filed June 21, 1881.

60. Allan M. Brandt, *The Cigarette Century: The Rise, Fall, and Deadly Persistence of the Product That Defined America* (New York: Basic Books, 2007), 28–31.

61. Scruggs, 348–350; Hinton A. Helper, *Centennial Souvenir of Lynchburg, Va.* (New York: South Publishing, 1886), 24, 66–81.

62. In 1886, Virginia Seminary and College (now the Virginia University of Lynchburg), was founded a quarter century after Lynchburg College held its final session. In 1891, Randolph-Macon Woman's College, now Randolph College, was chartered. In 1903, Virginia Christian College, now the University of Lynchburg, opened its doors. All three colleges were radical departures from the norms of American higher education—a Black coeducational college, a liberal arts college for women on par with institutions for men, and a coeducational liberal arts college, respectively.

63. Michael J. Schewel, "Local Politics in Lynchburg, Virginia in the 1880s," *Virginia Magazine of History and Biography*, April 1981, 174.

64. Charles Button, *Lynchburg Daily Virginian*, October 10, 1886, 2.

65. *Lynchburg Daily Virginian*, October 15, 1886, 2.

66. Lynchburg's would-be nemesis, General David Hunter, died on February 2, 1886.

67. Helper, 5, 41.

68. *Ibid.*, 5–6.

69. Katherine K. Preston, "Popular Music in the 'Gilded Age': Musicians' Gigs in Late Nineteenth-Century Washington, D.C.," *Popular Music* 4 (1984): 30.

70. Chambers, 260–261; *Lynchburg Daily Virginian*, October 12, 1886, 3. On May 30, 1883, five Lynchburg firemen were killed while fighting a massive fire on Main Street. Their funeral was held in the opera house, and by August, their memorial at the base of Court House Hill was in place. Christian, 344–347.

71. *Lynchburg Daily Virginian*, October 13, 1886, 1.

72. *Lynchburg Daily Virginian*, October 12, 1886, 3; October 13, 1886, 1.

73. *Ibid.*, October 14, 1.

74. *Ibid.*, October 15, 2.

75. Christian, 357–358.

Appendix B

1. Private Gage is buried in the Scott family cemetery at Locust Thicket House on Old Forest Road in Lynchburg, Virginia.

2. All of the casualties sustained by this regiment during the Lynchburg Campaign occurred near Liberty, Virginia, on June 19, 1864, during General Hunter's retreat from Lynchburg.

3. Private Thorn is buried in the Staunton National Cemetery in Staunton, Virginia.

4. The nine members of the Ninety-First Ohio Volunteer Infantry who died during the Lynchburg Campaign are buried outside the wall of the Quaker Cemetery in Lynchburg, Virginia. Their graves are marked with a bronze plaque placed there by the Taylor-Wilson Camp #10, Sons of Union Veterans of the Civil War.

5. The actual graves of these men are unknown, but a monument to their sacrifice is located on the campus of the University of Lynchburg near the area where they died.

6. Private Simpson is buried near the men of the Ninety-First Ohio Volunteer Infantry outside the wall of the Quaker Cemetery in Lynchburg, Virginia.

Bibliography

Manuscript Resources

Blinn, Charles Henry. "Journal of C.H. Blinn, Private Co. A, 1st Vermont Cavalry." 2 vols. Burlington: Silver Special Collections, University of Vermont Libraries.
    Volume 1 of this well-written and insightful journal describes in detail the creation of the Union POW camp at the Fair Ground in Lynchburg, Virginia, in June 1862.

Blunt, Ruth Holmes. "The Rise and Decline of Lynchburg Tobacco Warehouses." 1960.
    This is an unpublished manuscript in the collection of Jones Memorial Library that contains data on some of the pre–Civil War tobacco factories.

Byrd, Cecil K., ed. "Journal of Israel Cogshall, 1862–1863." *Indiana Magazine of History* 42, no. 1 (March 1946): 69–87.
    Cogshall, a Methodist minister, served as a chaplain to the men of the Nineteenth Michigan Volunteer Infantry from October 24, 1862, until September 9, 1863, during which time he kept a journal. Until 1994 when *They Died to Make Men Free: A History of the 19th Michigan Infantry in the Civil War* by William Anderson was published, there was very little contemporary material available on this regiment other than Cogshall's journal.

City of Lynchburg. "Minute Book of City Council, vol. 3, 1851–1864." Lynchburg: Jones Memorial Library.
    This valuable tool for the historian is a complete record of the regular and special meetings of the Lynchburg City Council. It illustrates how unprepared local leaders were in dealing with the war in general and the POW camp in particular.

Diuguid, George A. "Soldier Book Record of Burials, Confederate Section, Old City Cemetery, May 19, 1861 to September 19, 1869, Lynchburg, Virginia, Listed in Order of Burial." 2 vols. Copied from Original Books, November 15, 1994, at the Design Group, Lynchburg, Virginia, for the Southern Memorial Association. Lynchburg: Diuguid Funeral Service, 1994.
    Without this priceless manuscript in the collection of the Old City Cemetery, the history of Lynchburg in the Civil War era would be incomplete. It contains a wealth of data found nowhere else. "Soldier Book Record of Burials" is a two-volume manuscript. It contains meticulous records of the interments made by the firm of George A. Diuguid from 1861 to 1869, including the data on the size of the coffins provided by his workshop for both Confederate and Union dead.

Gill, George F. "Diary, 1862–1863." Louisville, Kentucky: The Filson Historical Society.
    Sergeant Gill was a member of I Company, First Kentucky Volunteer Infantry, who was taken prisoner during the Battle of Stones River, December 31, 1862–January 2, 1863, at Murfreesboro, Tennessee. On his journey to Libby Prison in Richmond, he made a brief stop in Lynchburg to collect rations.

Bibliography

Harding, Jeannie Cummings. "Retaliation with Restraint: Destruction of Private Property in the 1864 Shenandoah Valley Campaign." MA thesis, James Madison University, 2013.

    The chapter dealing with General David Hunter's raid on Lexington, Virginia, between June 11th and 14th is well researched and well written. There is an excellent balance between primary and secondary sources. The author presents the facts in an impartial manner, leaving the reader or scholar to draw their own conclusions.

Kraje, Marilyn S. "The Challenge to Care: Lucy Mina Otey and the Ladies' Relief Hospital in Lynchburg, Virginia during the Civil War." MA thesis, Lynchburg College, 2015.

    This is a detailed and well-informed study of the prototype of what a Civil War–era hospital was like, written by a nursing professional who is also a well-trained historian.

Matthews, James M. *The Statues at Large of the Confederate States of America, Passed at the Fourth Session of the First Congress: 1863–4. Carefully Collated with the Originals at Richmond.* Richmond: R.M. Smith, Printer to Congress, 1864.

    This was the Confederate equivalent to *The Congressional Record*.

Oakey, John Theodore, comp. "The Story of the Old Lynchburg College." Typed manuscript, Jones Memorial Library collection.

    This monograph is part of the Lynchburg sesquicentennial effort to gather data from persons who remembered Lynchburg's first college as well as information gleaned from the *Lynchburg Daily Virginian* and the *Methodist Protestant*. The foreword was written by Ann Norvell Otey Scott, the granddaughter of Lucy Mina Otey, the director of the Ladies' Relief Hospital.

Roberts, Ziba. "Diary." James S. Schoff Civil War Collection, William L. Clements Library, University of Michigan, Ann Arbor.

    Although this diary lacks the polish of Charles Blinn and the disarming candor of Michael VanBuskirk, it is packed with details of everyday life as a POW, especially food, which was Roberts's main concern—the purchase, preparation, and consumption of meals for and with his mess. He was also a patient at the "hospital" at the Fair Ground, and his critique of the care he received there is especially valuable.

Robinson, Daniel. "Belle Isle: Prison in the James River." MA thesis, Virginia Polytechnic Institute and State University, 1980.

    A clear, concise, and carefully crafted discussion of the failure of General Winder to provide adequate facilities for Union POWs. The mistakes made on Belle Isle were repeated at Andersonville with results beyond tragic.

Spencer, Alice DuPuy. *"I Even Remember Where the Puddles Were."* Edited by Joe Spencer. Lynchburg: Privately printed, 1997.

    Alice DuPuy Spencer (1905–1995) grew up in a house that was built after the Civil War on property adjoining the Fair Ground. On page 4 of her edited diary, she identifies the probable graves of the Union soldiers who were not buried in the City Cemetery. She refers to them as the "Civil War mounds."

Starbuck, Gregory. "Hearth and Home: The Civil War in Three Virginia Communities." MA thesis, Lynchburg College, 2014.

    This is a fascinating comparison of three cities—Winchester, Petersburg, and Lynchburg—and the immediate and long-term effects of the Civil War on each. Of particular interest is Lynchburg, which was neither occupied by Union troops nor physically damaged during the war. It emerged from the conflict resilient and ready to resume its place in the reunited nation.

Bibliography

United States Sanitary Commission. *Narrative of Privations and Suffering of United States Officers and Soldiers while Prisoners of War in the Hands of Rebel Authorities. Being the Report of a Commission of Inquiry, Appointed by the United States Sanitary Commission. With an Appendix, Containing the Testimony.* Philadelphia: King and Baird, Printers, 1864.

This is an exposé on the treatment of Union POWs that confirmed many of the stories that had appeared in the press since 1861. It also includes a series of candid reports on the Confederate POW camps in the North.

VanBuskirk, Michael Henry. "Diary, 1862–1864." SC1383. Bowling Green, KY: Special Collections Library, Western Kentucky University.

Without this straightforward account by this Indiana farmer's son of his ordeal from the moment of his capture until he boarded the train to Petersburg to be paroled for exchange, the story of the months at the Lynchburg Union POW camp would be only two dimensional at best.

The War of the Rebellion: A Compilation of the Official Records of the Union and Confederate Armies. Series I, 52 vols. Series II, 8 vols. Series III, 5 vols. Series IV, 4 vols. Washington, D.C.: Government Printing Office, 1880–1901.

This is a veritable treasure trove of information, and any work that aspires to deal with the Civil War without using it is incomplete.

Washington and Lee University. "Board of Trustees Meeting Minutes, August 4, 1864. Board of Trustees Meeting Minutes Book, February 21, 1843–September 1873." Board of Trustees Records, RG-2. Lexington, VA: Washington and Lee University Special Collections and Archives.

The entry for August 4, 1864, records how the faculty of Washington College, learning that Union general David Hunter was approaching Lexington with the intention of punishing the Virginia Military Institute for its role in the Confederate victory at New Market, risked the safety of their own institution when they chose to hide valuable scientific equipment and books from the Virginia Military Institute on their campus.

Newspapers

Chicago Tribune, 1865
Daily Dispatch (Richmond, VA), 1861–1865
Daily Intelligencer (Wheeling, WV), 1861
Daily Richmond Enquirer, 1861–1865
Daily Richmond Examiner, 1861–1863
Daily Richmond Whig, 1861–1865
Lynchburg Daily Virginian, 1861–1886
Lynchburg News, 1866–1886
Lynchburg Republican, 1861–1865

Published Memoirs

Abbott, Major Lemuel Abijah. *Personal Recollections and Civil War Diary 1864.* Burlington, VT: Free Press Printing Co., Printers, Binders, Stationers, 1908.

This is a detailed treatment of 1864 by a sergeant who was promoted to the rank of first lieutenant in Company E, Tenth Vermont Volunteer Infantry, shortly after one of the men in that unit, Private James Lockwood, vanished on a day when the regiment was not engaged in battle. Lockwood was taken prisoner while being treated for a head wound and died in Lynchburg as a POW.

Bibliography

Andrews, Henry Franklin. *The Hamlin Family, a Genealogy of James Hamlin of Barnstable, Massachusetts, Eldest Son of James Hamlin, the Immigrant, Who Came from London, England, and Settled in Barnstable, 1639.* Extra, IA: Published by the author, 1902.
    This is a useful work for gathering data on soldiers from Massachusetts who died in Lynchburg.

Bennett, Charles W., Jr., ed. *"Four Years with the Fifty-Fourth," the Military History of Franklin Bennett, 54th Pennsylvania Volunteer Regiment, 1861–1865.* Richmond, VA: Privately printed, 1985.
    Captain Bennett's edition of his great-grandfather's diary contains a concise day-by-day account of Hunter's bungled attempt to take Lynchburg in June 1864 by a private who had a keen eye for details.

Blackford, Susan L., comp., and Charles M. Blackford, ed. *Memoirs of Life In and Out of the Army in Virginia During the War between the States.* 2 vols. Lynchburg: Warwick House Publishing, 1996.
    This is a remarkable collection of letters and commentaries by a husband and wife who kept everything dealing with the war until a generation had passed and their narrative could be objective. It is the most complete picture of Lynchburg in the 1860s in print.

Cavada, Frederick F. *Libby Life: Experiences of a Prisoner of War in Richmond, Virginia, 1863–64.* Philadelphia: J.B. Lippincott, 1865.
    Captured at Gettysburg in July 1863, Lieutenant Colonel Fredrico Fernández Cavada described in detail his experiences in Richmond's Libby Prison. It is a chilling account made all the more unsettling by his periodic flashes of humor.

Coburn, J. Osborn. *Hell on Belle Isle: Diary of a Civil War POW.* Edited by Don Allison. Bryan, OH: Faded Banner Publications, 1997.
    This is a beautifully written account of a soldier who never lost hope even when he knew that all hope was gone. Between the lines of Sergeant Jacob Coburn's sensitive account of his slow decline, the reader is reminded of the total disregard for human dignity and life by those in charge of the Richmond prison system.

Cooper, Lieutenant Alonzo. *In and out of Rebel Prisons.* Oswego, NY: R.J. Oliphant, 1888.
    This is one of many personal narratives that contradicts the basic thesis presented in William Best Hesseltine's seminal work, *Civil War Prisons: A Study in War Psychology.*

Craighill, Edward Addison. *Confederate Surgeon: The Personal Recollections of E.A. Craighill.* Edited by Peter W. Houck. Lynchburg: H.E. Howard, 1989.
    This memoir, written by the youngest surgeon in Confederate service, is well composed and is particularly valuable because it presents fresh insights into the Battle of Lynchburg. Craighill's narrative dealing with the Lynchburg hospital system is especially valuable. The editor's notes add depth to the narrative because he too was a physician.

Dennett, John Richard. *The South as It Is, 1865–1866.* Edited with an introduction by Henry M. Christman. New York: Viking, 1967.
    J.R. Dennett was a writer for *The Nation,* which began publication in July 1865. Dennett arrived in Richmond on July 8, 1865, and penned the final paragraph of his travel diary in Boston on April 3, 1866. During those nine months, he traveled through the South painting vivid word pictures of a defeated people, but what is particularly important is that he visited Lynchburg as Brigadier General N.M. Curtis was replacing

Bibliography

Brevet Brigadier General J. Irvin Gregg as commander of the Lynchburg District. Dennett describes a city caught between times past and days yet to come.

Du Pont, Henry A. *The Campaign of 1864 in the Valley of Virginia, and the Expedition to Lynchburg.* New York: National Americana Society, 1925.
    The chief of artillery for the Army of West Virginia, then-captain Henry A. Du Pont, gives a balanced account of the events leading up to the Battle of Lynchburg and its aftermath.

Early, Jubal A. *A Memoir of the Last Year of the War for Independence in the Confederate States of America, Containing an Account of the Operations of His Command in the Years 1864 and 1865*, 2nd ed. Lynchburg: Charles Button, 1867.
    This is a detailed work by one of the leading Confederate commanders who became one of the main creators of the "Myth of the Lost Cause." He did not make any mention of using an empty train on the night of June 17, 1864, to fool Hunter into believing that Confederate troops were pouring into Lynchburg, and thus calls into question one of Lynchburg's cherished myths.

Egan, Michael. *The Flying, Gray-Haired Yank: or, The Adventures of a Volunteer.* Philadelphia: Hubbard Brothers, 1888.
    Michael Egan, the captain of Co. B, Fifteenth West Virginia Volunteer Infantry, was captured at Meadow Bluff, Virginia, on May 19, 1864, a week before his regiment joined General Hunter's ill-fated Lynchburg Campaign. He was briefly held in Lynchburg before being sent to Camp Oglethorpe in Macon, Georgia.

Ely, Alfred. *Journal of Alfred Ely, a Prisoner of War in Richmond.* Edited by Charles Lehman. New York: D. Appleton, 1862.
    Ely wrote a detailed account of the early months of incarceration endured by Union POWs as well as the total absence of any preparation by the Confederate government to deal with this problem.

Ferguson, Joseph. *Life-Struggles in Rebel Prisons: A Record of the Sufferings, Escapes, Adventures and Starvation of the Union Prisoners.* Philadelphia: James M. Ferguson, Publisher, 1865.
    A captain in the First New Jersey Volunteer Infantry, Joseph Ferguson gives a detailed account of the conditions under which officers were held in Lynchburg during the last year of the war.

Gaskill, Joseph W. *Footprints through Dixie: Everyday Life of the Man Under a Musket on the Firing Line and in the Trenches, 1862–1865.* Alliance, OH: J.W. Gaskill, 1919.
    From August 1862, when he mustered into Co. B of the 104th Ohio Volunteer Infantry at the age of nineteen as a private until he mustered out of the army as a corporal in June 1865, J.W. Gaskill marched through Tennessee, Kentucky, Georgia, and North Carolina. His narrative of his adventures as an enlisted man is at times poignant but always entertaining.

Grant, Ulysses S. *Personal Memoirs of U.S. Grant.* 2 vols. New York: Charles L. Webster, 1882.
    In the seventy chapters that compose this memoir Grant emerges as a humble, honest, unpretentious man who sought to "set the record straight" and leave a legacy for the country he served and saved. Grant ran a race with Death to finish his history, and he won. Thanks to his friend Mark Twain, who managed its publication, the biography provided a financial legacy for Grant's heirs.

Hadley, John Vestal. *Seven Months a Prisoner.* New York: Charles Scribner's Sons, 1898.
    First Lieutenant John Vestal Hadley of Company B of the Seventh Indiana Volunteer Infantry was taken prisoner on May 6, 1864, during the Battle of the Wilderness.

Bibliography

On his way to Macon, Georgia, he spent three nights in the fetid, lice-infested room reserved for officers in downtown Lynchburg. While he endured what he described as the "black hole of Calcutta," the enlisted men had the compensation of fresh air at the Fair Ground. They were bound for Andersonville and he for Macon, Georgia. Time did not soften Hadley's narrative of his experiences.

Halpine, Charles Grahame. *Baked Meats of the Funeral: A Collection of Essays, Poems [&c.] by Private Michael O'Reilly, Collected, Revised and Ed. by an Ex-Colonel.* New York: Carleton, Publisher, 1866.

    Colonel Halpine was a member of Major General David Hunter's staff during the 1864 Shenandoah Valley Campaign. His honest appraisal of the failure of Hunter's raid is a valuable addition to the sources of that attempt to seize Lynchburg, if only for one day.

Hobart, Harrison C. "Libby Prison—The Escape." In *War Papers, Wisconsin Commandery, Military Order of the Loyal Legion of the United States*, 4 vols., 1:394–409. Milwaukee: Burdick, Armitage and Allen, 1891.

    In 15 short pages, the author relates the ingenuity and bravery of the men who risked their lives to escape from the hellhole that was Libby Prison.

Hopwood, Josephus. *A Journey Through the Years.* St. Louis: Bethany Press, 1932.

    Private Josephus Hopwood of Company l, 7th Illinois Cavalry was taken prisoner twice. The first time he was quickly exchanged, but his second incarceration was for six months on Belle Isle. He recovered, finished his college education, and in 1903 founded Virginia Christian College—now the University of Lynchburg. In 1932 he dictated his memoir to his wife, Sarah LaRue Hopwood. Time softened his memories of his ordeal, but it shaped the whole course of his life.

Humphreys, Charles A. *Field, Camp, Hospital and Prison in the Civil War, 1863–1865.* Boston: Press of George H. Ellis, 1915.

    Chaplain to the Second Massachusetts Volunteer Cavalry, Charles Humphreys was captured near Aldie, Virginia, in July 1864, and sent to Lynchburg where he was housed in a tobacco factory. Humphreys gives a vivid and detailed account of his confinement and the penalty he paid for speaking his mind in a church service.

Humphreys, Milton W. *A History of the Lynchburg Campaign.* Charlottesville: Michie Company, Printers, 1924.

    Milton Wylie Humphreys left Washington College in Lexington, Virginia, when the Civil War began, and joined the 13th Virginia Light Artillery. In 1865, Sergeant Humphreys resumed his studies, completing his B.A. and earning his M.A. in 1869. He taught Greek and Latin at Washington College under President Robert E. Lee. With a doctorate from the University of Leipzig in Germany, he began a career that included Vanderbilt University, the University of Texas, and finally the University of Virginia where he taught from 1887 to 1915. Several years before his death in 1928, this distinguished classics scholar penned this work which is beautifully written from the standpoint of style, as well as being noted for its objectivity.

Isham, Asa B., Henry M. Davidson, and Henry B. Furness. *Prisoners of War and Military Prisons.* Cincinnati: Lyman and Cushing, 1890.

    Although the book does not mention the POW camp in Lynchburg, it contains a wealth of information on Libby Prison and Belle Isle. Its real strength lies in the fact that the twenty-six chapters are based on personal narratives. The final section, "Prison Life and Prisons in the South," is an excellent introduction to how the subject was viewed a generation after the end of the war.

Lincoln, Charles P. "Engagement at Thompson Station, Tennessee." In *Military Order of the Loyal Legion of the United States War Papers*, vol. 14. Washington, D.C.: Commandery of the District of Columbia, 1893.

Bibliography

Captain Lincoln's eyewitness account of the debacle that occurred on March 5, 1863, in Williamson County, Tennessee, contains the verisimilitude that is only possible when the author endured the frustration, humiliation, and abuse associated with defeat. The treatment Lincoln endured in the hands of the enemy led to his resignation and discharge on May 1, 1864, for disability.

Lynch, Charles H. *The Civil War Diary, 1862–1865, of Charles Lynch. 18th Connecticut Volunteers*. Hartford, CT: Case, Lockwood and Brainard, 1915.

This is an ordinary soldier's account of life in a crack regiment during the Civil War. Lynch's appraisal of General David Hunter is anything but favorable, and his account of the Lynchburg Campaign gives verisimilitude to an often-overlooked chapter in the history of the war.

Mattocks, Charles. *"Unspoiled Heart": The Journal of Charles Mattocks of the 17th Maine*. 3rd ed. Edited by Philip N. Racine. Knoxville: University of Tennessee Press, 1994.

Bowdoin College graduate and Medal of Honor recipient, Colonel Charles Mattocks was taken prisoner on May 5, 1864, during the Battle of the Wilderness and arrived in Lynchburg on May 7. Incarcerated in a tobacco factory that he called "Hotel de Yanks," he gives a detailed account of the prison where he spent ten days before being shipped to Macon, Georgia.

Northrop, John Worrell. *Chronicles from the Diary of a War Prisoner in Andersonville and Other Military Prisons of the South in 1864*. Wichita: Published by the author, 1904.

Captured on May 5, 1864, during the Battle of the Wilderness, Private Northrop was held briefly at the Fair Ground in Lynchburg before being shipped to Danville. He gives a description of the Lynchburg camp, as well as relating in detail conversations with civilians and soldiers who were sick of the war.

Putnam, George Haven. *A Prisoner of War in Virginia, 1864–65*. 3rd ed. New York: G.P. Putnam's Sons, 1914.

Brevet Major Putnam was a prisoner in Libby and Danville as the system created by General Winder was beginning to fall apart. His appendixes are very valuable for the data they contain.

Reid, Whitelaw. *After the War: A Southern Tour. May 1, 1865, to May 1, 1866*. New York: Moore, Wilstach, & Baldwin, 1866.

Arriving in Lynchburg in the fall of 1866, Whitelaw Reid, unlike John Dennett, was impressed by the speed with which the city and its environs had recovered from the effects of the recent conflict. He began his career as a war correspondent and eventually became the editor of the *New York Tribune* and, at the end of his life, American ambassador to France.

Roach, Alva C. *The Prisoner of War and How Treated. Containing a History of Colonel Streight's Expedition to the Rear of Bragg's Army, in the Spring of 1863, and a Correct Account of the Treatment and Condition of the Union Prisoners of War in the Rebel Prisons of the South, in 1863–4, Being the Actual Experience of a Union Officer during Twenty-Two Months' Imprisonment in Rebeldom. With Personal Adventures, Biographical Sketches, and History of Andersonville Prison Pen*. Indianapolis: Railroad City Publishing House, 1865.

This work is part memoir and part exposé of the conditions endured by Union POWs by one who was a keen observer as well as a survivor. Roach's book confirmed most of the rumors about the treatment of Union soldiers while in captivity—especially where a starvation diet rendered them unfit for further service if they survived to be paroled. Lieutenant Roach was held at Libby Prison before being shipped to Macon, and

Bibliography

he was able to interview comrades who witnessed the horrors of Belle Isle and Andersonville. Books like Roach's memoir helped shape the public perception of the Confederate POW camps.

Royall, Anne. *Mrs. Royall's Southern Tour, or Second Series of the Black Book.* Vol. 1. Washington, D.C.: Publisher unknown, 1830.

Noted for her candor and anti-clericalism, the indomitable Anne Royall is considered by many to be the first American female journalist. Her portrait of Lynchburg at the beginning of the two decades that transformed it into the metropolis of central Virginia is both positive and negative and therefore extremely valuable.

Smedley, Charles. *Life in Southern Prisons: From the Diary of Corporal Charles Smedley of Company G, 90th Regiment Penn'a Volunteers, Commencing a Few Days Before the Battle of the Wilderness, in Which He Was Taken Prisoner, in the Evening of the Fifth Month Fifth Day, 1864.* Lancaster, PA: Published by the Ladies' and Gentlemen's Fulton Aid Society, 1865.

Smedley gives a brief but detailed account of his four-day stay in the Lynchburg POW camp from May 9 to May 13, 1864. He was among those Union soldiers captured during the Battle of the Wilderness and sent to Lynchburg.

Sneden, Robert Knox. *Eye of the Storm.* Edited by Charles E. Bryan, Jr., and Nelson D. Langford. New York: Free Press, 2000.

A Canadian by birth, Sneden joined the Fortieth New York Volunteer Infantry—the Mozart Regiment—on September 30, 1861, and mustered into E Company that same day but later transferred to D Company. He kept a diary that he expanded to a 1,000-page memoir illustrated with over 500 watercolors and sketches, and they are part of the permanent collection of the Virginia Museum of Fine Arts. His maps and sketches of Richmond, made while he was a prisoner, are particularly valuable. He survived Andersonville. Saved by chance, this record of a soldier's survival is considered one of the most important Civil War–era memoirs in print. The Virginia Historical Society deserves praise for preserving it.

Stillwell, Leander. *The Story of a Common Soldier of Army Life in the Civil War, 1861–1855.* Erin, KS: Franklin Hudson Publishing, 1920.

Written at the end of a long and successful legal career, this memoir is honest, factual, and entertaining. Stillwell entered the service as a boy, but like so many of his comrades in arms, he returned home a man.

Strother, David Hunter. *A Virginia Yankee in the Civil War: The Diaries of David Hunter Strother.* Edited by Cecil D. Eby, Jr. Chapel Hill: University of North Carolina Press, 1961.

A kinsman of General David Hunter and a Virginian by birth, Strother chose to serve the United States instead of the Old Dominion during the Civil War. In his diaries, he records his frustrations and states his honest opinions on every topic, especially the events during the Lynchburg Campaign.

Strum, Jesse Tyler. *From a "Whirlpool of Death ... to Victory": Civil War Remembrances of Jesse Tyler Strum, 14th West Virginia Infantry.* Edited by Mary E. Johnson. Charleston: West Virginia History, 2002.

After a year in a local militia unit, Tyler Strum joined Company D of the Fourteenth West Virginia Volunteer Infantry and served until the end of the war. He lived in Kansas after the war and wrote a number of articles for local newspapers about his wartime service. This slim volume is a compilation of those entertaining articles. His regiment was part of General David Hunter's raid on Lynchburg; one man was killed, eleven were wounded, and four were either captured or missing.

Bibliography

Watson, George. "Captain George Watson's Account of His Mutilation in Battle, Captivity, and Suffering as a Prisoner of War, Together with Incidents in Connection Therewith." In *"This War Is a Terrible Thing": Civil War Letters of the National Guard, the 19th and 20th Pennsylvania Volunteers,* edited by James Durkin and Jennifer M. Whitcomb, 257–268. Glenside, PA: J. Michael Santarelli Publishing, 1994.

This work is important because it contains Watson's account of his wounding and capture during the Battle of the Wilderness on May 5, 1864—he survived a field amputation of his right leg up to his hip. He also wrote a detailed account of the time he spent as a patient in Lynchburg, especially in Crumpton's tobacco factory. He was a member of Company H of the Nineteenth Pennsylvania Volunteer Infantry. He died shortly before his sixty-eighth birthday.

Wilkeson, Frank. *Turned Inside Out: Recollections of a Private Soldier in the Army of the Potomac.* Lincoln: University of Nebraska Press, 1997.

This work is the antidote to memoirs written a generation after the end of the Civil War when time had blunted the sharp edges of memory. Wilkeson neither forgot nor forgave the incompetence of officers who sent men to certain death. Wilkeson saw, experienced, remembered, and preserved it all in scathing prose.

Wilson, Edward S. "The Lynchburg Campaign." In *Sketches of War History, 1861–1865: Papers Prepared for the Ohio Commandery of the Military Order of the Loyal Legion of the United States, 1890–1896.* Vol. 4. Edited by W.H. Chamberlain. Cincinnati: Robert Clarke, 1896.

As a young lieutenant, Wilson relates his service under Hunter and the failure of his commander to secure his objective during the Lynchburg Campaign.

Yoder, Jacob E. *The Fire of Liberty in Their Hearts: The Diary of Jacob E. Yoder of the Freedmen's Bureau School, Lynchburg, Virginia, 1866–1870.* Edited by Samuel L. Horst. Richmond: Library of Virginia, 1996.

The diary of a native of Gilbertsville, Montgomery County, Pennsylvania, who at the age of twenty-eight moved to Lynchburg to work with the Freedmen's Bureau as a teacher of African American children. For the next thirty-nine years until his death in 1905 at the age of sixty-seven, Yoder devoted his professional life to the education of Black children. It is a powerful diary, honest, straightforward, and impassioned.

Regimental Histories

Abbott, Stephen G. *The First Regiment New Hampshire Volunteers in the Great Rebellion.* Keene, NH: Sentinel Printing, 1890.

The author of this work, which is over 500 pages in length, was the chaplain of the regiment. Entirely too much time is consumed with background, but when the narrative reaches the main topic—the war—it is filled with vital information.

Adams, John G.B. *Reminiscences of the Nineteenth Massachusetts Regiment.* Boston: Wright & Potter, 1899.

Captain Adams wrote an entertaining account of his service in the Union Army from July 1861 to the end of the war when he was a paroled prisoner waiting to be exchanged. He was briefly a prisoner at Libby, but most of his incarceration was spent at Camp Oglethorpe in Macon, Georgia. One of his comrades died at the POW camp at the Fair Ground in Lynchburg.

Anderson, John. *The Fifty-Seventh Regiment of Massachusetts Volunteers in the War of the Rebellion. Army of the Potomac.* Boston: E.B. Stillings, 1896.

A tome of 512 pages, it gives a detailed history of the regiment, but it contains minor errors. For example, Private James J. Willard was listed as dying on May 6, 1864,

Bibliography

during the Battle of the Wilderness. Willard actually died on July 26, in a hospital in Lynchburg as a POW. This is simply an example of how difficult it was to keep track of casualties in the heat of battle.

Anderson, William M. *They Died to Make Men Free: A History of the 19th Michigan Infantry in the Civil War.* Dayton: Morningside House, 1994.
   This is an important reference because it deals with the deposition of Union prisoners at the camp at the Fair Ground in Lynchburg. It confirms the continued use of animal stalls for cold weather shelter.

Ayling, Augustus D., Adjutant General. *Register of Soldiers and Sailors of New Hampshire, 1861–1865.* Concord, NH: Ira C. Evans, Public Printer, 1893.
   This is an excellent reference for corroborating the data on the five soldiers from New Hampshire who died in Lynchburg as POWs.

Bacarella, Michael. *Lincoln's Foreign Legion, the 39th New York Infantry, the Garibaldi Guard.* Shippensburg, PA: White Mane Publishing, 1996.
   This is an excellent introduction to one of the most unusual units in the Union Army. One of its members died as a POW in one of the Lynchburg hospitals.

Bates, Samuel P. *History of Pennsylvania Volunteers, 1861–5: Prepared in Compliance with Acts of the Legislature.* 4 vols. Harrisburg: B. Singerly, State Printer, 1870.
   This is where many searches begin for data on Pennsylvanians who served in units from their home state, including the fifty-three who died as POWs in Lynchburg hospitals.

Beach, William H. *The First New York (Lincoln) Cavalry, from April 19, 1861 to July 7, 1865.* New York: Lincoln Cavalry Association, 1902.
   This regiment was part of the Army of West Virginia during Hunter's Lynchburg Campaign. It was part of the First Cavalry Division under General Alfred S. Duffie and the Second Brigade under Colonel L.E. Wynkoop. In this well-written history, only the death of one soldier is recorded during Hunter's Lynchburg Campaign.

Beaudry, Louis N. *Historic Records of the Fifth New York Cavalry, First Ira Harris Guard: Its Organization, Marches, Raids, Scouts, Engagements and General Services, during the Rebellion of 1861–1865, with Observations of the Author by the Way, Giving Sketches of the Armies of the Potomac and of the Shenandoah. Also, Interesting Accounts of Prison Life and of the Secret Service. Complete Lists of Its Officers and Men.* 2nd ed. Albany: S.R. Gray, 1865.
   Chaplain Beaudry wrote with an almost encyclopedic thoroughness. The reader has the pleasant experience of being lured from one topic to another. The lists are particularly useful to the student of Civil War history.

Beaudry, Louis N. *War Journal of Louis N. Beaudry, Fifth New York Cavalry, the Diary of a Union Chaplain, Commencing February 16, 1863.* Edited by Richard N. Beaudry. Jefferson, NC: McFarland, 1996.
   This edition of the three surviving war journals of Chaplain Beaudry demonstrates his keen eye for facts and his skill at weaving them into a fascinating narrative.

Bennett, Brian A. *Sons of Old Monroe: A Regimental History of Patrick O'Rorke's 140th New York Volunteer Infantry.* Dayton: Morningside House, 1992.
   This is a well-written and well-researched 649-page history of the regiment that won undying fame during the Battle of Gettysburg at Little Round Top when its beloved Colonel "Paddy" O'Rorke gave his life to save the regimental banner. Two of the members of this storied unit died in Lynchburg at Crumpton's tobacco factory in July 1864.

Bibliography

Bilby, Joseph G. *Three Rousing Cheers: A History of the Fifteenth New Jersey from Flemington to Appomattox.* Hightstown, NJ: Longstreet House, 1993.

As a Vietnam veteran, the author has empathy for the combat experiences of the men of the Fifteenth New Jersey which is missing from many modern works dealing with the Civil War. His description of the daily routine of ordinary soldiers echoes similar accounts published over a century later. One soldier from the regiment was killed by a civilian guard at the Lynchburg POW camp in October 1864.

Bonnell, John C., Jr. *Sabres in the Shenandoah: The 21st New York Cavalry, 1863–1866.* Shippensburg, PA: Beidel Printing House, 1996.

This is a well-researched and well-written account of the eventful days in May and June 1864, when the course of the Civil War might have been changed during Brigadier General David Hunter's Lynchburg Campaign. The Twenty-First New York Cavalry was part of Hunter's First Cavalry Division under the command of Brigadier General Alfred S. Duffié. Colonel R.F. Taylor was in command of the First Brigade, which included the Twenty-First New York Cavalry. From the ranks of that regiment, three soldiers and two officers were killed, three soldiers were wounded, and five soldiers were captured or missing.

Booth, Jim. *A Good and Holy Cause: A History of the 29th Ohio Veteran Volunteer Infantry, the Giddings Regiment.* Kingsville, OH: Jim Booth, 2011.

A journalist by profession, Booth fashioned a narrative that is informative because it is based on a rich trove of letters and journals and persuasive because he knew how to subtly use the right words. Scholars may argue about the causes of the Civil War, but there is no doubt that the men of the Twenty-Ninth Ohio were offering their lives for the cause of universal freedom. Three of them were among the men who died at the Lynchburg POW camp.

Bowen, James L. *History of the Thirty-Seventh Regiment Mass. Volunteers, in the Civil War of 1861–1865, with a Comprehensive Sketch of the Doings of Massachusetts as a State and of the Principal Campaigns of the War.* New York: Clark W. Bryan, 1884.

The genesis of this comprehensive history was a paper delivered in 1871. Over the decades, various members of the regiment contributed data until 1882 when former private James L. Bowen, a printer by trade, was given the task of completing the proposed book. It is well written and beautifully organized. It is 431 pages long with 51 pages of appendixes. One of the members of the regiment was wounded during the Battle of the Wilderness, and as a POW he died in July 1864 at the hospital located at Camp Davis in Lynchburg.

Boyce, Charles W. *A Brief History of the Twenty-Eighth Regiment New York State Volunteers, First Brigade, First Division, Twelfth Corps, Army of the Potomac, from the Author's Diary and Official Reports with the Muster-Roll of the Regiment....* Buffalo: C.W. Boyce, 1896.

A well-written and well-organized history of the regiment that seems more like a family than a military unit. It is based on journals, letters, and personal memoirs. A number of the men of the Twenty-Eighth New York were captured during General Stonewall Jackson's Valley Campaign in the spring of 1862, and thus they were among the first inmates in the Lynchburg POW camp. One of their number died at the Fair Ground in July 1862.

Brant, J.E. *History of the Eighty-Fifth Indiana Volunteer Infantry, Its Organization, Campaigns and Battles.* Bloomington, IN: Cravens Bros., Printers and Binders, 1902.

Stripped of everything but their basic uniforms, the men of the Eighty-Fifth Indiana Volunteer Infantry were taken prisoner on March 5, 1863, during the Battle of Thompson's Station. They endured a journey on foot and in open railcars from

Bibliography

Tennessee to Lynchburg. Lieutenant Colonel Brant recounts their trek and the fate of the men who died along the way of wounds or hypothermia.

Brown, Edmund Randolph. *The Twenty-Seventh Indiana Volunteer Infantry in the War of Rebellion, 1861–1865. First Division, 12th and 20th Corps. A History of Its Recruiting, Organization, Camp Life, Marches and Battles, Together with a Roster of the Men Composing It by a Member of Company C.* Monticello, IN: n.p., 1899.

In 644 pages, Brown covered every aspect of his regiment's history. His style is engaging because he loved his subject. Seven members of the Twenty-Seventh Indiana died in Lynchburg while POWs; one was buried near the camp and six in the City Cemetery.

Camper, Charles, and J.W. Kirkley. *Historical Record of the First Regiment, Maryland Infantry, with an Appendix Containing a Register of the Officers and Enlisted Men.* Washington, D.C.: Gibson Brothers, Printers, 1871.

Over 300 pages in length, the book contains a great deal of valuable data about the members of the regiment and every engagement in which they participated. Appendix D is particularly valuable because under each battle are listed the names of the men killed, wounded, or taken prisoner. Eleven members of the First Maryland died while POWs in Lynchburg. One was exhumed and sent to his parents in Baltimore, six were originally buried in the City Cemetery, and three were buried near the camp.

Cazeau, Theodore, *A Brief Account of the Thirteenth New York Volunteer Regiment, 1861–1863.*, Rochester: Historic Monograph Collection, Central Library of Rochester and Monroe County, 1925.

This privately printed twenty-page essay is an introduction to the regiment which was directly involved in Congressman Alfred Ely's capture and incarceration in Libby Prison. His exposé made readers north of the Mason-Dixon Line aware of the condition of Confederate prisons.

Child, William. *A History of the Fifth Regiment New Hampshire Volunteers in the American Civil War, 1861–1865 in Two Parts.* Bristol, NH: R.W. Musgrove, Printer, 1893.

This book is divided into two parts: the first part deals with regimental history, while the second part is devoted to rosters and statistics. One member of the unit died as a POW in one of the hospitals in Lynchburg on July 29, 1864.

Clark, Walter, ed. *Histories of the Several Regiments and Battalions from North Carolina in the Great War, 1861–65*, 5 vols. Goldsboro, NC: Nash Brothers, 1901.

This well written and researched multi-volume source contains valuable notes on the 42nd North Carolina Infantry, the unit created by Colonel George C. Gibbs to guard Union prisoners of war at Salisbury, North Carolina, and Lynchburg, Virginia.

Cogswell, Leander W. *A History of the Eleventh New Hampshire Regiment Volunteer Infantry in the Rebellion War, 1861–1865.* Concord, NH: Republican Press Association, Railroad Square, 1891.

This book of 785 pages contains both text and valuable rosters of the members of the regiment. One of their number was wounded on May 6, 1864, during the Battle of the Wilderness, subsequently captured, and died as a POW in Crumpton's tobacco factory, one of the Lynchburg hospitals.

Cook, Benjamin F. *History of the Twelfth Massachusetts Volunteers (Webster Regiment).* Boston: Twelfth (Webster) Regiment Association, 1882.

Only 167 pages long, the work is essentially a calendar of events with little or no analysis. However, Lieutenant Colonel Cook's book is valuable because of the wealth of data it contains. One of the members of the regiment who was wounded and captured during General Stonewall Jackson's Valley Campaign died on August 9, 1862, at the Fair Ground shortly before the auxiliary hospitals opened.

Bibliography

Crowninshield, Benjamin W., and Daniel Henry Gleason. *A History of the First Massachusetts Cavalry Volunteers with Roster and Statistics by D.H.L. Gleason.* Boston: Houghton, Mifflin, 1891.

This work is considered by many scholars to be one of the best regimental histories to appear before the end of the nineteenth century. Well written, reflective, insightful, and yet discreetly circumspect, it chronicles the life of the regiment from its inception to its final muster. One of its members was part of the occupying force in Lynchburg after the war and was killed in an altercation with a former Confederate soldier.

Driver, Robert J., and Kevin C. Ruffner. *1st Battalion Virginia Infantry, 39th Battalion Virginia Infantry, 24th Battalion, Virginia Partisan Rangers.* Lynchburg: H.E. Howard, 1996.

This work is part of a series published by H.E. Howard, Inc., which sought to make available to scholars and the general public modern histories of all the Virginia regiments that served the Confederacy.

Estabrook, Charles E., ed. *Wisconsin Losses in the Civil War: A List of the Names of Wisconsin Soldiers Killed in Action, Mortally Wounded or Dying from Other Causes in the Civil War.* Madison: Democrat Printers Company, State Printer, 1915.

This is a valuable reference, an early attempt to assemble and systematize data from a number of sources to provide the public with accurate information concerning the soldiers from Wisconsin who lost their lives fighting to save the Union.

Foster, John Y. *New Jersey and the Rebellion: A History of the Service of the Troops and People of New Jersey in Aid of the Union Cause.* Newark: Martin R. Dennis, 1868.

It is not a detailed work because it appeared within three years after the war's end; nonetheless, it was important. It seeks to provide the general reader with a rationale for the service and sacrifice of both military personnel and civilians.

Gould, Major John Mead. *History of the First-Tenth-Twenty-Ninth Maine Regiment in Service of the United States from May 3, 1861 to June 21, 1866, with the History of the Tenth Me. Battalion by Rev. Leonard G. Jordan.* Portland, ME: Stephen Berry, 1871.

This is a mammoth work—709 pages comprising 60 chapters. It is solid, detailed, and not very exciting but essential for anyone studying Maine's role in the Civil War. A total of eight men from these regiments died in Lynchburg as POWs.

Haines, Alanson A. *History of the Fifteenth Regiment New Jersey Volunteers.* New York: Jenkins & Thomas, Printers, 1883.

Chaplain Haines wrote a factual history of the regiment that is 388 pages in length and divided into 19 chapters. It includes a detailed roster. Corporal Charles Coward was shot and killed by a guard while a prisoner in the Lynchburg camp. There were only two such deaths recorded at the Fair Ground camp.

Haynes, E.M. *A History of the Tenth Regiment, VT Vols. with Biographical Sketches.* Rutland, VT: Tuttle Printers, 1894.

There are numerous biographical sketches with photographs of both officers and enlisted men in this history. The 504 pages are divided into seven chapters, and the book is well written. The narrative of the various engagements in which the regiment was involved is detailed, but it is the lives of the individual soldiers that catch the reader's attention. One of the members of the regiment, Private James E. Lockwood, died from a head wound received on May 7, 1864, during the Battle of the Wilderness. Barely 15, he was buried on August 8th in Lynchburg's City Cemetery.

Hewitt, William. *History of the Twelfth West Virginia Volunteer Infantry, the Part It Took in the War of Rebellion, 1861–1865.* Charleston: Twelfth West Virginia Infantry Association, 1892.

Bibliography

This work contains an excellent account of Hunter's raid through the valley, the Battle of Lynchburg, and the retreat to West Virginia. The Twelfth West Virginia was one of the first Union units to enter Lynchburg after Lee's surrender at Appomattox.

Higginson, Thomas Wentworth. *Massachusetts in the Army and Navy During the War of 1861–65*. 2 vols. Boston: Wright and Potter Printing Co., State Printers, 1896.

This reference work is the gateway to studying the participation of Massachusetts in the Civil War. Volume 1 is 647 pages long, and volume 2 is 805 pages. Each volume has an index. It is well written, although at times pedantic. It is a work for scholars, not Civil War history buffs.

Houghton, Edwin B. *The Campaigns of the Seventeenth Maine*. Portland, ME: Short & Loring, 1866.

Captain Houghton dated his preface March 1, 1866, which means that this work of 333 pages comprising 23 chapters and three appendixes was written before memories of army life and battles were softened by time. It is well written and worth reading because it obviously served as a model for later works of a similar nature.

Husk, Martin W. *The 111th New York Volunteer Infantry: A Civil War History*. Jefferson, NC: McFarland, 2010.

Using primary sources, Husk fashions a regimental history that is both readable and scholarly. The men speak for themselves as they muster into the regiment until the war finally comes to an end. The reader cannot help but be moved by appendix A. It is the story of 83 soldiers who were stripped of everything but their basic uniform and sent first to Libby and then to Salisbury. Only 29 survived the winter of 1864–65 to be paroled for exchange. One member of the regiment captured on May 5, 1864, died on June 30, 1864, in one of the Lynchburg hospitals and was buried in the City Cemetery.

Jackman, Lyman. *History of the Sixth New Hampshire Regiment in the War for the Union*. Concord, NH: Republican Press Association, Railroad Square, 1891.

Jackman's diary provides the framework for his narrative, but it is enriched by contributions from his fellow veterans. It is well written and quite readable. It is 630 pages long and contains a thorough roster. There are 21 chapters. One of the members of the regiment was wounded on May 6, 1864, during the Battle of the Wilderness, and died in one of the Lynchburg hospitals on June 2, 1864.

Jones, Wilbur D., Jr. *Giants in the Cornfield: The 27th Indiana Infantry*. Shippensburg, PA: White Mare Publishing, 1997.

This is a story of Private Michael Henry VanBuskirk's regiment and how it was forged from farm boys, who could plow a straight furrow, into soldiers, who were part of a unit that took whatever the enemy hurled at them and returned it without faltering. They were supposedly the tallest regiment in the army, and Jones fashions a narrative that tells how they lived up to that challenge. Six of their number were among the first POWs in the newly opened Lynchburg camp.

Keyes, Charles M., ed. *The Military History of the 123d Regiment Ohio Volunteer Infantry*. Sandusky, OH: Register Steam Press, 1874.

This slender volume of 196 pages is divided into 14 chapters. Chapter 5 is devoted to General David Hunter's Lynchburg Campaign because the 123rd Ohio Volunteer Regiment was part of the First Infantry Division under the Command of General Jeremiah Sullivan. Three men were killed on June 18th, and were among the unknown buried the following day. One of the final chapters is a very detailed roster. It is an easy read and filled with facts, not frills.

Kidd, James H. *Personal Recollections of a Cavalryman with Custer's Michigan Brigade in the Civil War*. Ionia, MI: Sentinel Printing, 1908.

Bibliography

Colonel Kidd covers the history of the first, fifth, sixth, and seventh cavalry regiments that composed Brigadier General George Armstrong Custer's brigade. The book is 476 pages long and is divided into 24 chapters with maps and illustrations. Not only is it filled with information, but the book is also well written and easy to read.

Lincoln, William S. *Life with the Thirty-Fourth Mass. Infantry in the War of the Rebellion.* Worcester, MA: Press of Noyes, Snow & Company, 1879.

Particularly useful in understanding why General Hunter failed to take Lynchburg in June 1864, this well-written history is the work of one who saw it from start to finish. During General Hunter's Lynchburg Campaign, seven soldiers were killed, and 42 were wounded, including 1 officer.

Lynch, Charles H. *The Civil War Diary, 1862–1865, of Charles Lynch, 18th Connecticut Volunteers.* Hartford, CT: Case, Lockwood and Bramard, 1915.

This is a memoir by an ordinary soldier who participated in Hunter's ill-fated raid that ended with his flight to West Virginia after his defeat at Lynchburg. It is the perfect companion to Chaplain W.C. Walker's history of the regiment.

Maharay, George S., ed. *Lights and Shadows of Army Life from Bull Run to Bentonville by Wm. B. Westervelt of the 27th New York Infantry and the 17th New York Veteran Zouaves.* Shippensburg, PA: Burd Street Press, 1998.

William Westervelt joined the Twenty-Seventh New York Volunteer Infantry, which was a two-year unit, in 1861, and so in 1863, he eventually joined the Seventeenth New York Veteran Zouaves and mustered out of the army in 1865 as a lieutenant. In 1886, he published his diary, but Maharay's edited version makes this fascinating journal—which contains a great deal about Virginia—accessible to the general reader as well as the scholar.

Marvin, Edwin E. *The Fifth Regiment, Connecticut Volunteers. A History Compiled from Diaries and Official Reports. Published for the Reunion Association of the Regiment.* Hartford, CT: Wiley, Waterman, and Eaton, 1889.

Captain Marvin of the F Company was chosen as the unit's historian and given the job of compiling a record of the regiment from its first day of service to its last. Using several diaries, he created a creditable history that does just that. One of the members of the Fifth Connecticut was taken prisoner during Stonewall Jackson's 1862 Valley Campaign and died in Lynchburg in July 1862.

McBride, John Randolph. *History of the Thirty-Third Indiana Veteran Volunteers During the Four Years of Civil War, from Sept. 16, 1861, to July 21, 1865; and Incidentally of Col. John Coburn's Second Brigade, Third Division, Twentieth Army Corps, Including Incidents of the Great Rebellion.* Indianapolis: W.B. Burford, 1900.

McBride describes in detail the inhuman treatment the men of the Thirty-Third Indiana Volunteer Infantry received after their capture during the Battle of Thompson's Station on March 5, 1863, especially their arduous journey from Tennessee to Lynchburg.

A Member of Company C. *The Twenty-Seventh Indiana Volunteer Infantry in the War of the Rebellion 1861 to 1865, First Division 12th and 20th Corps.* Gaithersburg: Butternut Press, 1899.

Unfortunately, the author of this 664-page well-written and detailed history of one of the outstanding regiments from Indiana is anonymous. The roster is particularly well done, offering the reader several ways of locating the data on a particular soldier. Having been captured during Stonewall Jackson's Valley Campaign in the spring of 1862, soldiers from the Twenty-Seventh Indiana were among the first inmates in the Lynchburg POW camp. Seven of them died at the Fair Ground during the first weeks the facility was opened.

Bibliography

Morrow, Robert F., Jr. *77th New York Volunteers, "Sojering" in the VI Corps.* Shippensburg, PA: White Mane Publishing, 2004.

With an engineer's precision, the author constructs a compelling narrative about one of the most active Union regiments. The Seventy-Seventh New York seemed to always be in the thick of the fight, whether in the Peninsular Campaign or protecting Washington City from Brigadier General Jubal A. Early. In 273 pages, the author uses firsthand accounts and excellent photographs to create verisimilitude. The men of the Seventy-Seventh New York were a "band of brothers" who met in reunion each year for half a century. One of the members of the unit, Corporal William Arnold, died at Crumpton's Tobacco Factory on September 22, 1864. (There were thirty-two hospitals in Lynchburg during the war.)

Mowrer, George H., comp. *History of the Organization and Service During the War of the Rebellion of Co. A 14th Pennsylvania Cavalry.* N.p., 1899.

This unit was part of the Army of West Virginia during General David Hunter's Lynchburg Campaign. Of the 11 men from the Fourteenth Pennsylvania who were killed on June 18, four were from A Company.

Murphey, Thomas G. *Four Years in the War: The History of the First Regiment of Delaware Veteran Infantry Volunteers.* Philadelphia: James S. Claxton, 1866.

Thorough and well written by the chaplain of the regiment, this 315-page work contains detailed descriptions of the involvement of the First Delaware in many of the major engagements of the war. One of its members, taken prisoner during the Battle of the Wilderness, died in Lynchburg on August 12, 1864, at Crumpton's tobacco factory.

Newcomer, C. Armour. *Cole's Cavalry; or Three Years in the Saddle in the Shenandoah Valley.* Freeport, NY: Books for Libraries Press, 1895.

Colonel Henry A. Cole was the commander of the First Maryland Cavalry, Potomac Home Brigade—hence the name. This work is short with no frills and only the basic facts. Cole's cavalry was part of the Army of West Virginia during General David Hunter's Lynchburg Campaign, but it suffered no casualties.

Northrop, John Worrell. *Chronicles from the Diary of a War Prisoner in Andersonville and Other Military Prisons of the South in 1864.* Wichita: Published and copyrighted by the author, 1904.

Private Northrop presents his readers with a detailed description of the camp at the Fair Ground during the last year of the war. After a five-day stay, he was shipped to Andersonville.

Osborn, Hartwell, et al. *Trials and Triumphs: The Record of the Fifty-Fifth Ohio Volunteer Infantry.* Chicago: A.C. McClurg, 1904.

Although this 364-page regimental history has no index, it is well written and well illustrated. It includes a chapter on the home front and especially the varied activities of the women's groups to support the soldiers in the field and their families back home. Four men from the Fifty-Fifth Ohio died in Lynchburg as POWs.

Payne, Edwin W. *History of the Thirty-Fourth Regiment of Illinois Volunteer Infantry.* Clinton, IA: Allen Printing Company, 1902.

Sergeant Payne wrote a credible 370-page history of the Rock River Rifles, a regiment whose service was in the western theater until late in the war. One of their number was taken prisoner during the Battle of Stones River on December 31, 1862, and died at Burton's tobacco factory in Lynchburg on January 24, 1863.

Peck, Theodore S. *Revised Roster of Vermont Volunteers Who Served in the Army and Navy of the United States During the War of the Rebellion, 1861–1864.* Montpelier, VT: Press of the Watchman Publishing, 1892.

Bibliography

This is a valuable reference for checking and confirming data on combatants from Vermont.

Pellicano, John M. *Conquer or Die, the 39th New York Volunteer Infantry: Garibaldi Guard, a Military History*. Flushing: Pellicano Publications, 1996.

A former officer with the New York Police Department, John Pellicano has written an entertaining but scholarly history of the Thirty-Ninth New York. Named for one of the creators of a united Italy, Giuseppe Garibaldi, the guard was a potentially volatile mixture of French, German, Hungarian, Italian, Portuguese, Spanish, and Swiss recruits who might fight with one another during a lull in hostilities but were always ready to engage the enemy together. One of their number died in Crumpton's tobacco factory in June 1864, from wounds received during the Battle of the Wilderness.

Phisterer, Frederick. *New York in the War of the Rebellion*. 6 vols. Albany: J.B. Lyon, 1912.

This is an excellent work with which to begin a study of the military units from New York. Data gleaned from these six volumes may be enhanced with information from memoirs, regimental histories, and secondary works.

Pierpont, Brigadier General Francis P. *Annual Report of the Adjutant General of the State of West Virginia for the Year Ending December 31, 1864*. Wheeling, WV: John F.M. Dermot, Public Printer, 1865.

Like similar reports issued by other states, this official document contains important data for the scholar.

Rawling, C.J. *History of the First Regiment of Virginia Infantry. A Narrative of the Military Movements in the Mountains of Virginia, in the Shenandoah Valley and East of the Blue Ridge During the War of the Rebellion, of the First Regiment Virginia Infantry Volunteers—Three Months' and Three Years' Service*. Philadelphia: J.B. Lippincott, 1887.

Raised as a Union regiment in western Virginia, it became the First West Virginia Volunteer Infantry Regiment and participated in General Hunter's failed attempt to take Lynchburg. Rawling gives a straightforward account of events as well as the rationale for Hunter's defeat.

Reader, Frank S. *History of the First West Virginia Cavalry, Formerly the Second Virginia Infantry, and of Battery G, First West Va., Light Artillery*. New Brighton, PA: Daily News, 1890.

Taken prisoner during General David Hunter's abortive raid on central Virginia, Private Reader and three companions escaped from the train that left Lynchburg on July 19, 1864, bound for Andersonville. The story of their cross-country flight that led them to the Union lines at Petersburg is exciting and well written.

Ritchie, David F. *Four Years in the First New York Light Artillery: The Papers of David F. Ritchie*. Edited by Norman L. Ritchie. Hamilton, NY: Edmonston Publishers, 1997.

Captain David Ritchie was not only an excellent artilleryman but also a war correspondent for the Utica, New York, *Morning Herald*. A keen observer of civilians as well as military personnel, he wrote with a style that was compelling and a vocabulary that reminds the reader that Ritchie practiced his craft at a time when the English language in the hands of a professional not only educated his readers but also entertained them. He entered the service as an infantry private and rose to the rank of artillery captain.

Secheverell, J. Hamp. *Journal History of the Twenty-Ninth Ohio Veteran Volunteers, 1861–1865: Its Victories and Its Reverses*. Cleveland: n.p., 1883.

Although this history is a compilation of a number of journals, it is well written

Bibliography

and thorough. Four members of the regiment died in Lynchburg and were buried in the City Cemetery.

Shaw, Horace H. *The First Maine Heavy Artillery, 1861–1865: A History of the Causes of War and Its Results to Our Country, with Organization, Company, and Individual Records*. Portland, ME: n.p., 1903.

Divided into four parts, the work traces with military precision the history of the regiment that lost more officers than any other unit in the Union Army. The casualty rate among the ranks was also very high.

Stevenson, James Hunter. *"Boots and Saddles," a History of the First Volunteer Cavalry of the War, Known as the First New York (Lincoln) Cavalry, and Also as the Sabre Regiment. Its Organization, Campaigns, and Battles*. Harrisburg: Patriot Publishing, 1879.

This book is as entertaining as its title. The First New York Cavalry was part of the Army of West Virginia and therefore participated in General David Hunter's Lynchburg Campaign. It is 388 pages in length and divided into 27 chapters.

Stryker, William, Adjutant General. *Record of Officers and Men of New Jersey in the Civil War, 1861–1865*. 2 vols. Trenton: John L. Murphy, Steam Book and Job Printer, 1876.

This is a valuable reference work containing the basic data on which to base a more thorough search of service personnel from New Jersey.

Sutton, J.J. *History of the Second Regiment West Virginia Cavalry Volunteers During the War of the Rebellion*. Portsmouth, OH: Privately printed, 1892.

This book is valuable for its treatment of the 1864 Shenandoah Valley Campaign, especially the Battle of Lynchburg.

Swinfen, David B. *Ruggles' Regiment: The 122nd New York Volunteers in the American Civil War*. Hanover, NH: University Press of New England, 1982.

Drawn from a number of sources, especially the diary of Private William Eugene Ruggles, it is at present the only history of the 122nd New York Volunteer Infantry in the Civil War. At the time of her death, Ruggles's daughter Reba was a resident of Craichie, Scotland, and her estate was left to the University of St. Andrews, and they granted permission for the publication of the diary. This work is of particular interest because it contains 22 sketches by Ruggles and Philip M. Ostrander, and they are reproduced with permission from the University of Dundee.

Tobie, Edward P. *History of the First Maine Cavalry, 1861–1865*. Boston: Press of Emery and Hughes, 1887.

Members of the First Maine Volunteer Cavalry were among the initial group of Union soldiers to enter the Lynchburg POW camp at the Fair Ground. Three of them were among the first to die at the camp and be buried in the City Cemetery. Tobie provides details about the opening of the camp that corroborate information found in other sources, including Blinn, Roberts, and VanBuskirk.

Turner, George H., ed. *Record of Service of Michigan Volunteers in the Civil War 1861–1865, 1st Michigan Cavalry*. Kalamazoo: Irling Bros. and Everard, 1905.

This is a volume in a series; each one provides the basic data on a specific regiment. Four members of this contingent died in Lynchburg as POWs.

Turner, Ronald R. *7th West Virginia Cavalry*. Manassas: Ronald R. Turner, 1989.

During the Battle of Lynchburg, the Seventh Volunteer West Virginia Cavalry was part of the Second Brigade of the Second Cavalry Division under the command of Colonel John Hunt Oley of the Seventh West Virginia Cavalry. During General David Hunter's Lynchburg Campaign, two soldiers from this regiment were killed, thirteen were wounded, and eight were listed as missing or captured.

Bibliography

Waite, Otis. *New Hampshire in the Great Rebellion: Histories of the Several New Hampshire Regiments and Biographical Notices of Many of the Prominent Actors in the Civil War of 1861–65*. Claremont, NH: Tracy, Chase, 1870.
   This mammoth volume of 678 pages includes data on 18 infantry regiments, the First Cavalry, the First Light Artillery, the First Heavy Artillery, Sharpshooters, and the Veterans' Battalion. There are a number of biographical sketches of prominent men and women who were involved in the war effort. Four soldiers from New Hampshire died in Lynchburg as POWs and were buried in the City Cemetery.

Waitt, Ernest L., ed. *History of the Nineteenth Regiment, Massachusetts Volunteer Infantry, 1861–1865*. Salem, MA: Salem Press, 1906.
   A committee which included John G.B. Adams collected data from surviving members, and Waitt fashioned a concise, unvarnished narrative of the unit's history. In June 1864, the remnants of the 19th Massachusetts were captured near Petersburg, Virginia. They were eventually sent to Lynchburg by rail and then marched to Danville, the next stop on their journey to Georgia.

Walker, William C. *History of the Eighteenth Regiment Conn. Volunteers in the War for the Union*. Norwich, CT: Published by the committee, 1885.
   Chaplain Walker gives a detailed account of Hunter's failure to take Lynchburg and his retreat to West Virginia. There is an emphasis on the fine performance of the men of the Eighteenth Connecticut Volunteer Infantry.

Welcher, Frank J., and Larry G. Ligget. *Coburn's Brigade, 85th Indiana, 33rd Indiana, 19th Michigan, and 22nd Wisconsin in the Western Civil War*. Carmel: Guild Press of Indiana, 1999.
   Eight men from Coburn's brigade died in Lynchburg as a result of the inhumane treatment they received after the Battle of Thompson's Station. *Coburn's Brigade* is a well-written and moving tribute to their valor against impossible odds and their suffering on the long journey to prison.

Wildes, Thomas F. *Record of the One Hundred and Sixteenth Regiment Ohio Infantry Volunteers in the War of the Rebellion*. Sandusky, OH: I.F. Mack and Brother, Printers, 1884.
   This is a well-written history of an Ohio regiment by an officer who cared for the welfare of the soldiers under his command. His recounting of the Shenandoah Campaign of 1864, especially Hunter's failure to execute General Grant's orders, is insightful and honest.

Wilmer, L. Allison, J.H. Jarrett, and George W.F. Vernon. *History and Roster of Maryland Volunteers, War of 1861–5*. 2 vols. Baltimore: Press of Guggenheimer, Weil, 1898.
   This is a valuable resource filled with information concerning the units from Maryland, as well as data on the personnel who served in them.

Windsor, A.H. *History of the Ninety-First Regiment, OVI*. Cincinnati: Gazette Steam Printing House, 1865.
   Written by the unit chaplain within months of the end of the war, this book is a measured and poignant tribute to the valor of the sons of Ohio who risked their lives so that their nation might survive. This is the history of a regiment that lost one officer and eight enlisted men during the Battle of Lynchburg in June 1864.

Journal Articles

Anderson, William M. "The Union Side of Thompson's Station." *Tennessee Historical Quarterly* 29, no. 4 (Winter 1970–71): 396–406.

Bibliography

This is a concise and well-written exposé of the incompetence of Brigadier General Charles C. Gilbert and the mistakes Colonel John Coburn made under very trying circumstances. Eight young soldiers from Indiana, Michigan, and Wisconsin died as POWs and were buried in the City Cemetery in Lynchburg, thanks to the debacle at Thompson's Station.

Byrne, Frank L. "Libby: A Study in Emotions." *Journal of Southern History* 24 (1958): 430–436.

This is a brief article based on unpublished manuscripts as well as published memoirs that only begins to explore the many facets of life and death at Libby Prison.

Danker, Donald F. "Imprisoned at Andersonville: The Diary of Albert Harry Shatzel, May 5, 1864–September 12, 1864." *Nebraska History* 38 (1957): 81–126.

Private Albert H. Shatzel, A Company, First Vermont Cavalry, was captured on May 5, 1864, during the Battle of the Wilderness. On his way to Andersonville, he spent two nights at the Lynchburg POW camp.

Faust, Drew Gilpin. "'The Dread Void of Uncertainty': Naming the Dead in the American Civil War." *Southern Cultures* 11, no. 2 (Summer 2005): 7–32.

In the 21st century, it is hard for the average reader to comprehend the immense sense of loss experienced by thousands of families—both Union and Confederate—who never knew the ultimate fate of a loved one listed as missing in action or presumed dead. Dr. Faust briefly but succinctly informs her reader of the pain suffered by those who never gained closure and how their suffering inspired the generations that followed to try and see that it never happened again.

Hesseltine, William Best. "Andersonville Revisited." *Georgia Review* 10, no. 1 (Spring 1956): 92–101.

This is Hesseltine's scathing review of MacKinlay Kantor's Pulitzer Prize–winning novel, *Andersonville*, which was published in 1955.

Hunt, Edward, ed. *Merchant's Magazine and Commercial Review* 32, June 1855.

This edition contains the statistics that placed Lynchburg in second place among the wealthiest cities in the United States based on per capita income.

Preston, Katherine K. "Popular Music in the 'Gilded Age': Musicians' Gigs in Late Nineteenth-Century Washington, D.C." *Popular Music* 4 (1984): 25–47.

This article contains data on Louis Weber and his popular band which played a number of concerts in Lynchburg during the city's centennial celebration in 1886.

Schewel, Michael. "Local Politics in Lynchburg, Virginia, in the 1880s." *Virginia Magazine of History and Biography* 89, no. 2 (April 1982): 170–180.

A telling account of that brief moment between the end of Reconstruction and the promulgation of the infamous Virginia Constitution of 1902, when the working classes—both Black and white—worked together to form a city council that was freely elected and truly representative of all the people of the Hill City.

Williamson, Raymond. "Lynchburg Paper Money of 1862." *Lynch's Ferry* 8, no. 1 (Lynchburg: Lynchburg Historical Foundation, 1995).

A Fellow of the American Numismatic Society, Mr. Williamson was the authority on the currency printed by order of the Lynchburg City Council during the Civil War.

Secondary Works

Ayres, Edward L. *The Thin Light of Freedom: The Civil War and Emancipation in the Heart of America*. New York: Norton, 2017.

Bibliography

While the main emphasis of this beautifully written book lies elsewhere, the author includes a short summary of General Hunter's Lynchburg Campaign (166–178) with copious endnotes which is an excellent introduction to the subject.

Baber, Lucy Harrison, and Evelyn Lee Moore. *Behind the Old Brick Wall: A Cemetery Story*. Lynchburg: Lynchburg Committee of the National Society of the Colonial Dames of America in the Commonwealth of Virginia, 1968.

Written by two highly respected antiquarians, this work contains important data on the Union burials in the Old City Cemetery.

Bell, James Pinkney. *Our Quaker Friends of Ye Olden Times*. Lynchburg: J.P. Bell, Company, Publishers, 1905.

This work was compiled by an antiquarian who was a descendant of some of Lynchburg's pioneer Quakers. Bell includes a wealth of material on the Society of Friends, including transcripts of the Cedar Creek Meeting in Hanover County, Virginia, and the South River Meeting in Campbell County, Virginia. It is also rich in data useful to historians and genealogists alike, information compiled by one, who as a boy, worshipped with the last members of the South River meeting.

Blackford, Charles M. *Campaign and Battle of Lynchburg, Va., Delivered by Request of the Garland-Rodes Camp of Confederate Veterans of Lynchburg, Virginia, June 18, 1901*. Lynchburg: J.P. Bell, 1901.

On June 18, 1901, the 35th anniversary of the Battle of Lynchburg, Captain Blackford read a paper for the Garland-Rodes Camp of Confederate Veterans on General Hunter's failure to take the Hill City. At the urging of the members present, he had his presentation published, and the slim paper-bound volume sold faster than it could be printed. The appendix, which Blackford added, is particularly valuable because it lists all the Lynchburg companies that served the Confederacy.

Blakey, Arch Frederic. *General John H. Winder, C.S.A.* Gainesville: University Press of Florida, 1990.

The author fashions a balanced treatment of a man who was the wrong candidate for a very important job that should have been assigned to a much younger man. It is a carefully crafted chronicle of a lackluster career that declined into a disaster, which cost the lives of too many soldiers.

Brandt, Allan M. *The Cigarette Century: The Rise, Fall, and Deadly Persistence of the Product That Defined America*. New York: Basic Books, 2007.

Although Brandt does not mention Lynchburg, Virginia, and its role in tobacco culture before the Civil War, he does discuss in detail the role played by the Bonsack cigarette rolling machine in ending Lynchburg's preeminence in the manufacturing of tobacco products before 1860.

Brown, Douglas Summers. *Lynchburg's Pioneer Quakers and Their Meeting House*. 2nd ed. Lynchburg: H.E. Howard, 1986.

Using extant records of the South River Meeting, Mrs. Brown wrote a balanced history of the Quaker presence in Lynchburg from 1757 until the meeting ceased to exist in the generation before the Civil War.

Brown, William M. *Marshall Lodge #39*. Staunton: McClure Printing Co., 1953.

Founded in 1793, Marshall Lodge #39 included in its membership many of the prominent business and professional men in antebellum Lynchburg. Unfortunately Dr. Brown's book must be used with caution because it contains no citations. If it is to be used as a reference, the data in question must be verified from another source.

Bruner, Robert F. *The Panic of 1857: Nationalism and Secession*. Charlottesville: Darden School of Business, University of Virginia, 2017.

Bibliography

This work by an economist deals with the effects of the financial crisis that crippled the industrial and agrarian sections of the United States—except the cotton- and tobacco-producing states—and helped embolden the leaders of South Carolina to secede from the Union in December 1860.

Bryant, William Cullen. *Prose Writings of William Cullen Bryant*, vol. 2, *Travels, Addresses and Comments*. Edited by Parke Godwin. New York: D. Appleton, 1889.

Bryant's 1842 tour of the South contains a description of a tobacco factory in Richmond, Virginia, in particular the steps used in producing plug tobacco. The process was identical to that performed in Lynchburg.

Casstevens, Frances H. *"Out of the Mouth of Hell": Civil War Prisons and Escapes*. Jefferson, NC: McFarland, 2011.

A general history of prisons, both Union and Confederate, it is well written and has an extensive bibliography. It is an excellent introduction to this increasingly pertinent aspect of Civil War studies.

Chambers, S. Allen. *Lynchburg: An Architectural History*. Charlottesville: University of Virginia Press, 1981.

This is the definitive work that traces the architectural history of the city from its humble origins on the banks of the James River to the skyscrapers of the 20th century. It is liberally illustrated and filled with data useful to the historian of any period in the city's past.

Christian, W. Aubrey. *Lynchburg and Its People*. Lynchburg: J.P. Bell, 1900.

A clergyman by profession, Christian wrote a history of Lynchburg primarily based on surviving local newspapers. It ends with December 1899. An index of names was added in 1967. Although a secondary source, it contains data that are found nowhere else because some of the newspapers on which it was based no longer exist.

Cohen, Stan. *Historic Springs of the Virginias*. Charleston, WV: Quarrier Press, 1981.

This is essentially an illustrated history of the natural springs in Virginia and West Virginia. It includes Bedford Alum Springs at New London, Virginia. After burying their fallen comrades, Hunter's troops rested and refilled their canteens there before marching toward Lynchburg.

Cornelius, Roberta D. *J.P. Bell's of Lynchburg, Virginia, Established in 1859*. Lynchburg: J.P. Bell, 1959.

This is a brief history of the printing firm which by the very nature of its products began diversifying the economy of Lynchburg in the decade before the Civil War.

Cunningham, Horace Herndon. *Doctors in Gray: The Confederate Medical Service*. Baton Rouge: Louisiana State University Press, 1958.

This is still considered the definitive work on the Confederate medical service and the medical personnel who often worked under impossible conditions but achieved remarkable results. However, the book fails to deal with the Lynchburg system or the critical role played by women in the hospitals of the South.

Driscoll, Charles E. *John Jay Terrell, MD, Civil War Doctor to Man and Horse*. Lynchburg: Warrick House Publishing, 2020.

A well-researched and well-crafted work by a retired physician who writes with professional knowledge about one of the pivotal figures in the history of central Virginia during the Civil War. Dr. Terrell's care of smallpox victims and horses suffering from glanders placed him at the forefront of both human and veterinary medicine.

Durden, Robert F. *The Dukes of Durham, 1865–1929*. Durham, NC: Duke University Press, 1987.

Bibliography

This work contains important data on the "arrangement" between James Bonsack and James B. Duke that led to the replacement of Lynchburg by Durham, North Carolina, as the "Tobacco City" at the end of the 19th century.

Dyer, Frederick H. *A Compendium of the War of the Rebellion*. 3 pts. Des Moines: Dyer Publishing, 1908.
This mammoth work of 1,796 pages has appeared in one-, two-, and three-volume versions and five editions since it was first published. It is divided into three parts: number and organization of the armies of the United States, chronological data on military actions, and regimental histories. The final part proved most useful in the completion of *Yankees in the Hill City*.

Faust, Drew Gilpin. *This Republic of Suffering: Death and the American Civil War*. New York: Vintage Books, 2008.
In this sensitive and beautifully written work, the modern reader is able to begin to understand the agony suffered by those who were forced to confront the loss of a loved one during the cruelest of wars. The importance of the system that evolved in Lynchburg, particularly the care shown to Union soldiers who died as prisoners, is easier to grasp after a careful reading of this book.

Fluharty, Linda Cunningham. *Civil War—West Virginia, Union Lives Lost*. Baton Rouge: Linda Cunningham Fluharty, 2004.
This is an extremely useful tool in tracing the transformation of Virginia units loyal to the Union into regiments from the sovereign state of West Virginia, especially the casualty data for the soldiers of the Mountain State.

Fogarty, Gerald P. *Commonwealth Catholicism: A History of the Catholic Church in Virginia*. Notre Dame: University of Notre Dame Press, 2001.
Father Fogarty deals with the role of the Sisters of Charity working in the military hospitals and the responsibility among the clergy in Lynchburg in regard to the burial of the dead on both sides.

Freehling, William W., and Craig M. Simpson. *Showdown in Virginia: The 1861 Convention and the Fate of the Union*. Charlottesville: University of Virginia Press, 2010.
With great care the authors examine the propaganda used to persuade the majority of voters that the Commonwealth had common cause with the cotton South. Only the representatives of the far western counties had the courage to resist and create a new state, West Virginia. Well-written, well-researched, and every vital fact is cited—in short, a first-class piece of scholarship.

Gallagher, Gary W., ed. *Struggle for the Shenandoah: Essays on the 1864 Valley Campaign*. Kent, OH: Kent State University Press, 1991.
This excellent collection of informative and well-written essays contains the following papers: Gary W. Gallagher, "Introduction" and "The Shenandoah Valley in 1864"; Jeffrey D. Wert, "Jubal A. Early and Confederate Leadership"; A. Wilson Greene, "Union Generalship in the 1864 Valley Campaign"; Robert K. Krick, "'The Cause of All My Disasters': Jubal A. Early and the Undisciplined Valley Campaign"; and Dennis E. Frye, "'I Resolved to Play a Bold Game': John S. Mosby as a Factor in the 1864 Valley Campaign."

Gilmer, Jeremy Francis. *Lynchburg and Vicinity*. Richmond: Confederate Engineer Bureau, 1864.
Major General J.F. Gilmer was the chief engineer of the Confederate army, and using the maps of Lynchburg, Virginia, produced by his department, it is possible to locate all the places cited in *Yankees in the Hill City*.

Glenn, Justin. *The Washingtons: A Family History*. Vol. 1, *Seven Generations of the Presidential Branch*. El Dorado, CA: Savas Beatie, 2014–2015.

Bibliography

This is a carefully researched but at times hard to follow genealogy of the Washington family that includes the first president.

Goldfield, David R. *Urban Growth in the Age of Sectionalism: Virginia, 1847–1861.* Baton Rouge: Louisiana State University Press, 1977.

Although this work's main foci are Richmond and Norfolk, there are references to Lynchburg, especially the rivalry between the Hill City and the Capital City.

Gwynne, Samuel C. *Hymns of the Republic.* New York: Scribner's, 2019.

This recent work deals with the last year of the war, and unlike so many authors, Gwynne understands the role that Lynchburg played in those last critical months of the Civil War.

Hanchett, William. *Irish: Charles G. Halpine in Civil War America.* Syracuse: Syracuse University Press, 1970.

This is a thorough and entertaining biography of Major Charles Halpine, assistant adjutant general to General David Hunter during his ill-fated raid into central Virginia. Halpine saw it all and, in time, recorded his impressions of the whole sad affair under his pseudonym, Miles O'Reilly.

Haskins, Charles H., and William I. Hull. *A History of Higher Education in Pennsylvania.* Washington, D.C.: Government Printing Office, 1902.

This work contains a concise history of Madison College in Uniontown, Pennsylvania, from its founding to its untimely end on the eve of the Civil War.

Helper, Hinton A. *Centennial Souvenir of Lynchburg, Va.* New York: South Publishing, 1886.

Although it is only 5" × 6½" and a mere 96 pages, this pocket-size guide to Lynchburg during the centennial of its incorporation as a town is packed with information for the visitor; it is also a testament to a community that has moved beyond the trauma of the Civil War. It is a snapshot of a city that is not on the edge of the yesterday but the brink of tomorrow.

Hesseltine, William Best. *Civil War Prisons: A Study in War Psychology.* Columbus: Ohio State University Press, 1998.

First published in 1930, this is the seminal work that began the modern debate on Civil War prisons. As William Blair states in his excellent foreword to this edition, Hesseltine's thesis is dated in part because he did not have access to the data that are available to current students of the period. This is particularly true in regard to the Lynchburg POW camp.

Hobbs, Thomas Gibson, Jr. *The Canal on the James: An Illustrated Guide to the James River and Kanawha Canal.* Compiled by Nancy Blackwell Marion and edited by Mary Molyneux and Thomas G. Ledford. Lynchburg: Blackwell, 2009.

This is the definitive work on the canal that was to have fulfilled George Washington's dream of a link between the Atlantic Ocean and the Ohio River.

Houck, Peter W. *A Prototype of a Confederate Hospital Center in Lynchburg, Virginia.* Lynchburg: Warwick House Publishing, 1986.

Written by a practicing physician rather than a historian, what the book lacks in organization is more than compensated by the valuable data it contains concerning the second largest hospital center in the Upper South after the huge Chimborazo complex in Richmond.

Jeffrey, William H. *Richmond Prisons 1861–1862.* St. Johnsbury, VT: Republican Press, 1893.

The author's lack of organization does not detract from the fact that there is a great deal of valuable information about how the system cobbled together by General Winder functioned until it was overwhelmed by sheer numbers and incompetent subordinates.

Kellogg, Robert H. *Life and Death in Rebel Prisons.* Hartford, CT: L. Stebbins, 1865.

Although this work deals with Andersonville, the reader is able to better understand how the system fashioned by General Winder degenerated into the nightmare that was Camp Sumter.

King, Edward. *The Great South.* Hartford, CT: American Publishing, 1875.

Less than a decade after J.R. Dennett and Whitelaw Reid visited Lynchburg, Edward King visited the Hill City during his tour of the South—a journey that he chronicled in a work of more than 800 pages. Illustrated by James Wells Champney, *The Great South* became a classic. King, like Reid, was charmed by "Old Lynchburg."

Maher, Mary Denis. *To Bind Up the Wounds: Catholic Sister Nurses in the Civil War.* Baton Rouge: Louisiana State University Press, 1989.

Catholic nuns, widows, and married women were the only females allowed to nurse in military hospitals in both the North and the South. Trained to provide skilled care, the Sisters of Charity rendered exemplary service wherever they were sent. They were also ambassadors for their church. Sister Mary Denis Maher's slim, well-written volume is packed with vital data for the student of Civil War medicine.

Markham, Jerald H. *The Diuguid Records, 1861–1865, and Biographical Sketches.* Westminster, MD: Heritage Books, 2007.

This volume builds on the work begun in *Behind the Old Brick Wall*, and it contains an amazing amount of data but very few citations. Without footnotes or endnotes, the reader must try and find the sources on which the author relied. However, by creating a chart listing the names of all the soldiers, both North and South, using the data in the "Diuguid Soldiers Book," he confirms the fact that soldiers were placed in a hospital based on the availability of a bed and not the color of their uniform. Thus, POWs were integrated into the hospital system and not treated in a separate facility.

Miller, Edward A., Jr. *Lincoln's Abolitionist General.* Columbia: University of South Carolina Press, 1997.

A balanced and well-written biography of Brigadier General David Hunter who might have shortened the war by at least six months if he had followed orders and not concentrated on his own agenda. General Jubal Early is given credit for saving Lynchburg, but that accolade truly belongs to the incompetent Union general David Hunter who spent so many hours burning the Virginia Military Institute and those private dwellings that displeased him that he lost the advantage of time and, with it, Lynchburg.

Morris, George S., and Susan L. Foutz. *Lynchburg in the Civil War: The City, the People, the Battle.* Lynchburg, VA: H.E. Howard, 1984.

This is a useful instruction to Lynchburg in the 1860s, but its real value lies in the charts, maps, and muster rolls it contains.

Naisawald, L. van Loan. *The Battle of Lynchburg: Seize Lynchburg—if Only for a Single Day.* Lynchburg: Warwick House Publishing, 2004.

Only a professional soldier with knowledge of all matters military could write an analysis of the events leading up to the Battle of Lynchburg, the engagement itself, and its aftermath. There are only 78 pages of densely written text, but every word is weighed and measured; however, the one serious weakness of the book is that the endnotes are not in standard form.

Parker, Sandra V. *Richmond's Civil War Prisons.* Lynchburg: H.E. Howard, 1990.

This is the best work on the entire network of prisons in Richmond from the early months of 1861 to the evacuation of Richmond in April 1865. It is well written and well researched.

Bibliography

Pickenpaugh, Roger. *Captives in Blue: The Civil War Prisons of the Confederacy.* Tuscaloosa: University of Alabama Press, 2013.
  Well researched and beautifully written by someone who appreciates and understands his subject, this work contains correct information about the Lynchburg camp.

Pond, George E. *Campaigns of the Civil War,* vol. 11, *The Shenandoah Valley in 1864.* New York: Charles Scribner's Sons, 1883.
  This work gives a thorough treatment of Lynchburg's involvement in a campaign waged by Union forces in the breadbasket of the Confederacy.

Potter, Clifton, and Dorothy Potter. *Lynchburg: "The Most Interesting Spot."* 2nd ed. Lynchburg: Beric Press, 1985.
  The first edition of this work was published in 1976 to provide an easy-to-read textbook to be used in the city schools. It includes a number of the cherished "legends" of the Hill City, including how General Early alarmed General Hunter and saved the city using an empty train.

Robert, Joseph Clarke. *The Story of Tobacco in America.* Chapel Hill: University of North Carolina Press, 1967.
  First published by Alfred A. Knopf in 1949, the book broadens the focus of Robert's earlier work, *The Tobacco Kingdom,* to encompass the history of James I's "precious stink," which saved England's first successful colony down to the 20th century.

Robert, Joseph Clarke. *The Tobacco Kingdom: Plantation, Market, and Factory in Virginia and North Carolina, 1800–1860.* Gloucester, MA: Peter Smith, 1965.
  First published in 1938 by Duke University Press, this work has stood the test of time. It contains a wealth of material gleaned from countless sources that are cited with meticulous care.

Roll of Honor, Names of Soldiers Who Died in Defense of the American Union Interred in National Cemeteries at Antietam (Maryland) and at Arlington (Additional), Culpeper Court-House, Cold Harbor, Winchester, Staunton, and Various Scattered Localities in Virginia. 27 vols. Washington, D.C.: Government Printing Office, 1866–1871.
  This is an invaluable resource that contains data from numerous sources arranged in a manner that is easy to use.

Sanders, Charles W., Jr. *While in the Hands of the Enemy: Military Prisons in the Civil War.* Baton Rouge: Louisiana State University Press, 2005.
  Although a fairly recent work, the author devotes only a paragraph to the first weeks of the existence of the camp in Lynchburg for Union prisoners.

Scruggs, Phillip Lightfoot. *The History of Lynchburg, Virginia, 1786–1946.* Lynchburg: J.B. Bell, 1971.
  Although well written—the author was a professional journalist—the book does not have a proper bibliography, an index, footnotes, or endnotes. However, it does contain one short paragraph about Union POWs, which attempts to present the facts known in 1971 about this forgotten chapter in Lynchburg's history.

Snow, Richard. *A Guide Book of Flying Eagle and Indian Head Cents.* Atlanta: Whitman Publishing, 2007.
  This is the standard work on small United States cents from 1856 to 1909 by the recognized authority on the subject.

Speer, Lonnie R. *Portals to Hell: Military Prisons of the Civil War.* Mechanicsburg, PA: Stackpole Books, 1997.
  Although the work is useful as an introduction to the subject of prisons during the Civil War, the data on Lynchburg are minimal at best and not correct.

Bibliography

Springer, Paul J., and Glenn Robins. *Transforming Civil War Prisons: Lincoln, Lieber, and the Politics of Captivity*. New York: Routledge, 2015.
   What it lacks in writing style is compensated by the wealth of information this slender volume contains. That said, there is no mention of Lynchburg.

Stillé, Charles J. *History of the United States Sanitary Commission Being the General Report of Its Work During the War of the Rebellion*. New York: Hurd and Houghton, 1868.
   This is an essential volume for anyone who wishes to explore the fate of Union soldiers taken prisoner during the Civil War—both those who survived and those who did not.

Taxey, Don. *The U.S. Mint and Coinage*. New York: Arco Publishing, 1966.
   This is a scholarly study of the United States Mint and its evolution, as well as a detailed treatment of the design and production of its products.

Tripp, Steven Elliott. *Yankee Town, Southern City: Race and Class Relations in Civil War Lynchburg*. New York: New York University Press, 1997.
   Without a doubt, this is the best work dealing with the Hill City before, during, and after the Civil War. The scholarship is solid, the narrative engaging, and the conclusions compelling.

Wade, Richard C. *Slavery in the Cities: The South, 1820–1860*. New York: Oxford University Press, 1964.
   The section dealing with the tobacco industry in Virginia is useful, particularly the firsthand accounts of the processing of the "golden leaf" for market.

Walker, Gary C. *Hunter's Fiery Raid Through Virginia Valleys* [retitled from *Yankee Soldiers in Virginia Valleys: Hunter's Raid*]. Roanoke: A&W Enterprise, 1989.
   This well-written account of the adventures and misadventures of Brigadier General David "Black Dave" Hunter covers the Lynchburg fiasco in great detail—chapter 10, "Friday, June 17–Saturday, June 18" alone is 71 pages long, and the depth of detail is amazing. However, this book has one glaring flaw. Although there are copious citations, they are useless because they are not done in proper form. The serious student of the Lynchburg Campaign must play detective to use Walker as a source.

Waugh, Joan, and Gary G. Gallagher, eds. *Wars Within a War: Controversy and Conflict Over the American Civil War*. Chapel Hill: University of North Carolina Press, 2009.
   Each one of the 12 chapters in this book is the work of a recognized scholar in the field of American Civil War studies. Drew Gilpin Faust's essay, "Battle over the Bodies: Burying and Reburying the Civil War Dead, 1865–1871," is particularly valuable because it details events that were in sharp contrast to the respect shown to the Union dead in Lynchburg.

Welcher, Frank J., and Larry G. Ligget. *Coburn's Brigade, 85th Indiana, 33rd Indiana, 19th Michigan, and 22nd Wisconsin in the Western Civil War*. Carmel: Guild Press of Indiana, 1999.
   Although there is no mention of Lynchburg, eight soldiers from the regiments covered in this volume died in Lynchburg hospitals as a result of the inhumane treatment they received at the Battle of Thompson's Station. This work is well written. Frank Welcher is considered the authority on the involvement of Indiana in the Civil War.

Wiley, Lib. *Alongside the River: A History of Lynchburg's Congregations*. Lynchburg: Lynchburg Bicentennial Committee, 1986.
   This slender volume contains the basic facts about the numerous churches whose ministers provided proper burial services for the fallen from both armies.

Bibliography

Williams, Richard G., Jr. *The Battle of Waynesboro.* Charleston, SC: History Press, 2014.
    This work is part of the Civil War Sesquicentennial Series. The Virginia Central Railroad, which linked Covington to Richmond, passed through Staunton, Waynesboro, and Charlottesville and was vital to the shipment of supplies, the wounded, and POWs from the Lower Shenandoah Valley to the cities of the Upper South. This is a well-written account of the pivotal role Waynesboro played in the course of the war. The first prisoners in the Lynchburg POW camp were bivouacked in Waynesboro near the tracks of the Central Virginia Railroad after their capture during the 1862 Shenandoah Valley Campaign.

Woodward, Joseph Janvier. *Outlines of the Chief Camp Diseases of the United States Armies as Observed During the Present War.* Philadelphia: J.B. Lippincott, 1863.
    Dr. Woodward was the army assistant surgeon when this essential tool for the doctor in the hospital or the field was published. It was written for the layperson as well as the professional so that both might benefit from its sage advice.

Yancey, Rosa Faulkner. *Lynchburg and Its Neighbors.* Richmond, VA: J.W. Ferguson and Sons, 1935.
    The most gifted local genealogist and antiquarian of her generation, Mrs. Yancey devoted several years to the completion of this work. It is not without biases but is a valuable source of data on all aspects of the history of Lynchburg and its surrounding counties.

Index

Acker, Pvt. Sidney E.A. 77, 165
Aiken's Landing, VA 41, 72, 73
Albemarle Female Institute 81, 178*n*
Aldie, VA 86, 190
Alexander, Capt. George W. 42
Allen, Pvt. Benjamin 164
Allison, Lt. William H., CSA 73
Almy, Cpl. Frank M. 165
Amherst County, VA 10, 12, 19, 20, 105, 127, 137
Amherst Court House 103, 104, 105, 109
Amory, Lt. Charles W. 87, 179*n*
Anderson, Jefferson 139
Anderson, Maj. Robert 22
Andersonville, GA 6, 43, 51, 75, 76, 86, 87, 97, 117, 120, 122, 171*n*, 175*n*, 178*n*, 186, 190, 191, 192, 200, 201, 204, 209
"Andersonville" (film) 3.
Andersonville (novel) 3, 171*n*
Andrews, Pvt. Charles E. 150
Annapolis, MD 49, 67, 98, 125, 151
Appomattox, VA 1, 7, 124, 125, 195, 198
Appomattox Campaign 125
Army of Northern Virginia, CSA 100, 121, 123, 124, 125
Army of the Shenandoah 100, 101, 102, 103, 110, 111, 112, 115, 116
Arnold, Cpl. William 163, 200
Ashby, Gen. Turner, CSA 58
Averell, Gen. William W. 102, 103, 104, 105, 107, 108, 111

Bader, Pvt. Henry 150
Baldwin University 173*n*
Ballard, Pvt. Joseph 162
Ballard, Sgt. Patterson 169
Barber, Pvt. William 167
Bardsley, Pvt. John G. 157
Barker, Pvt. John H. 144
Barney, Pvt. John P. 161
Barnum, Pvt. Isaac 157

Barr, 1st Lt. James 169
Barrett, Pvt. Merritt C. 151
Beardsley, Pvt. John G. 169
Beauregard, Gen. P.G.T. 22, 25
Beckwith, Pvt. George 154
Bedford County, VA 10, 105, 111, 127
Beechner, Pvt. John 152
Bell, Cpl. John 168
Belle Isle 1, 5, 38, 40, 41, 42, 43, 47, 48, 49, 50, 51, 57, 67, 72, 73, 77, 85, 95, 174*ns*, 175*ns*, 186, 188, 190, 192
Berry, Pvt. James 151
Beyer, Edward iv, 19, 20
Big Lick, VA, (Roanoke) 138
Big Otter River 111, 112
Biggers, Abram 137
Black Codes 132, 133
Blackburn's Ford, Battle of 34
Blackford, Charles M. 21, 115, 129, 142, 172*ns*, 182*ns*, 183*n*, 188*n*, 205
Blackford, Susan 172*ns*, 183*ns*, 188*n*
Blackford, William M. 23
Blackwater Creek 54
Blair, Pvt. George 168
Blinn, Pvt. Charles 57, 58, 59, 61, 63-70, 175*n*, 176*ns*, 177*ns*, 185, 186, 202
Bobson, Pvt. Allen 158
Bonsack, James A. 138, 183*n*, 184*n*, 205, 207
Booker, David E. 94, 172*n*
Booker, James M. 94, 172*n*
Booker, William T. 94, 129
Boose, Sgt. Moses 154
Bossieux, Lt. Virginius 43, 47, 48
Bowen, James I. 195
Bowen, Pvt. Robert 157
Bower, Pvt. Joseph 143
Bower, Pvt. Marquis 71, 147, 177*n*
Bowles, Pvt. Almon E. 163
Boyce, Charles W. 195
Boyce, Pvt. John 156

Index

Boyd, Pvt. James A. 168
Boyd, Pvt. William C 151
Branch, William D. 124
Bragg, Gen. Braxton, CSA 43, 111, 191
Brant, Lt. Col. Jefferson 178, 195-196
Brant, Pvt. Joseph 167
Breckenridge, Gen. John C., CSA 102
Breen, Cpl. Dennis 166
Bremer, Pvt. Andrew 148
Bristol, VA 14, 131
Brommel, Pvt. H. Fritz 148
Bronson, Pvt. Lewis C. 151
Brown, Douglas Summers 205
Brown, Edmund R. 196
Brown, John 23, 30, 31, 173*n*
Brown, William M. 172*n*, 205
Brownsburg, VA 103
Bryant, William Cullen 20, 172*n*, 206
Buchanan, Pres. James 31, 138
Buchanan, VA 102, 104, 105, 107, 108, 110
Budd, Pvt. Sebring 163
Buell, Lt. Col. George P. 136
Bull Run, 1st Battle of 25, 34, 199
Bull Run, 2nd Battle of 83, 199
Burdett, Pvt. Henderson F. 156
Burnside, Gen. Ambrose 78
Burr, Pvt. Joel L. 162
Butler, Gen. Benjamin 49, 73, 75, 174*n*
Butler University 83
Button, Charles 17, 56, 57, 63, 119, 120, 134, 140, 141, 176*ns*, 182*ns*, 184*n*, 189
Buzzards' Roost 25, 120, 123, 127, 128, 136, 142, 183*n*

Calas, Pvt. Frederick 154
Calhoun, Pvt. George S. 149
Camp Davis 24, 54, 87, 93, 94, 120, 123, 133, 154, 155, 156, 158, 159, 195
Camp Nicholls 93, 94, 96
Camp Oglethorpe, GA 51, 118, 120, 189, 193
Camp Parole, MD 125
Camp Paxton, WV 53, 54
Camp Sumter, GA 3, 4, 51, 75, 117, 120, 209; *see also* Andersonville, GA
Campbell County, VA 10, 19, 127, 205
Canada 10, 28
Carden, Pvt. Patrick 166
Carl, Pvt. Frank W. 153
Carr's Tobacco Warehouse 46
Carter, Pvt. James 169
Castle Godwin 38
Castle Pinckney, SC 36, 88

Castle Thunder 1, 5, 42, 46
Cavada, Lt. Col. Frederick 43, 44, 173*n*, 174*ns*, 175, 188
Cedar Creek 11, 101, 205
Centennial 136, 139, 140, 141, 142, 184*n*, 204
Ceredo, WV 53
Chalron, Pvt. Peter 166
Charles Town, WV 50
Charleston, SC 4, 22, 31, 32, 36, 88, 113, 173, 176
Charleston, WV 111, 182
Charlottesville, VA 14, 16, 60, 61, 63, 81, 102, 108, 109, 110, 111, 114, 115, 116, 129, 171*n*, 173*n*, 180*n*, 181*n*, 183*n*, 212
Chateau de Tonnerre 42
Chicago Tribune 125, 183*n*, 187
Chorarty, Pvt. Henry 145
Christian, Aubrey 23, 119, 171*ns*, 172*ns*, 175*n*, 179*ns*, 182*ns*, 183*ns*, 184*ns*, 206
Christian burial 1, 7, 177, 207, 211
Christian's Tobacco Factory 94, 152, 172*n*
City Cemetery (Lynchburg VA) 27, 66, 67, 68, 72, 73, 77, 87, 91, 120, 134, 143-166, 176*n*, 177*n*, 183*ns*, 185, 186, 196, 197, 198, 202, 203, 204, 205
City Council (Lynchburg VA) 5, 6, 24, 26, 55, 90, 122, 124, 137, 139, 176*n*, 185, 204
City Point, VA 41, 43, 47, 73, 75, 122
Clarkson, Col. John, CSA 53
Clearnott, Pvt. Joseph 160
Coburn, Sgt. Jacob 50, 51, 175*n*, 188
Coburn, Col. John 74, 177, 199, 203-204, 211
Cocks, Pvt. John H. 145
Coffren, Pvt. Sebra F. 157
Cold Harbor 102, 111, 210
College Hospital (Lynchburg VA) 63, 86, 87, 89, 90, 92, 95, 96, 98, 99, 154-157, 159-162
Collierville, TN 50
Collins, Pvt. James 163
Columbia, SC 4, 83
Columbia, TN 74
Condon, Pvt. Elijah 154
Conn, Cpl. Daniel 167
Connelley, Pvt. James 155
Coonts, Pvt. Philip 170
Cooper, Pvt. Eugene 160
Coulter, Pvt. George M. 168
Counsel, Pvt. James D. 167
counterfeit currency 27, 48, 53, 63

214

Index

Courthouse (Lynchburg VA) 14, 15, 16, 18, 191
Coward, Pvt. Charles A. 77, 163, 197
Cox, Samuel K. 16, 17
Crabtree, Pvt. Martin 166
Craighill, Dr. Edward 98, 99, 180n, 188
Crane, Stephen 80
Creigh, David Stuart 103
Crew and Pemberton Prison 46
Crimean War 91, 110
Cronshaw, Pvt. John 163
Crook, Gen. George B. 103, 104, 107
Crumpton's Tobacco Factory 87, 95, 97, 151, 153-165, 172n, 192, 194, 196, 200, 201
CT 5th Vol. Inf. 199
CT 18th Vol. Inf. 106, 107, 108, 115, 116, 181n, 191, 199, 203
Cumberland Gap 9
Cumberland Presbyterian Church 16, 172n
"Curl's Row" 136
Curtis, Pvt. Albert M. 168
Curtis, Gen. Newton Martin 129, 130, 136, 188

Dafoe, Pvt. Edward 157
Dahlgren, Col. Ulrich 47
Daily Intelligencer 53, 175n, 187
Danville, VA 4, 44, 76, 82, 84, 86, 88, 89, 95, 123, 137, 139, 191, 203
Daugherty, Pvt. Daniel 170
Davis, Pvt. Charles C. 154
Davis, Pres. Jefferson, CSA 5, 33, 35, 41, 43, 49, 55, 73, 75, 91, 174, 175
DE 1st Vol. Inf. 161, 200
Dearing, Gen. James 125
Decker, Pvt. Alonzo 167
Delano, Pvt. Levi G. 146
Dennett, John Richard 130, 131, 183n, 188, 189, 191, 209
Derr, 2nd Lt. Samuel A. 160
De Villiers, Col. Charles A. 35, 36
Dickey, Pvt. William 168
Dilcher, Pvt. Henry 160
District of Columbia 136, 190
Diuguid, George A. 6, 67, 134, 183n, 185
Diuguid, Samson 67
Diuguid Funeral Service 6, 27, 67, 73, 87, 91, 119, 134
Diuguid Funeral Service *see* Lynchburg
"Diuguid Soldiers Book or DSB" 87, 143-165, 148, 151, 155, 176n, 177ns, 178ns, 179ns, 185, 209

Dix, Gen. John A. 40
Dix-Hill Cartel 4, 7, 40, 41, 42, 43, 47, 71, 72, 73, 75, 122
Dockham, Pvt. George A. 150
Donahue, Pvt. Peter F. 145
Donald, Pvt. John 162
Doniphan, the Rev. Alexander 17
Douthat, Capt. Henry C., CSA 109
Dow, Gen. Neal 51
Dowling, Pvt. Patrick 66, 177n, 144
Dublin, VA 52
Duffié, Gen. Alfred N. 103, 104, 105, 107, 108, 109, 110, 194, 195
Duke, James B. 138, 206-207
Dulaney, Pvt. Daniel 170
Duncan, Col. Alender P. 127
Dunlap, Pvt. William H. 167
Dunn, Sgt. Samuel 168
DuPont, Capt. Henry 104, 181ns, 189
Durbin, Pvt. John W. 169
Durham, NC 138, 139, 206, 207

Early, Bishop John 18
Early, Jubal A. 8, 60, 109, 111, 113, 114, 115, 117, 123, 182n, 189, 200, 207, 209, 210
Eckenrode, Dr. H.J. 92
education 15, 16, 18, 29, 126, 129, 130, 136, 137, 139, 142, 171n, 172n, 184n, 190, 193, 208
Edward, Henry 139
Ellis, Pvt. Nathan D. 168
Ellison, Andrew 14, 15
Ellison, William 15
Elson, Pvt. Albert 167
Ellsworth, Pvt. Isaac 147
Ely, Alfred 34, 35, 36, 37, 173ns, 189, 196
Emack, Lt. George M., CSA 39
emancipation 11, 28, 29, 128, 130, 204
Emmert, Pvt. Philip 149
Eustice, Pvt. William 153

Fair Ground (Lynchburg VA) 3, 6, 7, 24, 37, 38, 54, 55, 56, 57, 62-68, 68, 70, 71, 72, 75, 76, 77, 78, 81-86, 89, 94, 99, 111, 116, 117, 120, 121, 123, 125, 130, 135, 138, 140-151, 160, 161, 177n, 185, 186, 190, 191
Fairbanks, Pvt. Forrest G. 156
Fairfield, VA 103
Farlow, Pvt. Robert 159
Farmville, VA 124, 127
Federal Burial Corps 134, 135
Ferdun, Pvt. George E. 150

215

Index

Fergason, Pvt. John L. 153
Ferguson, Lt. Joseph 84, 85, 86, 174*n*, 179*n*, 189
Ferguson's Tobacco Factory 95, 98, 153, 172*n*
Fifteenth Amendment 136
Firestone, Pvt. Martin D. 168
First National Bank (Lynchburg VA) 129
Fisher, Pvt. William 168
Fitzpatrick, Lt. Terrance 124
Floyd, Gen. John B., CSA 52, 53, 175*n*
Forbes, Cpl. Daniel 158
Forest Road 54, 175*n*, 184*n*
Forrest, Gen. N.B., CSA 50
Forsberg, Augustus 140
Fort Monroe, VA 74
Fort Moultrie, SC 31
Fort Sumter, SC 6, 22, 31, 75, 113
Fourteenth Amendment 133, 135, 183*n*
Fowler, Sgt. Thomas 156
Frankenheimer, John 3
Franklin, TN 74
Frederick County, VA 59, 100
Freedmen's Bureau 126, 127, 130, 132, 133, 136, 193
Freedmen's Bureau Act 126
Freischmann, Pvt. Charles 148
Fremont, Gen. John C. 60, 61
Frier, Pvt. Joseph 146
Fugitive Slave Act of 1793 28
Fugitive Slave Act of 1850 28
Fullmer, Pvt. Isaiah 155

Gache, Fr. Louis-Hippolyte 96
Gage, Pvt. Charles B. 167, 184
Galt, Capt John, CSA 55, 56, 63, 65, 68, 72, 73
Gamble, George 97, 98, 180*n*
Garfield, Pvt. Henry D. 145
Gatton, Pvt. George W. 145
Gatton, Pvt. Jefferson 155
Gefner, Pvt. Joseph 169
General Order No. 28 174*n*
General Order No. 29 101, 174
General Order No. 42 125
General Order No. 61 136
General Order No. 111 73, 74
General Order No. 252 41, 75
Gephart, Pvt. Ernest 166
Gibbon, Gen. John 124, 125, 183*n*
Gibbs, Col George C., CSA 5, 6, 7, 36, 37, 38, 40, 41, 43, 51, 55, 56, 57, 62, 63, 64, 65, 66, 69, 71, 72, 78, 81, 89, 173*n*s, 196
Gibbs, Pvt. Therone 154

Gilbert, Gen. Charles C. 74, 204
Gilham, Cordelia 104
Gilham, Maj. William, CSA 104
Gilson, Pvt. Richard 160
Glass, E.C. High School 8, 142
Gleanor's Tobacco Factory 42
Glover, Pvt. John F. 156
Goggins, Pvt. Andrew A. 161
Gordon, Gen. John D., CSA 116
Gordonsville, VA. 76, 81, 83, 84, 86, 97
Gosley, Pvt. Hugh S. 146
Goswell, Pvt. William 166
Graham, Pvt. Louis 168
Grant, Gen. Ulysses S. 7, 8, 41, 77, 100, 101, 102, 108, 121, 124, 175*n*, 180*n*, 183*n*, 189, 203
Green, Pvt. William A. 155, 169
"Greenbacks" 48, 82, 131
Greene, Lt. Israel 30
Greenville, VA 103
Gregg, Gen. J. Irvin 127-130, 136, 189
Groft, Pvt. John 168
Guardhouse (Lynchburg VA) 88
Guggenheimer, Nathaniel 23
Guldner, Pvt. Nicholas 146
Guyandotte, WV 52, 53, 54, 55, 66, 175*n*

Hadley, Lt. John V. 83, 84, 179*n*, 189
Hall, Pvt. David L. 168
Hall, Pvt. Fleming 146
Halleck, Gen. Henry W. 74, 103
Halpine, Col. Charles G. 106, 113, 180*n*, 181*n*, 190, 208
Halsey, Pvt. Joseph C. 154
Hamilton, Maj. Andrew G. 46
Hamilton, Pvt. Evander B. 159
Hammond, Pvt. Leroy 161
Hardison, Pvt. Hiram P. 149
Harpers Ferry, WV 22, 23, 30
Harps, Pvt. David S. 145
Harrison, Pvt. Battael V. 167
Harrison, Pvt. Solomon 169
Harrisonburg, VA 60, 61, 101
Hart, Capt., CSA 112
Hartmann, Pvt. August C. 147
Hartmann, Capt. John B. 164
Harwood's Tobacco Factory 33
Hawkins, Pvt. William 169
Hayes, Col. Rutherford B. 113
Heald, Sgt. John S. 88, 89
Hedenthall, Pvt. Joseph 168
Hennessy, Pvt. Michael 157
Henrico County Jail 38
Hernandez, Pvt. Juan 154

Index

"Heroes of America" 121
Herring, Pvt. Daniel 149
Hess, Pvt. Henry 149
Hesseltine, W.B. 2, 3, 4, 171*ns*, 188, 204, 208
Hill, Gen. A.P., CSA 79
Hill, Gen. D.H., CSA 40
Hillegas, Pvt. Nathaniel 168
Hitt, Cpl. Joseph W. 170
Hoback, Cpl. Alexander 169
Hollins University 16, 173*n*
Hollywood Cemetery 19
Hooker, Gen. Joseph 78
Hopwood, Josephus 18, 48, 49, 50, 175*ns*, 190
Hopwood, Sarah LaRue 18, 172*n*, 175*ns*, 190
Horseford Road 125
"Hotel de Yanks" 82, 83, 191
Houdon, Jean-Antoine 107
Howard, Gen. Oliver O. 126
Howard's Warehouse 35-38, 173*n*
Hudson, Pvt. Alanson 168
Hueninston, Pvt. Newton P. 149
Hull, Pvt. Edmund J. 168
Humphreys, Chap. Charles A. 86, 87, 88, 98, 179*ns*, 190
Humphreys, Cpl. Gabriel 164
Humphreys, Milton W. 181*ns*, 190
Hunsaker, Pvt. George 164
Hunter, Gen. David 7, 8, 60, 88, 98, 100-117, 180*ns*, 184*n*, 187, 189, 191, 192, 193, 199, 208, 209, 210, 211
Hurt, William W. 91, 179*n*
Huson, Calvin, Jr. 34, 36, 37
Hutter, Ada 116
Hutter, Maj. George C. 112, 116
Hutter, Harriet 113, 116

IL 7th Vol. Cav. 50, 175*n*, 190
IL 34th Vol. Inf. 151, 200
Imboden, Gen. John D., CSA 102, 109, 112
IN 7th Vol. Inf. 83, 189
IN 14th Vol. Inf. 144
IN 27th Vol. Inf. 57-60, 144, 146-151, 196, 198, 199
IN 33rd Vol. Inf. 74, 152, 177, 199, 203, 211
IN 85th Vol. Inf. 152, 178, 195, 203, 211
Isaac, Pvt. Peter 149

Jackson, Alexander D. 18
Jackson, Gen. Thomas J., CSA 6, 26, 30, 37, 55, 56, 58, 60, 63, 72, 100, 108, 195, 196, 199
Jackson St. High School (Black) 137
James River 4, 5, 12, 13, 15, 19, 20, 32, 34, 40, 41, 44, 47, 49, 52, 72, 84, 104, 107, 108, 110, 117, 120, 136, 186, 206, 208
James River and Kanawha Canal 5, 13, 16, 25, 30, 32, 38, 45, 52, 54, 107, 117, 120, 123, 125, 136, 137, 171*n*, 208
James River Bateaux 5, 12, 13
James River Company 13
Jefferson, Thomas 29, 102
Jefferson Barracks 50
Jeffries, Capt. Thomas D. 42, 73
Jenkins, Col. Albert G., CSA 53
John Brown's Stable 143, 144
Johnson, Pres. Andrew 126, 131-133, 135
Johnte, Cpl. John George 148
Jolly, Pvt. James D. 166
Jones, Pvt. Jesse 156
Jones, Pvt. Owen R. 152
Jones, Gen. William E., CSA 102
Jones, Pvt. William H. 147
Jones Memorial Library ix, 172*n*, 176*n*, 179*n*, 185, 186
Jubilee (Freedmen) 125

Kantor, MacKinlay 3, 204
Kayser, Pvt. John S. 170
Keller, Pvt. Delevan 157
Kelley, QM Sgt. John 154
Kenneke, Pvt. Harman A. 167
Kenner, Capt. Henry C. 98, 162
Kettering, Pvt. Samuel 150
Kettle, Pvt. John W. 145
Kiehl, Pvt. Cyrus 168
Kilpatrick, Gen. Judson 47
Kinerson, Pvt. Albert 151
King, Sgt. Henry B. 117, 166
King, Pvt. William 170
King, Pvt. William C. 145
Knight-Capron Library ix
Kyle, Pvt. Joseph F. 163

Lacey, Capt. Robert S. 126, 127
Ladies Relief Hospital 91, 92, 94, 99, 125, 179*n*, 186
Lambden, Pvt. John 144
Lanman, Charles 37, 173*n*
Lannen, Pvt. Dennis 146
Lapier, Pvt. John B. 153
Laurel Hill Cemetery 19
Leach, Sgt. William 147
Leadbeater, Pvt. Leonard 169

217

Index

Lee, Gov. Fitzhugh 142
Lee, John B. 119
Lee, Gen. Robert E., CSA 5, 30, 33, 72, 102, 112, 114, 115, 121, 123, 124, 142, 190
Lemon, Pvt. Robert 170
Lennox, Pvt. Samuel 153
Leonard, Pvt. Frank 162
Letcher, Gov. John 22, 31, 32, 106, 108
Levy, Cpl. Joseph M. 168
Lewisburg, WV 111
Lexington, VA 8, 16, 18, 102-112, 181*n*, 186, 187, 190
Libby, Luther 38
Libby and Son, Ship Chandlers and Groceries 38
Libby Prison 1, 5, 38-45, 47, 51, 69, 72, 73, 81, 82, 85, 95, 173*n*, 174*ns*, 175*ns*, 177, 185, 188, 190, 191, 193, 196, 198, 204
Liberty (Bedford) VA 105, 107, 110, 111, 112, 116, 184*n*
lice 44, 49, 50, 62, 68, 69, 97, 190
Ligon and Co. Tobacco Factory 34
Lincoln, Pres. Abraham 21, 22, 26, 32, 35, 41, 43, 75, 100, 125, 126, 131, 133, 171*n*
Lincoln, Lt.-Col. William S. 109, 114, 181*ns*, 182*ns*, 199, 110
Linsly Military Institute 107
Little Otter Creek 116
Little Otter River 111
Lockwood, Pvt. James E. 161, 187, 197
Love, Pvt. Andrew 159
Ludlow, Lt. Col. William H. 74
Lynch, Pvt. Charles 106, 181*ns*, 191, 199
Lynch, John 9, 14, 18, 67, 183*n*
Lynchburg and Danville RR 137
Lynchburg and New River RR 13-14
Lynchburg and Salem Turnpike 54, 64, 112
Lynchburg and Tennessee RR 14
Lynchburg College (new) 18, 172
Lynchburg College (old) 17, 18, 22, 90, 172*n*, 179*n*, 184*n*, 186
Lynchburg Daily Virginian 14, 17, 21, 52, 53, 55, 56, 63, 119, 123, 140, 141, 171*n*, 175*ns* 176*ns*, 177*ns*, 179*ns*, 182*ns*, 183*ns*, 184*ns*, 186
Lynchburg Emigration Society 130
Lynchburg Female Orphan Asylum 138, 142
Lynchburg High School (White) 137

Lynchburg National Bank 129
Lynchburg Republican 63, 123, 187
Lynchburg-Salem Turnpike 54, 64, 112

MA 1st Vol. Cav. 165, 197
MA 2*nd* Vol. Cav. 86
MA 2*nd* Vol. Inf. 69
MA 12th Vol. Inf. 151, 161, 196
MA 34th Vol. Inf. 109, 117, 153, 155, 166
MA 37th Vol. Inf. 155
MA 54th Vol. Inf. 114
MA 57th Vol. Inf. 159, 193
Mackenzie, Gen. Ranald S. 124, 125, 127, 136
Macon, GA 4, 18, 51, 86, 118, 120, 122, 189, 190, 191, 193
manumission 29, 75
Marsh, Sgt. Simon 168
Marshall, Dr. M. Ernest x
Marshall Lodge 39, 17, 172*n*, 205
Marshall Theater 28
Martin, Pvt. Francis 166
Martin, Pvt. John R. 167
Martinsburg, WV 104
Mason, Pvt. Asa 152
Mason-Dixon Line 3, 16, 17, 67, 120, 196
Masonic Hall (Lynchburg VA) 24
Massie's Tobacco Factory 77, 153, 156, 163
Mathews, Pvt. James L. 170
Matson, Pvt. James 167
Mattocks, Maj. Charles 81, 82, 83, 178*ns*, 191
Mayo's Tobacco Factory 38
McBaird, Pvt. James 152
McCausland, Gen. John, CSA 103, 104, 105, 107, 108, 110, 112, 181*n*
McClellan, Gen. George B. 26
McCluskey, Pvt. John 159
McCormick, Capt. Edward, CSA 62, 63, 65, 68
McCort, Pvt. James 148
McCowen, 1st Sgt. Israel T. 167
McDonald, Pvt. Savage 168
McDowell, Gen. Irvin 25, 26
McGill, Pvt. Samuel 162
McGinnis, Pvt. John C. 152Oh
McIntosh, Pvt. Frank 159
McKee, Pvt. Samuel L. 168
McKinley, Capt. William 104, 113
McLean, Wilbur 124
McPherson, Pvt. Thomas 170
McVey, Pvt. James 154

Index

McWilliams, Pvt. James 168
MD 1st PHB Vol. Cav. 160
MD 1st Vol. Inf. 144-151, 160, 196
MD 3rd Vol. Inf. 150
MD 2nd ES Vol. Inf. 168
MD 2nd PHB Vol. Inf. 159, 166
ME 1st He. Arty 202
ME 1st Vet. Vol. Inf. 164, 197
ME 1st Vol. Cav. 146, 149, 150176, 202, 207
ME 3rd Vol. Inf. 154, 157, 158
ME 7th Vol. Inf. 155
ME 10th Vol. Inf. 147-150, 197
ME 13th Vol. Inf. 51
ME 17th Vol. Inf. 81, 178ns, 191, 198
ME 31st Vol. Inf. 161
Meade, Gen. George 78
Medal of Honor 83, 103, 191
Memphis, TN 50
Methodist Episcopal Church 16
Methodist Protestant Church 16, 17
Mexico 28
MI 1st Vol. Cav. 144, 145, 156, 157, 163, 202
MI 3rd Vol. Cav. 82
MI 5th Vol. Inf. 154
MI 6th Vol. Cav. 50, 154, 156, 160, 199
MI 7th Vol. Cav. 160, 199
MI 8th Vol. Inf. 156
MI 11th Vol. Cav. 77, 165
MI 19th Vol. Inf. 151, 152, 185, 194, 203, 211
MI 21st Vol. Inf. 152
MI 26th Vol. Inf. 155
Middletown, VA. 58, 100, 101
Military District One 135
Miller, Samuel 138
Miller Park 138, 140, 141, 142
Mitchell, Jacob D. 23
Monk, Pvt. Henry 147
Monteith, Pvt. William 163
Montgomery, Capt. Norris, CSA 41, 42, 174n
Moore, Lt.-Col. James M. 133
Moore, Pvt. John T. 150
Moore, Sur. Gen. Samuel Preston, CSA 92
Morse, Pvt. Jacob H. 159
Morse, Pvt. William 167
Mosby's Rangers 86, 179n, 207
Moss, Pvt. Jacob 164
Mt. Jackson, VA. 60, 101
Mulford, Maj. John E. 75
Mumford, William B. 73

Munson, Pvt. Enos 148
Murfee, James T. 18
Murphy, Pvt. Patrick 147

Napoleon I 95
Nashville, Battle of 121
NC 2nd M. Vol. Inf. 153
NC 42nd Inf. C.S.A. 6, 37, 41, 55, 57, 64, 72, 173n, 196
Neal, Pvt. James L. 156
Neifergold, Pvt. Francis 168
Nelson County, VA 12, 127
New London, VA 18, 112, 206
New Market, Battle of 100, 101, 102, 187
New River RR 14
Newtown, VA. 58
NH 1st Vol. Cav. 163, 193, 194, 203
NH 5th Vol. Inf. 160, 194, 196
NH 6th Vol. Inf. 153, 158, 194, 196, 198
NH 11th Vol. Inf. 158, 195, 196
Nicholls, Gen. Francis T., CSA 111
Nichols, Cpl. Langdon H. 149
Nightingale, Florence 91
NJ 1st Vol. Inf. 84, 86, 189, 202
NJ 3rd Vol. Cav. 164, 202
NJ 4th Vol. Inf. 164, 202
NJ 10th Vol. Inf. 77, 163, 164, 202
NJ 15th Vol. Inf. 163, 195, 197, 202
Norfolk and Western RR 138
North Garden Depot, VA 62, 108, 114
Northrop, Pvt. John 76, 77, 178ns, 191, 200
Notman, John 19
NY 1st Vol. Cav. 134, 194, 202
NY 1st Vol. Dragoons 156
NY 1st Vol. Lt. Arty. 149, 201
NY 4th Vol. Cav. 146
NY 5th Vol. Cav. 153, 159, 160, 194
NY 5th Vol. He. Arty. 164, 166
NY 7th Vol. He. Arty. 158
NY 8th Vol. Cav. 153
NY 8th Vol., Inf. 145, 147, 148
NY 11th Vol. Lt. Arty. 78
NY 13th Vol. Inf. 34, 173, 196
NY 14th Vol. He Arty. 154
NY 15th Vol. Cav. 155, 157, 158, 166
NY 21st Vol. Cav. 167, 195
NY 27th Vo. Inf. 199
NY 28th Vol. Inf. 57-61, 150, 195
NY 39th Vol. Inf. 154, 194, 201
NY 40th Vol. Inf. 80, 192
NY 45th Vol. Inf. 147
NY 48th Vol Inf. 46

Index

NY 50th Engineers 134
NY 54th Vol. Inf. 143, 145
NY 60th Vol. Inf. 91
NY 61st Vol. Inf. 154
NY 63rd Vol. Inf. 162
NY 64th Vol. Inf. 143
NY 65th Vol. Inf. 163
NY 66th Vol. Inf. 176
NY 77th Vol. Inf. 113, 163, 200
NY 111th Vol. Inf. 155, 157, 198
NY 121ST Vol. Inf. 156
NY 126th Vol. Inf. 160
NY 140th Vol. Inf. 153, 156, 159, 194
NY 146th Vol. Inf. 161, 162, 163
NY 147th Vol. Inf. 157, 161, 162, 163

Oakwood Cemetery 45
Oberlin College, OH 167
OH 4th Vol. Inf. 147
OH 5th Vol. Inf. 148
OH 8th Vol. Cav. 167
OH 11th Vol. Inf. 36
OH 12th Vol. Inf. 167
OH 23rd Vol. Inf. 167
OH 25th Vol. Inf. 144, 177*n*
OH 27th Vol. Inf. 158
OH 29th Vol. Inf. 145, 147, 149, 157, 195, 201
OH 34th Vol. Inf. 167
OH 34th MT. Vol. Inf. 160, 167
OH 36th Vol. M Inf. 167
OH 55th Vol. Inf. 149, 151, 153, 200
OH 62*nd* Vol Inf. 149
OH 66th Vol. Inf. 71, 145-148, 150
OH 67th Vol Inf. 146
OH 91st Vol. Inf. 112, 167, 184, 203
OH 104th Vol. Inf. 189
OH 116th Vol. Inf. 88, 154, 155, 159, 168, 179*n*, 203
OH 122nd Vol. Inf. 160, 161
OH 123rd Vol, Inf. 168, 198
OH 135th Vol. Inf. 158
OH 152*nd* Vol. Inf. 111
Ohio State University 2, 3, 171*n*, 208
Old Dominion Iron and Nail Works 40
Olf, Pvt. John 160
Opera House 140, 184*n*
Orange and Alex. R.R. 14, 54, 56, 62, 105, 108, 109, 114, 115
Orange County, VA. 46, 76, 81
Orange County Courthouse 76, 81
O'Reilly, Miles *see* Halpine, Col. C.G.
Orton, Pvt. Martin 167
O'Shaughnessy, Pvt. Michael 146

Otey, Lucy Wilhelmina Norvell 91, 92, 179*ns*, 186
Otey, Capt. Van R., CSA 88, 179*ns*
Ould, Col. Robert, CSA 75
Owen, Dr. William O. 91, 94, 96, 119

Parker, Pvt. John B. 158
Pasteur, Louis 44
Pate, Capt. H. Clay, CSA 52
Peaks of Otter, VA 110, 111
Peatt, Pvt. Henry 144
Peck, Pvt. Arthur 169
PA In. Vol. Lt. Arty. 145
PA 5th Vol. Cav. 124
PA 6th Res. Vol. Inf. 161
PA 6th Vol. Cav 158
PA 11th Vol. Inf. 154
PA 14th Vol. Cav. 168, 200
PA 19th Vol. Inf. 180, 193
PA 20th Vol. Inf 193
PA 25th Vol. Inf. 144
PA 27th Vol. Inf. 144
PA 29th Vol. Inf. 145, 146
PA 46th Vol. Inf. 145, 148
PA 48th Vol. Inf. 156
PA 54th Vol. Inf. 168, 182*n*, 188
PA 72*nd* Vol. Inf. 159
PA 88th Vol. Inf. 154
PA 90th Vol. Inf. 97, 178*n*, 180*n*, 193
PA 110th Vol. Inf. 159
PA 111th Vol. Inf. 148
PA 114th Vol. Inf. 43
PA 116th Vol. Inf. 162
PA 140th Vol. Inf. 157
PA 148th Vol. Inf. 155
PA 149th Vol. Inf. 161
PA 150th Vol. Inf. 162
PA 183rd Vol. Inf. 159
Pest House Hospital 90, 92, 94, 95, 96, 99, 180*n*
Petersburg, VA 4, 14, 20, 37, 52, 54, 55, 72, 73, 115, 119, 123, 134, 186, 187, 201, 203
Phillips, Pvt. Theophilus C. 157
Pickenpaugh, Roger 4, 171*n*, 173*n*, 210
Piedmont, Battle of 88, 102, 103, 110
Pike, Pvt. William H. 149
Pitcher, Pvt. Horace M. 151
Platenburgh, Pvt. Peter 155
Pogan, Pvt. Robert 157
Pond, Lt. George E. 114, 181*ns*, 182*n*, 210
Pope, Gen. John 78
Poplar Grove Federal Cemetery 119, 134, 143, 183*n*

Index

Port Republic, VA 63, 101
Porte Crayon *see* Strother, D.H.
Potter, Dr. Dorothy T. x, 182*n*, 210
Potter, Dr. Edmund D. x, 70
Pottowatomie, KS, Massacre 30, 173*n*
Powell, Col. William H. 112
Praynard, Pvt. James P. 161
Preacher, Pvt. Bruno 150
Presbyterian Cemetery 18
Prince, Pvt. John E. 170
Proudfoot, Pvt. Francis 170
Pugh, Pvt. John H. 169
Putnam, Col. David 111

Quakers 9, 10, 11, 12, 14, 205

Rand, Pvt. Jasper 158
Randall, Pvt. William 168
Randles, Pvt. Charles 144
Randolph, George W., CSA 65, 73
Rapp, Pvt. Levi 161
Rawling, Pvt. Charles J. 115, 180*n*, 181*ns*, 182*n*, 201
Reader, Pvt. Frank 97, 117, 180*n*, 182*n*, 201
Reconstruction 90, 99, 107, 126, 127, 130, 131, 132, 133, 136, 204
Reconstruction Act of 1867 135
Red Badge of Courage 80
Redman, Pvt. John 160
Reed, Pvt. Charles E. 151
Reel, Pvt. Hiram 169
Reid, Whitelaw 131, 183*n*, 191, 209
Remington, Sgt. Francis A. 152
Rexroad, Pvt. Morgan 170
RI 1st Vol. Lt. Arty. 162
Rice, Gen. James Clay 83
Rice, Pvt. Micajot I. 157
Richmond and Petersburg RR 52
Richmond Junto 11, 12, 20, 31
Richmond Prison Association 34, 35
Richmond Dispatch 43 72, 173*ns*, 174*ns*, 175*ns*, 177*ns*, 181*n*
Rider, Sgt. John 156, 158
RMWC/Randolph College 18, 184*n*
Roach, Lt. Alva C. 95, 174*n*, 180*n*, 191, 192
Robins, Glenn 4, 171*n*, 211
Roberts, Pvt. Daniel S. 150
Roberts, Pvt. Ziba 57-66, 68, 69, 70, 72, 176*ns*, 177*ns*, 186, 202
Robertson, James I. Jr. x
Robinson, Daniel 186
Robinson, Capt. Horace 153

Robinson, Cpl. John 143, 160
Robinson, Pvt. Richard 152
Robison, Pvt. Charles 146
Rockbridge County, VA 106
Rockbridge Gazette 108
Rockfish Gap, VA 60
Rodes, Gen. Robert E., CSA 116
Rodgers, Capt., CSA 71
Rogers, Pvt. Lawson H. 161
Rose, Robert 12
Rose, Col. Thomas E. 46
Rosecrans, Gen. William S. 74
Ross, Erasmus, CSA 39
Royall, Anne 19, 172*n*, 192
Ruck, Pvt. Cyrus 162
Rucker, Anthony 12
Rucker, Benjamin 12
Rucker, Pvt. John W. 144, 177*n*
Rude's Hill 101
Runner, Pvt. George 170
Rust, Pvt. William 169

Sailor's Creek, Battle of 83
Saint Louis, MO 50
Salem, VA 16, 138, 140
Salisbury Prison, NC 6, 37, 38, 55, 56, 64, 76, 173*n*, 174*n*, 196, 198
Sandusky House ix, 98, 112, 113, 115, 116, 117, 179*n*
Sanitary Commission 3, 119, 134, 174*ns*, 175*ns*, 187, 211
Sargent, Sgt. Cyrus B. 168
Schaum, Pvt. Rudolph G. 147
Schneider, Cpl. Henry 168
Schofield, Gen. John M. 135, 136
Schwartz, Pvt. William 156
Scott, Anne Norvell Otey 91, 179*n*, 186
scurvy 66, 68, 151
Sears, Pvt. William A. 155
Seven Days Battle 40
Sheehan, Pvt. Michael 162
Shelbyville, TN 75
Sheridan, Gen. Philip 60, 61, 102, 121, 123, 124
Sherman, Pvt. Richard 156
Sherman, Gen. William T. 121
Shields, Cpl. William C. 167
Shockoe Hill Cemetery 36
Shum, Pvt. Albert 167
Sigel, Gen. Franz 100, 102
Sigler, Pvt. John W. 170
Silver Grays 27, 76
Simpson, Pvt. Roberts J. 169, 184
Sisters of Charity 96, 207, 209

Index

Slaughter, Charles M. 21
slavery and slaves 4, 5, 6, 10, 11, 12, 15, 16, 19, 20, 22, 23, 28, 29, 30, 32, 35, 39, 41, 42, 44, 45, 46, 47, 63, 64, 67, 68, 75, 82, 84, 85, 86, 87, 89, 92, 93, 94, 97, 98, 104, 110, 112, 113, 116, 119, 120, 125, 126, 128, 130, 131, 132, 135, 137, 139, 172n, 173ns, 211
Sly, Pvt. Hiram 145
smallpox 49, 68, 89, 94, 95, 96, 206
Smedley, Cpl. Charles 76, 77, 178ns, 192
Smith, Prof. Col. Francis H., CSA. 104
Smith, Pvt. Francis M. 170
Smith, Pvt. Harrison H. 164
Smith, Pvt. Henry S. 169
Smith, Pvt. John 167
Smith, Pvt. Wallace 91, 143
Smith, Pvt. William 153
Sneden, Pvt. Robert K. 39, 46, 192, 174n, 175n, 192
Society of Friends *see* Quakers
South River Meeting 11, 12, 60, 112, 205
Southside RR 14, 52, 54, 56, 71, 72, 83, 84, 85, 86, 115, 122, 138
Special Orders No. 145 65
Speed, John M. 21, 122
Speer, Lonnie 3, 4, 171n, 174n, 210
Spotsylvania Court House, battle of 80, 83, 84, 155
Sprague, Pvt. Thomas 147
Springer, Paul J. 4, 83, 171, 211
Springhill Cemetery 18, 19
Stahel, Gen. Julius 103
Stanton, Edwin M. 40, 74, 100
Stanton, Elizabeth Cady 79
Stanton, Pvt. Silas 167
State, Pvt. William H. 158
Staunton, VA 16, 60, 61, 88, 89, 101, 102, 103, 105, 109, 111
Steen, Pvt. John W. 167
Steiber, Pvt. Lewis 167
Steward, Pvt. James M. 170
Stewart, Pvt. John 146
Stiles, Sgt. Colvin 167
Stone's River, Battle of 185, 200
Stout, Pvt. George H. 158
Stow, Sgt. Stephen L. 160
Stowell, Pvt. Carlos A. 162
Strasburg, VA. 66
Stratton, Pvt. Moses C. 162
Strausbaugh, Pvt. Isaac 168
Steele's Tavern, VA 103
Strepler, Pvt. Jacob 144
Strikle, Cpl. John M. 156

Strother, Col. David H. 105, 107, 109, 110, 111, 113, 115, 180ns, 181ns, 182ns, 192; *see also* Porte Crayon
Stroup, 1st. Lt. George B. 167
Stuart, Gen. J.E.B. 30
Sullivan, Gen. Jeremiah C. 103, 107, 198
Summerdean, VA 103
Sutton, Pvt. Peter J. 163
Swanger, Pvt. James J. 168
Swisher, Pvt. John H. 148, 177

Taylor, Pvt. Joseph 144
Taylor's Tobacco Factory 38
Teasville (Waynesboro), VA 60
Tenth Amendment 133, 183n
Terrell, Dr. John J. 95, 96, 175n, 180n, 182n, 206
Thirteenth Amendment 132, 133
Thomas, 2nd Lt. David J. 169
Thomas, Gen. George Henry 79, 121
Thompson, Pvt. David 159
Thompson, Cpl. John 166
Thompson's Station, Battle of 74, 75, 195, 199, 203, 204, 211
Thorn, Pvt. Robert W. 167, 184n
Thornburg, Cpl. W.H. 167
Thornton, Pvt. David M.C. 156
Thorp, Cpl. Nathan 161
Tin Bridge 115
"Tin Shingles" 136
Tingley, Pvt. James 168
"Tobacco City" 6, 9, 20, 138, 207
tobacco: factories/warehouses, 7, 12, 19, 20, 35-38, 42, 46, 68, 75, 81, 86, 87, 88, 92, 93, 94, 111, 117120, 122, 127, 128, 130, 139, 173n, 185; hospitals 91, 93, 97, 99; restrictions on planting 92
Todd, Lt. David H., CSA 34-35, 173n
Tourtellotte, Sgt. Chester A. 161
Townshend, Pvt. Calvin W. 167
Treaty of Guadalupe Hidalgo 1848, 28
Trieschman, Pvt. Charles F. 148
Tripp, Pvt. Ezra G. 155
Trumbull, Lyman 133
Tullahoma, TN 74
"The Tunnel" 45, 46, 47, 48, 187
Turner, Nat 11, 30
Turner, Pvt. Richard R., CSA 39
Turner, Capt. Thomas Pratt, CSA 39, 41, 42, 72, 73, 81, 121, 177n
Tye River Gap 109

Underground Railroad 29
Union Hotel (Lynchburg VA) 91

Index

United States Colored Troops 135, 158
US 1st Cavalry 164
US 4th Cavalry 98, 162
US 4th Infantry 162
US 11th Infantry 162
University of Lynchburg 18, 178*n*, 179*n*, 184*n*, 190
University of Virginia 2, 140, 190

VA and TN RR 14, 15, 52, 54, 111, 152
VA Central RR 14, 60, 61, 102, 111, 212
VA Gen. Assembly 11, 12, 13, 14, 17, 29, 30, 31, 92, 129, 136, 139
VA 7th Vol. Cav., CSA 58
VA 21st Vol. Inf., CSA 59, 64
Van Buskirk, Cpl. Michael Henry 57, 58, 59, 61, 63, 65, 68-72, 176*ns*, 177*ns*, 186, 187
Van Horn, Pvt. Gilbert 168
Van Lew, Eliza Baker 36
Van Lew, Elizabeth 46
Van Order, Pvt. Kimble 155
Vicksburg, MS 41, 50
Vinyard, Cpl. Harvey 148, 177*n*
Virginia Christian College 18, 175*n*, 179*n*, 184*n*, 190
Virginia Constitution 29, 136, 204
Virginia Military Institute 8, 17, 18, 39, 100, 101, 104, 105, 106, 107, 108, 181*n*, 187, 209; Washington's statue 107, 111
Virginia University of Lynchburg 184*n*
VT 1st Vol. Cav. 57, 58, 59, 61, 144, 149, 151
VT 1st Vol. He. Arty. 162
VT 5th Vol. Inf. 164
VT 6th Vol. Inf. 162
VT 8th Vol. Inf. 150
VT 10th Vol. Inf. 161

Wade's Tobacco Factory 81, 84, 85, 86, 178
Walker, Chap. William 107, 108, 115, 181*ns*, 182*ns*, 203
Waller, Sgt. Coleman B. 169
Walton, Pvt. John W. 144
Warwick, Pvt. Alfred 164
Warwick House Hotel/Hospital 91, 128, 143
Washington, George 13, 95, 107, 111, 208
Washington and Lee University 2, 140, 181*n*, 187, 190
Washington College 107, 187, 190
Watkins, Pvt. John 170

Watson, Capt. George W. 97, 98, 180*ns*, 193
Waynesboro, VA 60, 61, 102, 109, 176*n*, 212
Waynesboro, Battle of 176*n*, 212
Wayside Hospital 94
Weber, Louis 140, 204
Weeks, Pvt. Joseph 150
Weik, Pvt. John 145
Welsh, Pvt. John 164
Wendle, Cpl. Jonathan L. 168
Wentz, Cpl. William 169
West Point 5, 30, 33, 39, 78, 100, 101, 103, 125
Weyers Cave, VA 61
Wheeler, Pvt. George E. 151, 154
Wheeling Convention 22, 32
Wheeling, WV 53, 107, 176*n*, 187, 201
White, Col. C.B. 104
White, Pvt. James 170
Whitlock's Warehouse 42
WI 3rd Vol. Inf. 147, 197, 204
WI 7th Vol Inf. 153, 197, 204
WI 22nd Vol. Inf. 152, 197, 203, 204, 211
Wickham, Q.M. Sgt. John S. 158
Wilcox, Gen. Orlando B. 136
Wilcox, Pvt. William S. 146
Wilderness, Battle of 76, 79, 80, 81, 83, 84, 97, 178*n*, 189, 191-198, 200, 201, 204
Wildes, Lt.-Col. Thomas F. 114, 179*n*, 180*n*, 181*n*, 182*n*, 203
Wilkeson, Lt. Frank 78, 79, 80, 83, 178*ns*, 193
Willard, Pvt. James J. 159, 193, 194
Wilson, Lt. Edward S. 112, 180*n*, 182*ns*, 193
Winchester, VA. 58, 59, 60, 123, 186, 210
Winder, Gen. John, CSA 5, 6, 33-43, 45, 47, 51, 54, 55, 64, 65, 66, 68, 73, 75, 78, 177*n*, 186, 191, 206, 209
Winder, Capt. Sidney, CSA 75
Wirz, Capt. Henry, CSA 41, 42, 43, 51, 73, 75
Wise, Gov. Henry 30, 31, 32
Witham, Pvt. Charles W. 148
Withers, Lt. Col. John, CSA 65
Wolford, Sgt. Reyless 168
Wood, Pvt. Samuel D. 155
Woodrum, Pvt. James 169
Woodstock, VA. 59, 60
Woodward, Pvt. Seth A. 166
WPA of VA—History Inventory 91
Wray, Cpl. Thomas C. 159
WV 1st Vol. Cav. 145, 169

223

Index

WV 1st Vol. Inf. 146, 169
WV 1st Vol. Lt. Arty. 66, 144, 156, 157, 169
WV 2nd Vol. Cav. 169
WV 3rd Vol. Cav. 169
WV 5th Vol. Cav. 180n, 182n
WV 5th Vol. Inf. 53, 117, 158, 169
WV 7th Vol. Cav. 155, 169
WV 9th Vol. Inf. 53, 54, 164, 169
WV 11th Vol. Inf. 156, 158, 169
WV 12th Vol. Inf. 170
WV 14th Vol. Inf. 170
WV 15th Vol Inf. 117, 156, 170

Yankee Square 67, 135, 144-151, 161
Yoder, Jacob E. 132, 133, 136, 137, 183ns, 193
York, Sgt. Calvin B. 152
Younger, Pvt. John 150

Zeigler, Col. John 53
Ziegler, Pvt. Franz 147
Zimmerman, Pvt. Charles 149
Zulker, Pvt. Benjamin C. 164

www.ingramcontent.com/pod-product-compliance
Lightning Source LLC
Chambersburg PA
CBHW032040300426
44117CB00009B/1131